Contents

About the Authors   v
Foreword   vii
Acknowledgements   ix

1. Counselling in Health Care Settings   1
2. Theoretical Concepts   9
3. Beliefs about Illness and Counselling   18
4. Reframing and Creating Balance in Patient Beliefs   31
5. Counselling Tasks in Health Care   40
6. Exploring and Defining Problems in Counselling   47
7. Principles and Aims of Counselling, and the Structure of the Session   60
8. Genograms   70
9. Confidentiality and Secrets   79
10. Giving Information   87
11. Giving 'Bad News'   97
12. Counselling for Loss and Terminal Care   109
13. Bereavement Counselling   119
14. Counselling the 'Worried-well' and Patients with Intractable Health Worries   129
15. Models of Consultation and Collaboration   140
16. Moving on from Feeling Stuck in Counselling   155
17. Counselling for the Prevention of Ill Health   166
18. Language Use and Stereotyping of Gender-Specific Diseases   175
19. Work Stress and Staff Support   185

    References   192
    Index   195

About the Authors

Robert Bor is Professor of Psychology at City University, London, and a Chartered Clinical, Counselling and Health Psychologist. He trained in the practice and teaching of family therapy at the Tavistock Clinic, is a member of the Tavistock Society of Psychotherapists, and is a UKCP Registered Systemic Therapist. He is a clinical member of the Institute of Family Therapy, London, a member of the American Family Therapy Academy and the American Association for Marriage and Family Therapy, as well as the Collaborative Family Health Care Coalition. He works in hospital, community and primary care settings, and extensively with acute and chronically ill patients and their families. He acts as a consultant to medical and nursing colleagues about their work with challenging or 'heart-sink' patients, and teaches communication skills to medical students. He has published widely on the impact of illness on families and serves on the editorial board of numerous international journals. He also has an interest in aviation psychology and is a qualified pilot. He is a Churchill Fellow.

Riva Miller has a background in medical social work. She trained as a family therapist at the Tavistock Clinic, at the Institute of Family Therapy and with the Milan Associates in Italy. She has always worked in a medical setting with people who are chronically ill. She currently holds several positions as a practitioner, manager, teacher and consultant, as a family therapist in the Haemophilia Centre and as HIV co-ordinator at the Royal Free Hospital, London. She is Honorary Senior Lecturer in the Royal Free Hospital School of Medicine. Since 1985 she has held a consultancy at the North London Blood Transfusion Service helping to consider ethical issues and instigate counselling policies. She has acted as an advisor for the World Health Organization since 1988 and run many workshops on their behalf on HIV infection. Her particular interests and expertise are in integrating systemic approaches to treatment and care in busy medical settings. She is also a UKCP Registered Systemic Therapist.

Martha Latz is a graduate of Nova Southeastern University Marital and Family Therapy Program in South Florida where she specialized in Medical Family Therapy work. Her publications have focused on developing skills within both traditional psychotherapies and the collaborative medical model. Currently in private practice and an adjunct professor at Nova Southeastern, she supervises Family Therapy graduate students in clinical applications of therapy skills. Her recent research has focused on working with acute and chronic female cardiac patients to promote more effective communication between patients and health care professionals. She is a clinical member of the American Association for Marriage and Family Therapy and a designated AAMFT approved supervisor. A member of the Society of Teachers of Family Medicine and Collaborative Family Health Care Coalition, she presents papers regularly at national and international conferences.

Heather Salt is a Chartered Consultant Clinical Psychologist and Head of the Health Psychology Unit at Northwick Park Hospital, London. She has also been a consultant lecturer in Health and Counselling Psychology at City University, London, and an Honorary Lecturer at the Royal Free Hospital School of Medicine. She has worked in an acute medical setting for many years and also has experience of primary care and community health psychology. She has an interest in organizational stress and psychoneuro-immunology. In her current research she is investigating team functioning and stress for health care professionals. She has numerous publications to her name.

Foreword

The movement to apply systems approaches to medical problems takes a leap forward with the publication of this book. Bor, Miller, Latz and Salt provide us with a broad, comprehensive and integrative approach to working with the psychosocial challenges faced by patients with acute or chronic illness or disability.

This movement to apply systems theory to health care settings started with the development of family systems theory during the 1950s. Early family therapists, such as Auerswald, Bowen, Minuchin, Weakland, Whitaker and Wynne, all envisioned that systems theory would be applied to both health and mental health problems. As physicians, they saw the relevance of systemic approaches to health care problems. But family therapy, psychology, social work and counselling defined themselves in reaction to the traditional medical model, opposing pathology-based explanations for psychosocial problems and also opposing the power base of psychiatrists and other physicians in most health care systems. And so, the mind–body split predominated from the 1960s through the 1980s in both medicine and mental health care.

Of course, a small but significant number of family therapists, behavioural medicine psychologists, family-oriented medical social workers, consult–liaison psychiatrists, family nurses and others did work in medical settings over these decades, in spite of the difficulties, because of their commitment to treating problems at the interface between mind and body. These early health care counsellors, many of them trained by the pioneers of family therapy, embraced the alternative medical model proposed by internist George Engel – the biopsychosocial model (1977), a model that also had its roots in systems theory. Family systems theory was merged with the biopsychosocial model to provide a conceptual framework for this enterprise (McDaniel, Hepworth and Doherty, 1992). Many talented people provided us with case examples to illuminate and inspire our work. The journal *Families, Systems & Health*, and others, published research about the systemic approach to biopsychosocial health care. Now, with this volume, we have a pragmatic manual that operationalizes the biopsychosocial systems approach to counselling and psychotherapy.

Managed care companies in the US, and health care agencies in the UK and elsewhere, frequently cite the need for training counsellors to work in health care settings. Every few weeks, I am called by one of them requesting a psychologist, counsellor or social worker who knows how to work in primary care, for example. Rarely am I able to refer someone who is truly knowledgeable. It is a reality of where we are in the development of this field. This book may change that reality. Administrators want trained professionals because they know from experience that counsellors untrained in health care, however effective they may be in other contexts, cannot easily parachute into a health care setting with their favourite counselling or psychotherapy skills in hand and land successfully. Health care has its own culture, its own rituals, its own practices, that require counsellors to adapt the style and even the substance of their treatment to be effective. *Counselling in Health Care Settings* provides us with a guide to the territory, so we may enter easily and provide services effectively. From health beliefs to gender issues, from genograms to grief sessions, from confidentiality to collaboration, this volume provides an overview of the issues that are special to working in health care as a counsellor or therapist. It will enable us to train a new generation of counsellors who can enter the system educated and knowledgable about the skills and challenges involved in working with people who are physically ill, their families, and the other health professionals who treat them.

As Mary Catherine Bateson said: 'The richest knowledge of the tree includes both myth and botany.' Illness is a threat to one's sense of agency and communion (McDaniel, Hepworth and Doherty, 1992), but it is also a 'call to consciousness' to deepen the awareness of life. Counselling in health care settings offers opportunities for healing and growth to patients, families and health care providers. It gives us as professionals the chance to contribute to humane, comprehensive and socially responsible approaches to health and illness. We all are indebted to the authors for providing us with a blueprint for this important work.

Susan H. McDaniel PhD
Professor of Psychiatry and Family Medicine
University of Rochester, New York

Acknowledgements

We have been fortunate in having supportive and inspiring colleagues in the many different settings in which we have each worked. Collaborative practice has been enormously important and has provided a secure base from which our ideas have developed.

These ideas would be no more than textbook theories without the opportunity to work with patients and their families in different clinical settings. We are grateful to all of them for sharing their own experiences and stories with us at different stages of illness. Their experiences have both moved and inspired us, but most of all taught us new ideas which we have then been able to put to the service of those we have counselled. Indeed, many of the ideas in this book have come from the feedback given to us by our patients about our practice, with an emphasis on what they have found helpful.

Special thanks go to Madeleine Sugden and David Johnston who helped to prepare the manuscript. We are also grateful to Linda Papadopoulos and Penny Stanion who shared with us some of their experience of using genograms in counselling sessions. Dr David Miller was very generous with his time and his ideas about work stress and staff support.

Naomi Roth, our editor at Cassell Publishers, has been a constant source of support and encouragement for which we are most grateful.

This book is dedicated to our patients and their families, as well as to our own families.

CHAPTER 1

Counselling in Health Care Settings

INTRODUCTION

Illness is at one level a private and individual matter. At another level, it has implications for family and social relationships. In spite of many significant advances in the diagnosis and treatment of medical conditions, a degree of ill health invariably affects most people in their life-time. Some may have to endure life-long and chronic ill health. Not only does illness evoke fears and anxieties – be they about pain, suffering, loss of functioning or death – but it also directly affects relationships. Partners may become carers; children may be called on to provide care and support; hospitalization may lead to periods of separation from the family and dependence on professional carers.

Counselling can help people to cope with and adjust to new and unwelcome circumstances. It can also help other family members to adapt to the changes brought about by illness, whether it is an acute episode or a chronic, life-long (inherited) or life-threatening condition. The notion of 'needing counselling', however, can inadvertently create a problem and undermine an individual's ability to cope and adapt, because of the associations between mental health and illness. Some unique and specific issues arise in health care settings which must be recognized by counsellors when working with people who are ill and their families. Some examples of questions we have been asked by counsellors will help to open up some of these issues for further scrutiny:

- Where does a counsellor fit into a multidisciplinary health care team?
- If we cannot cure patients of their medical condition, what is the role and task of the counsellor?
- Does the counsellor need to have detailed knowledge of a medical condition in order to counsel someone about it?
- Should counsellors give information to patients about medical conditions and treatment?
- How do confidentiality rules apply in health care settings?

- How can I work in a setting where privacy and time boundaries may be lacking?
- What do we do when the doctor asks us to see a patient who refuses to take his/her medication?
- How do I work with a person who has been referred for counselling but does not want it?
- How do you work with family members?
- How should we approach a patient who has just been given bad news by a doctor?
- What is the counsellor's role in dealing with loss and bereavement?

This book aims to address some of these questions by providing the reader with the theory and skills to effectively counsel patients and families affected by illness in a range of health care settings.

THE FIELD OF COUNSELLING IN HEALTH CARE SETTINGS

Counselling and medicine have always been closely connected: Freud himself was a medically qualified doctor. The relationship between psychotherapy and medicine has not, however, been without complications. The mind–body debate and the entry of non-medically trained counsellors and psychotherapists into the medical arena have presented a series of challenges, some of which are hotly debated by practitioners. A separate speciality of medical psychotherapy and medical counselling has emerged in recent years at the intersection of medical practice and the growing mental health fields of counselling, psychotherapy, clinical psychology, counselling psychology and health psychology.

Recently there has been tremendous growth in the amount of published professional literature which examines the role of psychological processes in the prevention, onset and treatment of physical illness. A variety of health care professionals have begun to work in this field, providing psychotherapeutic services to those with medical problems. Physicians, surgeons, nurses and other health care professionals have started to recognize that the skills of psychotherapists and counsellors can be fruitfully employed in dealing with a wide range of problems in different areas. This book especially focuses on two of these:

- Working with patients[1] and their families, to help them to cope with illness, and
- Acting as a consultant to medical and nursing staff about psychological aspects of patient care.

Collaboration will become increasingly important, as indicated by the growth in the number of psychotherapists and counsellors working in primary health care, clinics, hospitals, wards, nursing and medical schools, and even in health care management. This is an era of increasing specialization in medicine. Guidelines, however, are needed for focused and contextually appropriate counselling that can be used across specialities and be effective in new situations and with a range of problems. Increasing complexity in health care (new technology, medico-legal concerns, changing resources) necessitates effective communication between health care providers and patients and their relatives.

Patients may live longer with a chronic illness; this in turn may have an impact not only on the relationship between the patient and his family,[2] but also between the patient and health care providers. All health care providers are expected to be effective communicators, able to counsel their patients about their problems, investigations and treatment, and to prevent illness. Furthermore, in an era in which medico-legal issues are becoming prominent in health care, with litigation a more common outcome, counselling and psychotherapeutic skills could be central in reducing the risk of adverse outcomes and, if possible, avoiding litigation. While counselling and communications skills have always been central to the provision of medical care, it is clear that they have assumed a new level of importance. Counsellors and psychotherapists, whose specialist understanding of communication and relationship problems is well recognized, are now increasingly sought to work in health care settings with medically ill patients and their families.

In general, counselling and psychotherapy approaches taught in colleges and universities tend to favour individualistic approaches and theories, such as cognitive-behavioural and psychodynamic approaches. They also mostly address the application of these ideas in mental health or private practice settings. This book was first conceived in an effort to provide psychotherapists, counsellors, psychologists and other allied health care professionals with a theoretical base and a guide for the practice of counselling in relation to illness in health care settings. Our experience of working in different health care settings brought to our attention the limitations of training and the lack of practical guidelines for counsellors. We felt it would be helpful to describe our ideas about counselling after many years of clinical practice, close collaboration and carrying out and publishing research. We have attempted to address the following questions:

- What does a trained counsellor need to know about practising in a health care setting?
- How can we describe a framework of practice which is likely to complement the reader's preferred approach to therapy rather than be at variance with it?

The following chapters describe more fully:

- *A systemic perspective* which takes into account not only the individual patient, but also his or her family and the context or setting in which counselling takes place.
- *An approach to counselling* that can be used across the medical and allied disciplines, enhancing the quality of collaboration between practitioners.
- *A description of the skills and practice of medical counselling* against a background of individual and family life cycles, illness typologies and different definitions of the problem.
- *A framework for medical counselling* based on a tried and tested approach that has been used for many years in different health care settings.
- *A framework or map* which the counsellor can use with confidence when responding to diverse problems, one which can be applied with a good measure of flexibility.
- *A model of time-limited counselling* which offers useful information to patients, helps them to deal with the implications of this information, and provides emotional support or devises psychotherapeutic interventions.

- *Ideas and skills for dealing with diverse issues and problems* such as health promotion, loss and bereavement, and confidentiality.

COUNSELLING SETTINGS

Counselling takes place in all health care settings including general practice surgeries, family-planning clinics, accident and emergency departments, out-patient clinics, hospital wards and health education departments. In some settings, such as infertility, oncology and HIV/AIDS, there may be specialist counsellors. The requirements of each setting need to be incorporated into the counselling process in order for it to be effective and relevant. This includes taking into account time-limited interventions, and working with acute and chronic illnesses in counselling settings such as open wards and out-patient clinics.

BELIEFS ABOUT THE PSYCHOLOGICAL CARE OF PATIENTS WITH HEALTH CARE PROBLEMS

This book describes the tasks of counsellors working in health care settings and some of the beliefs that inform our practice. These beliefs, which influence our approach to counselling, come from our experience of working with patients with a wide range of health-related problems and their families, and with different medical teams and groups of professionals. The ideas also come from the authors' training in and experience of using different, although complementary, psychotherapeutic approaches. The main therapeutic approaches which inform our practice are: family-systems, constructivist, cognitive-behavioural and attachment theory. Some of these beliefs can be summarized as follows:

- It is helpful to recognize that problems can arise at different points in the course of illness, or pre-existing psychological problems be exacerbated by the stress associated with illness.
- Health-related problems have implications for relationships and attachments between the patient, family members and health care providers.
- The 'family' is the patient's most important social system. Our definition of family incorporates not only blood relatives but also close social relationships.
- It is important to be mindful of both the social context of the patient and the context in which counselling is provided. Context gives meaning to the psychological problem and, to a large extent, determines the range of possible solutions to it.
- Health care settings are different from the traditional counselling setting. There is a different pace to the work and different views about confidentiality, working practices, length of sessions and duration of counselling. It is essential to be adaptable and to respect the demands and constraints of health care settings.
- There are many approaches to counselling which can be used to equal effect. Whichever approach is used, a 'map' helps to conceptualize problems and their possible resolution.
- It is useful to have clear goals and objectives for counselling sessions in health care

settings. These can be linked to the definition of the problem (or changes in the definition of the problem), considering for whom it is a problem and a plan for working towards its resolution. There need be no predetermined or inflexible ideas about what would be the best solution in a particular case. However, an understanding of psychotherapeutic theory guides the counsellor in thinking about the onset of the problem, exploring the definition of the problem and formulating a treatment plan.

- In some circumstances, counsellors may have to explain their actions to others in a court of law, and theory and research may be important aspects of this.
- Lack of training in psychological theories or vague theoretical ideas can lead to confusion in counselling sessions for both the patient and counsellor.
- The counsellor's task is to help patients identify what meaning this particular illness has for them and to discuss the consequences of this (Wright *et al.* 1996). Our concern is to avoid situations in which patients may feel pushed to see things in the way we see them, or where we inadvertently disqualify their ideas or feelings.
- Lastly, patients are encouraged to collaborate in the process of counselling. This is a major departure from the traditional hierarchical configuration in counselling in which the counsellor is seen to have power and control. One consequence is that counsellors now have to accept greater challenges and more uncertainty in their practice. Some may also find the practice of this approach less stressful and more rewarding as responsibility is shared with patients.

A SOLUTION-FOCUSED COUNSELLING APPROACH

We describe a solution-focused counselling approach which has been found to be well suited to working in health care settings, particularly with people who have a physical illness. A solution-focused approach is useful for understanding the context of the evolution, maintenance and resolution of psychological problems. This ensures that attempts to treat psychological problems do not inadvertently lead to their exacerbation, or jeopardize the position of the counsellor in the health care setting. We use an integrative counselling model, drawing on ideas from complementary frameworks of systemic theory and practice. We endeavour to be flexible and responsive to the ideas and beliefs of the patient and other health care providers.

Progress in counselling in health care settings can be jeopardized by (a) a lack of skill or insufficient understanding of psychotherapeutic theory, (b) persistence with an idea or intervention in spite of feedback from the patient (and/or his social or family system) that this is not helpful, or (c) inattention to the difficulties of the counsellor's role in relation to doctors, nurses and health service managers.

Counselling and psychotherapy can imply weekly or more frequent sessions with a trained counsellor over many years. While this may be necessary or helpful for some patients, there is also a place for information or advice-giving in counselling in health care settings, as well as briefer periods of contact with the counsellor. Indeed, effective solution-focused counselling can sometimes be conducted in a single session or through consultations with other professionals caring for the patient which may obviate the need for a face-to-face contact between the patient and the counsellor.

The traditional medical model of diagnosis has an individual orientation.

Indications of problems are looked for *inside* the person and treatment is directed exclusively at the person as the intervention target. A systemic approach encourages the counsellor to look beyond the apparent problem and consider the wider social context of the patient when assessing or treating him.

A basic tenet of the solution-focused systemic approach is that all behaviour is part of an interactive process, whether at home, at work, or in a counselling session. Reciprocity in relationships implies that if something happens to one member of the family, it will affect the rest of the family who, in turn, will affect the behaviour of that individual. This means that behaviour cannot be studied in isolation, without taking into account the situation in which it occurs. The counsellor may influence the patient whose reactions, in turn, have an effect on the counsellor. Counselling is not a process of 'doing something to someone'. It is best described as an interactive process. Although there are many definitions of counselling and psychotherapy, it is necessary to clarify our definition:

> Counselling is an interaction in a therapeutic setting, focusing primarily on a conversation about relationships, beliefs and behaviour (including feelings), through which the patient's perceived problem is elucidated and framed or reframed in a fitting or useful way, and in which new solutions are generated and the problem takes on a new meaning.

An over-emphasis on counselling in health care settings may inadvertently cause some patients to believe they have a psychological problem. The approach described in this book starts out from the premise that problems first need to be identified and defined by patients or health care providers. An assumption on the part of the counsellor that all medically ill patients require or will benefit from counselling is unfounded. This view can be detrimental to the patient, the position of the counsellor in the system, and to how others view the practice of counselling. Many psychological problems in health care settings are adequately assessed and managed, and in some cases prevented, in the course of comprehensive medical care.

Counsellors may increasingly have opportunities to become involved in patient care due to the increasing workloads of health care providers and the constraints arising from pressures of time; increasing costs of diagnostic tests, investigations and treatment regimes; and evidence of benefit to some patients and their care-takers from counselling in some settings and for certain problems. There may also be a pressure to treat the patient's problems in the shortest possible time. The conventional fifty-minute counselling session may not always be appropriate, although the number of sessions may also be fewer than with a conventional open-ended contract. Solution-focused counselling can sometimes extend over a longer period, with sessions being held at greater intervals. A clearly mapped-out plan of action with the patient may itself be a major psychotherapeutic intervention for a patient who is dying, uncertain, anxious or bewildered.

CONCLUSION

This book is written mainly for counsellors, therapists, social workers and psychologists working within a health care setting with people suffering from a medical illness. The emphasis is on working with adult patients and their families, and collaboratively with other health care professionals. Readers wishing to acquire a more advanced understanding of how to counsel children are referred to an exellent text by Edwards and Davis (1998) entitled *Counselling Children with Chronic Medical Conditions.*

The ideas presented in this text can also be used by other health care professionals such as doctors, nurses, physiotherapists, occupational therapists and dieticians to help address some of their patients' problems. Our main focus is on developing an understanding of:

• How physical illness affects people and their family relationships.
• The roles and tasks of counsellors working with these patients and their families.
• How context or setting affects the counsellor's role and approaches to care and treatment.
• The dynamics of interprofessional consultation and liaisons.
• How the counsellor can practise effectively and creatively, even in some complicated and emotionally intense clinical situations.

Patients increasingly expect health care providers not only to be experts in their chosen field, such as medicine or nursing, but also to have the sensitivity and skills to discuss complex treatment and care issues. Conversational and problem-solving skills are highly relevant in this regard. However, there is some difference between being, on the one hand, a counsellor and, on the other, having counselling skills. Almost all health care professionals counsel in the course of their work. They constantly interact with patients, giving information, clarifying treatment options and helping people adjust to new and sometimes unwelcome circumstances. Psychotherapists, counsellors and psychologists, on the other hand, are expected to have advanced training and qualifications in their field. There are likely to be occasions when any health care provider sees the need to refer a patient to a counsellor in the same way as a doctor may refer medical problems to a specialist colleague. The special problems that arise in health care settings, coupled with time constraints in some clinical situations and the powerful feelings evoked by this work, may challenge people's existing counselling maps or frameworks. This book attempts to address some of these issues, conveying an approach to counselling people with medical problems when working in health care settings that has been applied and developed in several clinical and training settings through a range of social and clinical problems.

No counselling approach described in published literature teaches one 'what to say when'. Instead, counsellors and trainees in counselling can be introduced to new (either more or less expansive) ways of examining psychological problems and can incorporate an ever-widening range of concepts and skills in their practice map. The ideas in this book are not specifically intended to challenge a counsellor's preferred counselling approach – be it Kleinian, Jungian, client-centred, cognitive, behavioural, systemic, or any other. The aim is to extend the repertoire of ideas and skills available to counsellors, and to enhance their practice by reflecting on some of the unique and specific challenges of working as a counsellor in a health care setting.

Although most of our experience has been gained in developed countries with relatively good health and social services, we have also been directly involved in the application of many of these approaches in other settings where there is poverty, deprivation and minimal care. The ideas and cases may help to illustrate some of the dilemmas faced by those affected by health-related problems and by others in the systems which they inhabit – family, lovers, medical workers, nurses and others. They may also demonstrate how solutions can sometimes be found through more open communication and by applying different methods when confronted by new and complex problems.

Chapter 2 describes the theoretical ideas which underpin the skills outlined in the rest of the book. We highlight the importance of beliefs about illness, treatment and counselling in Chapter 3. A method for reframing unhelpful beliefs is covered in Chapter 4, which leads to a description of the main tasks in counselling in health care settings in Chapter 5. This counselling process is best facilitated by a detailed exploration of the 'problem' (Chapter 6) and a clear understanding of the aims and principles of counselling, and the structure of sessions (Chapter 7). The use of genograms or family trees in counselling is described in Chapter 8. The importance of patient confidentiality cannot be stressed too highly. However, this is not without its complications, and we address these issues in Chapter 9. The counsellor's role in giving information to patients is addressed in Chapter 10, and in giving 'bad news' in Chapter 11. Issues arising from terminal care, loss and bereavement are considered in Chapters 12 and 13. The 'worried-well' and those with intractable health worries can be an enormous drain on resources and the patience of health care staff. Chapter 14 conveys some ideas for counselling these patients. This paves the way for a more detailed exposition of collaborative practice between counsellors and health care professionals (Chapter 15). At some stage, every counsellor feels stuck in their work with patients. Possible sources are listed in Chapter 16, as are some ideas for over-coming an impasse. The importance of preventive counselling and promoting health through counselling is addressed in Chapter 17. Language is at the heart of counselling and it is essential that counsellors pay attention to gender-related issues which arise in the course of illness and health care (Chapter 18). Lastly, we recognize the enormous physical and emotional demands on all health care workers. Chapter 19 describes the counsellor's role in supporting colleagues and in preventing stress and burnout.

NOTES

1   We use the term 'patient' rather than 'client' or 'counsellee' to refer to these people because we work in hospital and clinic settings. This should not be taken to mean that the person is necessarily physically ill.

2   The personal pronoun 'he' rather than 'he/she' has been used throughout the book to refer to counsellors and patients. This does not reflect any bias on the part of the authors, but is merely a convenient pronoun.

CHAPTER 2

Theoretical Concepts

INTRODUCTION

Some conceptual ideas about practising as a counsellor in a health care setting are described in this chapter. An ability to approach each new case and problem with a receptive openness and to recognize that each patient will require different therapeutic approaches and procedures is important. This attitude needs to be balanced with a level of competence in tried and tested counselling approaches and interventions.

An important distinction needs to be made between professional work with the patient (counselling) and work with other professionals caring for the patient (consultation and collaboration). Counselling in a health care setting should always involve both. This is a basic tenet of a biopsychosocial systems perspective (Engel 1977; McDaniel *et al.* 1992) which stresses the interaction and interrelatedness between disease, individual, family, health care providers and other biopsychosocial systems. A minimum of three systems are involved in dealing with a medical problem: patient, family and clinician (Figure 2.1).

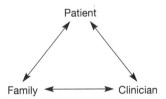

Figure 2.1 Minimum fundamental unit of health

Doherty and Baird (1983) referred to this triangle as the minimal fundamental unit of health. The participation of a counsellor and the inclusion of the illness as a part of the interactional system results in a more comprehensive depiction of transactions and is illustrated in Figure 2.2.

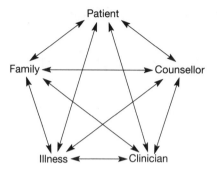

Figure 2.2 Pentagon depicting transactions which include a counsellor in the system

As the counsellor has to attend to issues involving himself, the patient, family, clinician and illness, within a given yet ever evolving context, it is more accurate to illustrate the complex interactions within the counselling context as follows:

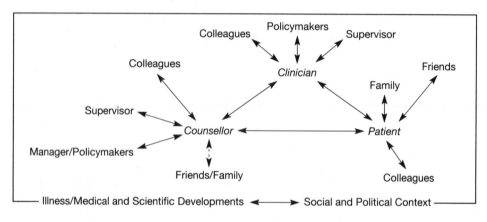

Figure 2.3

Using this framework helps to avoid the notion that a human problem is discrete, either physical or psychosocial. Instead, all problems are viewed as having biopsychosocial consequences. Psychosocial problems have physical components or features and physical problems have psychosocial ramifications. Interprofessional liaison is needed to ensure that problems (and solutions) are managed collaboratively. Providers of care, including counsellors, are viewed as part of, rather than apart from, the treatment system. This directly challenges the view that counsellors can remain neutral observers of their patients, detached from the psychological process. In these settings, counsellors may be confronted with complex interactions between different members of the system which develop into an intense emotional climate, especially in the face of pending or actual loss. This system can include a wide range of beliefs about illness and personal resilience which influence how people cope with other processes.

CONSIDERATIONS FOR COUNSELLORS WORKING WITH MEDICALLY ILL PATIENTS

We have identified ten main considerations for the counsellor which reflect the unique and specific features of therapeutic work with medically ill patients. These are derived from different theories of counselling and psychotherapy (including psychodynamic, systemic, person-centred, cognitive-behavioural and personal construct, among others) and our own clinical experience. The considerations are as follows.

Biopsychosocial approach

The application of a biopsychosocial approach (integrating biological, psychological and social features) to counselling has been extensively illustrated by McDaniel *et al.* (1992). There is a need for the counsellor to work collaboratively and without undue emphasis on either biological or psychological processes (to the detriment of the other). Social, medical and psychological events and processes are viewed as being interconnected and all require the ongoing attention of the counsellor. There is sometimes a tendency to over-emphasize psychological and social processes, whereas biomedical events may be equally relevant and themselves give rise to psychological problems.

Context

It is important to understand the context in which problems are identified or treated. The setting or context may be an in- or out-patient clinic, a GP surgery, a ward or a private practice setting. Each will influence or constrain the amount of time available for the patient, the degree of privacy in counselling sessions and sometimes also the psychotherapeutic approach used. The context determines how problems are viewed, what can be done about them and who should be involved in treatment and care. Systemic counsellors have been closely associated with the development and application of the contextual therapies and conceptual ideas pertaining to counselling and context advanced by Selvini Palazzoli and her co-workers (1980a).

Beliefs

Beliefs about health and illness are central to an understanding of how people are affected by illness, how they may respond to their care and treatment, and how they are likely to cope. The cognitive-behavioural and personal construct approaches emphasize the relevance of cognitions and beliefs in the onset, maintenance and treatment of psychological problems. Wright *et al.* (1996) distinguish between constraining and facilitative beliefs in relation to health and illness. Constraining beliefs maintain problems and impede the search for new options or alternatives. Facilitative beliefs expand possibilities for solutions. Beliefs are directly linked to behaviour. If a patient does not believe, for example, that a particular prescribed medication is likely to help his condition, it is less likely that he will comply with the treatment regime.

Attachment

The connection between attachment anxieties later in life and secure or insecure attachments to parents in infancy and childhood (Bowlby 1975) helps us to understand how people relate to one another. The advent of illness can intensify, challenge or alter these patterns of attachment. Not only does illness have the potential to threaten existing attachments (especially where there is the possibility of death), but illness can also give rise to new attachments, such as in the patient–health care provider relationship. John Byng-Hall (1995) has provided a solid foundation for understanding attachment in human relationships, especially in the context of changing family relationships.

Typology of illness

An understanding of the main characteristics of an illness is important in order to determine how a person may be affected. Rolland (1994) distinguished between four dimensions: onset, course, outcome and degree of incapacitation. It is not necessary to have an extensive understanding of a particular illness in order to offer counselling to an affected person, but it is important to appreciate the time phase (especially if it is a chronic illness) and practical consequences of the condition. This also helps to determine the possible ramifications for the patient's relationships.

Development and life cycle

Developmental and life-cycle issues determine how an individual, couple or family are affected by illness. For an individual, this will depend on whether the person is a newly born infant, child, adolescent, adult, and so on. Couples and families also progress through a series of developmental phases and each may imply or lead to changes in relationships between people. A newly wed couple, reconstituted family, or couple facing the 'empty nest' may each be affected differently in response to illness in the family. Carter and McGoldrick (1989) and Edwards and Davis (1998) have written extensively about the psychological impact of health problems at different stages of individual, couple and family development.

Curiosity and questions

Counselling proceeds in many different ways. Reflection and interpretation are probably most commonly associated with the process of counselling. However, the clinical interview, using carefully thought-out questions, provides an important source of information for the counsellor (Tomm 1987). Questions are a main catalyst for patient change and healing. Different types of questions can be used to link comments on behaviour, beliefs, feelings and ideas about the future. The purpose of such questions is to heighten the counsellor's sense of curiosity (Cecchin 1987) and to avoid becoming judgemental or having a fixed view of the patient and the problem, rather than a desire to uncover a single 'truth'. Circular, reflexive and hypothetical or future-oriented questions (see Chapter 7) provide the patient and his family with the opportunity to view themselves in the context of relationships and to recognize different perspectives of the problem.

Language, narratives and meanings

Narrative therapy, which draws on the language and stories of the patient, helps to reveal meanings about problems and how problems come to be viewed as such. It can be used when working with the full range of somatic symptoms (Anderson and Goolishian 1988). The narrative approach avoids stigmatizing or blaming the patient and also uses language to help resolve or alleviate problems associated with health-related issues (Griffith and Griffith 1994). Different groups of professionals are taught to think about psychological problems in different and seemingly incompatible ways. Ailments of the mind and body are often conceptualized differently by counsellors, psychotherapists and family therapists, as they are by doctors, nurses and other health care providers. One result has been that some counsellors do not have patients referred to them who are suffering from a 'real' medical or psychological problem. Similarly, some counsellors may not think to explore 'medical' meanings associated with psychological problems. The problem becomes more complex when treating patients whose symptoms appear to lie at the intersection of the two. This includes those suffering from somatoform disorders, such as non-electrical seizures, persistent headaches or conversion paralysis.

Cognition and behaviour

The direct (and circular) relationship between cognition (thought) and behaviour (action) is central to an understanding of how problems are maintained and can be resolved. Many psychological problems or symptoms associated with health-related problems can be effectively treated with cognitive-behavioural therapy (Beck 1976). Cognitive-behaviour therapy is especially useful when treating patients suffering from anxiety, depression, insomnia and other problems typically seen in mental health care settings, as well as for pain management and chronic fatigue syndrome. Identifying early experiences, dysfunctional assumptions, critical incidents, negative automatic thoughts and other factors which may maintain the problem are first steps towards its resolution. Thinking errors or cognitive distortions are often implicated in mood-related problems stemming from ill health, hospitalization or fear of undergoing medical procedures. For patients referred for counselling because of a fear of physical pain or separation from the family, behavioural methods (such as desensitization) can be used to ameliorate some symptoms.

Time and timing

Illness brings into sharp focus issues about time and longevity. The prospect of a shortened life-span, or one in which quality of life is drastically curtailed, is often a source of psychological distress. Long-term counselling approaches may be neither desirable nor feasible in a context in which there is high demand for psychological care or where patients cannot regularly attend counselling sessions over a prolonged period because of their illness. Counsellors who work in health care settings may be required to be flexible and improvise, thereby remaining responsive to the patient's needs. Decisions have to be made about which problems can be treated and the duration of counselling.

One consequence may be the need to focus more on issues of timing in counselling. Some patients may not require a lengthy lead-in to counselling; they may be willing and able to work at a deep level from the outset. Others, by virtue of their views about counselling, their problem, how they view themselves as coping and the natural employment of defences, may never benefit from the range of psychotherapeutic interventions that could otherwise have been employed. The challenge in these settings is for the counsellor to either work more quickly and intensively, or more slowly and cautiously. It is important to keep in mind how the patient and others view progress and outcome in counselling, as this will influence whether the patient continues in treatment and whether the counsellor continues to receive referrals from the medical team. Some constraints may also relate to the physical setting, such as a lack of privacy or nowhere to sit comfortably with the patient while he receives treatment (for example, through a drip), and these may affect when sessions can be arranged and how long they last.

LEVELS OF COUNSELLING

It is useful to distinguish between different levels of counselling in order to illustrate the range of activities carried out by counsellors and also to help identify what 'mode' the counsellor may be engaged in at a particular time. Each level suggests a different relationship with the patient. For example, contrary to some beliefs, both lay and informed, about counselling, it is sometimes necessary for the counsellor to give information about treatment and care. This is usually in highly specialized fields where dedicated counsellors are part of a multidisciplinary team. The best known specialities which have a tradition of employing counsellors are oncology, HIV/AIDS, infertility, multiple sclerosis, haemophilia, spinal injury and paediatrics. The different levels of counselling should be viewed as a continuum rather than as discrete and unrelated activities:

- *Information-giving*: the provision of factual information and advice about medical conditions, laboratory tests, treatments, drug trials, disease prevention and health promotion, among others.
- *Implications counselling*: a discussion with the patient and/or others which addresses the implications of the information for the individual or family, and his personal circumstances.
- *Supportive counselling*: in which the emotional consequences of the information and its implications can be identified and addressed in a supportive and caring environment.
- *Psychotherapeutic counselling*: focuses on healing, psychological adjustment, coping and problem resolution.

The titles of 'counsellor' or 'psychotherapist' are largely interchangeable. Professional training, the preferences of other colleagues and the tasks undertaken may influence which professional title or 'hat' is chosen. It is reasonable to argue that in health care settings all counselling work involves psychotherapy, and vice versa. However, those trained to only undertake information-giving and implications counselling should not treat patients using psychotherapeutic approaches and techniques without further training and supervision. Untrained and unsupervised counsellors may be ineffective or even damaging to the patient.

STAGES OF COUNSELLING IN HEALTH CARE SETTINGS

Most counsellors are comfortable exploring issues and concerns with patients without too much reliance on a structure or agenda. There is wide variation in how sessions are conducted and managed, usually in response to the needs and concerns of the patient, where the patient is seen, the context in which the counsellor works, and the counsellor's professional training. In health care settings where patients are physically ill, counsellors must be able to respond to and cope with a high level of unpredictability and emotional intensity. Ideally, a range of issues needs to be covered with patients in a first session, in a reasonably logical manner, progressing from one issue to the next.

The special circumstances and features of counselling in health care settings may mean that an initial consultation is the only direct patient contact in some cases (see Chapter 15). Consequently, the counsellor needs to be adept in making an assessment and intervening all in the same session. Unlike in some other settings, patients may not benefit from follow-up because they may not want or need further sessions. They may opt to be treated elsewhere and receive psychological support in another setting, they may recover and be discharged, or they may become more unwell and even die. Flexibility is required to ensure that the patient's needs are highlighted and met. This is also achieved by collaborative practice, as described below.

PRACTICAL HINTS FOR IMPROVING COLLABORATION IN HEALTH CARE SETTINGS

Whatever theoretical approach the counsellor uses, he will be challenged by the dynamics that exist within any health care setting and by those that are unique to a particular setting. It is helpful to strive to work collaboratively in order to be valued as a team member.

The 'rules' for collaborative and effective practice in health care settings vary from one context to another. Opportunities to reflect on practice in a wide range of health care settings through collaborative work, case discussions, peer supervision, consultation and research have highlighted some ways to enhance practice without straying beyond the boundaries of professional competence. Some ideas that have helped to achieve this are listed below.

- *Make no assumptions* about what constitutes a problem, for whom it is a problem, how people should cope with illness or disability, or how they should relate to one another. Also, do not assume that they understand their illness, its implications, treatment and so on.
- *Practise collaboratively* as part of a team. Dispel the myth that counsellors always have their own agenda and 'get on their high horse' in order to assert their views and opinion.

- *Be humble* but communicate directly. Learn from others and be tentative if you are unsure. Do not overstate the importance of counselling – patients rarely live or die by what happens in counselling, and medical and nursing concerns should take precedence. Refer patients to other colleagues where appropriate, but do not be reticent to offer directives if indicated.
- *Learn about health care issues* by attending case meetings and lectures, sitting in with doctors when they consult with patients, learning the language of the health care staff, and acquiring and developing an interest in anthropology and sociology so as to learn more about the health care setting.
- *Be curious*: adopt a stance of receptive openness and ask questions. Avoid making assumptions and becoming prescriptive.
- *Be flexible* about where you see patients, when you see them, your working hours, and approaches used in counselling for which there may be a special demand in a health care setting (cognitive-behavioural and family therapy). Work at the patient's pace and determine whether the problem is best solved by open-ended, exploratory counselling or by problem-focused counselling.
- *Be time conscious*: aim to achieve the most within the time constraints. Learn how to do counselling briefly. When feeding back to other colleagues, either verbally or in a letter, be succinct and to the point; avoid wordy and lengthy reports and unfocused discussions about patients.
- *Be proactive* by not waiting for problems to occur. Waiting for patients to identify and talk about their problems and fears may make it too late to help in any practical way, or the patient may believe that you too are colluding with his denial of the problem.
- *Where appropriate, give information*: counselling should be more a dialogue than a monologue. Do not be afraid to give information or suggest who the patient can talk to if he requires more specialist information (although doctors and nurses must be consulted if the information required is about medical concerns).
- *Practise defensively*: patients are increasingly conscious of their rights and what they can expect from health care professionals and in the course of their treatment. In some cases this can lead to litigation or a complaint to hospital/clinic managers or your professional body. The likelihood of this being done is reduced if (a) you refrain from making unrealistic claims, (b) you defer to doctors or nurses when in doubt about how to deal with a problem, (c) you keep factual notes of what happens in sessions but limit your opinions to what has been deduced from observations of behaviour, i.e. have evidence, and (d) you are curious and only offer ideas and opinions tentatively. Be accountable to your profession, colleagues and managers of the institution or setting in which you practise by giving feedback about your work and related problems without necessarily breaching patient confidentiality.
- *Be practical*: as counsellors we are sometimes longwinded and over-cerebral in response to patient problems. Learn to make rapid decisions, take small risks and think imaginatively, yet practically, about possible solutions.
- *Respect patients' defences*, which may serve to protect them. Talk about what you observe with the patient, but it is not always necessary to confront or directly challenge their defences. Counter any suggestion of blame for illness from either the patient or family members.
- *Sustain realistic hope*: therapeutic neutrality sometimes interferes with our ability to

offer supportive and comforting words to the patient and others. By focusing on practical issues it may be possible to give a message of some realistic hope without denying the gravity of the situation. Similarly, it is important not to shy away from discussing issues about death, dying, disfigurement, loss and pain when it is obvious that these need to be openly addressed. Help the patient to see a future and to participate in decision-making for it.

- *Suggest participation in rituals*, or create rituals which help people to focus on a particular issue or event (a birth or a death). Rituals give meaning to events, help to amplify feelings in a focused way and in a supportive context, and are a part of everyday life. Counsellors can help their patients create personally meaningful rituals to help them cope better with their circumstances, and some even participate in these with their patients and their family.
- *Help patients to gain a sense of mastery over their situations* by involving them in decisions. Work toward increasing their choices or options. Avoid fostering too much dependence as this may be counter-productive.
- *Evaluate your practice*: it is good practice to audit and evaluate your work. This can also help in the maintenance and development of your counselling service. Decisions about health care delivery are increasingly made on evidence-based practice. Evaluation and audit of counselling practice should be initiated by counsellors, as otherwise there is a danger that others will take charge of the evaluation process.
- *Dress according to the context*: unlike doctors and nurses, counsellors do not have a uniform or any props (stethoscopes or white coats) to identify them. Even so, most hospitals and clinics are rather conservative establishments and expect conservative and formal attire. Expectations may be different for counsellors working in community and outreach settings.
- *Teach others*: the accusation that some counsellors do not help other health care professionals to understand more about the psychological process and counselling is not without foundation. Offer to give seminars, invite colleagues to case discussions, collaborate in research and offer to see patients jointly with another professional colleague. Foster a climate of openness about your work; this may help others to understand better what you do with patients and may lead them to be more supportive of your service.

CONCLUSION

Different theoretical approaches contribute complementary ideas to the practice of counselling in health care settings. The emphasis in counselling should be on developing an integrative approach which brings together different ideas and skills in a unifying conceptual framework, rather than an eclecticism which may seem confusing or muddled in practice. The approach described in this book is mainly derived from family-systems theory, with an emphasis on solution-focused counselling. Experience has taught us to be receptive to ideas developed outside our main theoretical framework and to integrate these into our practice.

CHAPTER 3

Beliefs about Illness and Counselling

INTRODUCTION

This chapter provides a brief overview of the construction of meaning systems by individuals, families and cultural groups. Meaning systems can be understood as a collection of verbal and non-verbal communications that explain, give meaning to and understanding for personal, family and social experiences. The specific meaning system explored here is the illness meaning system and its impact on patients, family members and health care professionals in medical experiences.

THEORETICAL BACKGROUND

Meaning systems can be understood as constructions or co-constructions which include societal, cultural, moral and religious values held by individuals, families, and social and cultural groups. These groups typically hold common values, e.g. specific beliefs about appropriate and inappropriate behaviours of individuals and family members. Such values can address social and cultural actions, encounters with professionals and relationships with others. This chapter explores different ways that these constructions of illness meaning systems affect patients, their families, counsellors and health care professionals.

In addition to illness meaning systems, which include individually held under-standings about symptoms, illness, diagnosis, procedures and treatment plans, every health care experience involves generally held understandings. Headaches, colds or coughs, for example, often invoke familial or cultural understandings, e.g. 'Feed a cold, starve a fever', or a lump in the breast could indicate cancer. Patients and their families express their understanding of the illness experience to health care professionals through words, sounds and non-verbalizations such as facial expressions and gestures. Each verbalization or non-verbalization about a patient's expressed understanding of illness invites a response from all involved family members, counsellors and health care professionals. Patients often reflect behaviours of isolation, anger and confusion with emotional outbursts as a demonstration of how they view their illness.

Each convention for making sense of illness encompasses a specific social or cultural group sense of illness. This can involve rituals, special foods, or religious beliefs of other members of a patient's group. The beliefs of patients about their bodies can connect them to or disconnect them from medical experiences in many ways. The perceived relationship between body and mind varies from culture to culture. Western culture, for example, often views patients' bodies as separate from patients' thoughts or emotions; non-Western societies often view patients' bodies as linked with and connected to other members within their cultural group. Chinese traditions may think of patients' bodies and illnesses as expressing harmony or disharmony with their environment. The Navaho culture views a person's body as a landscape and illness as scars on the landscape; when a tribal member becomes ill, this may be not only a reflection/expression of physical illness but may be also connected with the pollution of Mother Earth (Kleinman 1988).

Other cultures also have symbolic representations for their members' bodies and bodily illnesses, which are dealt with in a manner congruent with the symbol. For example, the Aborigines of Australia view a member's skin as a sacred symbol. The skin is named and becomes a means of identification with, and status within, the group. To the Aborigines, a member's illnesses will mar his identification and affect his status or position as, for example, hunter or tracker, affecting the performance of his functions (Kleinman 1988). In some industrialized countries with well-developed health care services, a person's body is often viewed as a machine; if a part is worn, e.g. a patient's heart valve leaks, it can be replaced with a porcine or mechanical one. These examples illustrate how a variety of different meaning systems can offer counsellors and health care professionals latitude in interpretations that explain patient, family and group feelings, as well as perceptions and processes about illness and its impact.

Subtle pieces of information encoded within local and universal illness meaning systems are useful for designing patients' treatment and recovery plans. This subtle information can be thought of as idiosyncratic illness indicators, unique to patients and their families. These communicate information about a patient's past family illness history; past symptom recognition, treatment and coping skills; current health concerns; and current coping skills with illness (see Chapter 8 on genograms).

Idiosyncratic illness communications are often unique to a particular patient and family, with cultural and societal connections to words, behaviours, gestures and special foods – every culture has its own form of 'chicken soup'. Such communications fit a particular family's need in any specific situation. The following is an example of this:

Risotto is an Italian rice dish found in a variety of versions throughout Italy. In one Italian family, all members knew when a family member came down with a cold or fever from the flu, all because the smell of cooking risotto would fill the house. The risotto would be made with chicken broth for a cold or vegetable broth for a fever. Its only known bio-medical curative property was psychological in nature, prompting family support, soothing words, loving gestures and a good meal. The patient's cold or fever still had to run its full course but the entire family shared the psychosocial benefits of this specially prepared meal. The risotto, an ethnic food, held additional meanings and psychosocial benefits for this particular family.

Subtle forms of idiosyncratic illness communication are present in all families and become pronounced in interactions with health care professionals when patients present as ill. These communications can become so pronounced that they may interfere with information-gathering in a health care setting. When this occurs, the direct attention of a counsellor is needed because of potentially detrimental or emotionally damaging effects for patients and their family members. The following is an illustration of how a family's and health care professional's local, universal and idiosyncratic illness communications affected a health care situation.

An infant was rushed to the hospital by her mother and grandmother. The baby's father followed in another car. The health care team had difficulty gathering information essential for giving the infant proper medical assistance because the mother and grandmother were exchanging heated words over who should provide the answers. Both women were trying to answer the nurse's questions.

The Asian nurse was aware that the younger woman was the baby's mother. However, the nurse's cultural and social background trained her to ignore the mother's input in favour of the grandmother's information while the attending doctor was conducting an examination. The father arrived just as the nurse said that only the infant's parents were allowed in the treatment room with the baby. The mother, father and grandmother went in with the baby and they continued to fight among themselves. The physician noted that the baby showed additional signs of distress each time the mother's voice was raised in response to a statement of the grandmother's that it was because of the father's questionable heritage that her granddaughter inherited ill health.

At this point the physician ordered all the adults out of the room and turned his attention back to the infant. The infant's condition was serious enough to warrant being admitted to the hospital. The nurse returned to inform the parents of their daughter's condition and the treatment plan. The young couple engaged in another fight. The baby's mother began screaming, crying and hitting the father on his chest. Both were yelling at the grandmother to stay out of their decisions because they were the baby's parents, while she was only the baby's grandmother.

The attending physician and the nurse witnessed the adults' behaviour. The mother continued to pound on the father's chest and the father tried to restrain the baby's mother. The health care team members did not hear the verbal exchange because they were too far away. The physician told the nurse to call the family protection agency and report this apparent abuse situation. The parents and grandmother were then told to keep quiet and the physician told them that the baby's condition was serious and required admission to the hospital.

The mother again began crying, shaking and pounding on the father's chest, with the grandmother crying loudly in the background. This situation was emotionally out of control, adding additional strain to the family members. The infant received medical attention; however, the family protection professional said that the father had to leave the hospital and both parents were not allowed to see their daughter. The grandmother was allowed to see her granddaughter and the mother was ordered by the family protection professional to move back into her mother's home. The father was not to live with or see his baby or the baby's mother until they received counselling to handle their anger and physical displays. The family protection professional referred the couple to a medical counsellor two weeks after their initial medical crisis. The couple at the time of the first visit were still living apart and the mother had full responsibility for her daughter's medical care.

This situation was filled with all the participants' verbal and non-verbal communications from their local, universal and idiosyncratic illness meaning systems. Each participant had their own ideas about illness as well as appropriate behaviour and were unaware of how each other's systems subtly began to impact on the health care situation. In other words, the parents, grandmother, nurse and physician each held their own interpretations of what was happening during the infant's medical emergency.

The parents and grandmother came to the hospital already deeply involved in their established family history, with patterns of subtle communication with each other, past medical history, current health concerns, and past and present coping skills. The health care professionals were unaware of how this family interacted daily with each other or how their world-views affected what they did. The health care professionals were also unaware of how their own meaning systems, and cultural, societal and professional values could affect this family in a less than helpful manner.

However, this family and the health care professionals held enough universally held meanings and verbal and non-verbal communications in common to impart information about illness as well as behaviour. Each of the participants was trying to work in a collaborative manner without acknowledging that a new relationship with its own idiosyncratic communications had been formed during the baby's medical emergency. The new relationship and communications were a blending, first, of the patient–family–nurse; second, of the patient–family–nurse–physician; third, of the patient–family–nurse–physician–family protection agency. Note that:

- Some members in the health care relationship were less able to communicate effectively with other participants through their words and actions.
- Each member's level of skill in making verbal or non-verbal communications clearly influenced other participants' behaviours and the degree of support received, and created unnecessary distance by conveying emotions such as anger.
- Each member was affected by the other participants' meaning systems in this health care situation.
- A more self-reflective and referential meaning system would have been useful for this young couple and their daughter, to help them cope with their medical experience.

A counsellor, by being self-reflective and referential, enters a relationship with patients and their families through their meaning system and world-view. This is where an understanding perspective begins. The counsellor can offer other health care professionals different interpretations and alternative considerations about patients, their families' interactions and illness meaning systems to reduce emotional stress for all involved.

An effective health care experience provides patients and their families with the assurance that their concerns and experiences are legitimate. In the previous illustration, a counsellor's ability would have been useful to interpret the separate and inclusive meaning systems of the patient, the family and the health care professionals. A counsellor could have pointed out to the health care professionals that this family's current concerns and coping skills were reactions to their immediate health care situation. Attentive interventions could help bridge the gap between the different perspectives of the family, nurse and doctor. The counsellor could then have worked with the family protection professional to determine if the couple's perceived anger or abusive responses were chronic, warranting immediate interventions, or simply the result of ineffective coping skills for managing a crisis situation.

Trained counsellors can alert colleagues such as doctors and nurses to the different illness meaning systems that influence patient and family communications about illness, and can promote awareness that no one way of communicating is better than another. Acknowledging differences makes it easier to separate patients' psychological reactions to biomedical symptoms from psychopathological displays that warrant intervention. This can greatly improve the medical experiences shared by patients, their families and health care professionals.

STIGMA AND DISCRIMINATION

Some diseases carry a moral illness stigma arising from widely held cultural or moral values. This fosters a lower biomedical priority for some illnesses, particularly when there is a belief that the disease is 'self-inflicted', such as lung cancer from cigarette smoking, coronary heart disease from diet or lifestyle, and HIV disease from unprotected intercourse or the sharing of contaminated intravenous needles by drug users. When illnesses are implied to be self-inflicted, confined to a specific gender (see Chapter 18), or have a stigma attached, the stresses of the health care experience increase.

Illness discrimination and stigmas tend to go unrecognized but their effect is felt by all involved. The result is often isolation of patients from their families and social groups, and families from their sick members, other family members, social groups and health care resources. This complicates the whole process of diagnosis and treatment, leading to compliance, a false sense of security, unfounded fears, symptom ignorance or delayed health care, which eventually create major health care concerns. Idiosyncratic illness symptoms go largely unrecognized. The repercussions may be treatment non-compliance, miscommunication in health care consultations, hypochondria and misunderstandings of patients' behaviours.

Counsellors and health care professionals can form new relationships with patients and their families by developing unique illness meaning systems which include all participants in health care settings. These newly formed health care relationship illness meaning systems are a blending of each participant's individual meaning system. This blended meaning system can help clarify perceptions about the reactions of patients, family members and health care professionals to health problems. For example, a patient may lack current coping skills due to previously disastrous medical experiences which resulted from varied perceptions about correct behaviour. Often, these unrecognized perceptions result in additional stress for the health care professional, which in turn raises the level of emotional stress for patients and their families. This in turn affects subsequent patients who are diagnosed, treated, and living with illnesses that carry stigmas, which in turn increases their stress level and pain.

The following example of a patient and health care team working together with a counsellor shows how meaning systems can work together to provide satisfactory health care for patients.

Patient: I had no idea this was going to happen to me. This was a big shock and that's why – I was . . . I feel so angry. I didn't even have a chance to do anything to investigate it or to prepare myself or to say no, I want this doctor, I want that doctor. I went in for tests and woke up with tubes and stuff . . . wh-where was I? That's my anger. Everyone made choices for me.

Counsellor: So you think that if you had been able to talk right after the surgery, that it would have been different for you?

Patient: It would've – yes, because every time I wanted to say something about it [she is referring to her surgery], I would get shut up. You've got to be glad you're alive. Look at it, you could have been dead, you could've been in a box, you could've been this – I know I could have been all these things, but that doesn't mean that I don't have feelings, as to the way it [her surgery] occurred and I recovered.

Counsellor: Umm hmm.

Patient: That's why I'm upset. You know what I'm saying? I'm not saying that the end result was not beneficial to me. Of course it is. I'd have to be a moron to say that it was not beneficial as far as I'm concerned. But maybe – maybe because I've been in psychotherapy before. Okay, that I understand certain things . . . I have to say things . . . that gotta come out. And if they don't come out, they choke me. And pills aren't the answer. I'll come away from you with hope back here [she points to her heart]. And then the rest is up to me. I had to make the time, I had to make the effort, it's my job – it's my life and my body and my mind. You can't be with me seven days a week and certainly not forever. But this is a temporary thing, I think, just to get me on my feet which I appreciate. Don't get me wrong. But I have to still do the work.

Counsellor: Mm hmm. I must say you have really been doing the work by going through it and sharing your experience.

Patient: I try very hard. [cries]

Counsellor: You've been going through it.

This patient needed to process the meaning of her medical experience, which is very important to her, because these unexpressed feelings were impeding her recovery. She was left with feelings of loss of control and dissatisfaction until the counsellor allowed her to express her feelings. During the interview the counsellor discovered that this patient had a legitimate reason for being dissatisfied. In the following extract, the patient refers to her scar and her reactions to it.

Patient: Now, I don't like him. I don't like me. I don't like the way I look. I hate this scar. The doctors tell me, 'You're lucky to be alive.' I say, yes . . . but I feel unlucky. You know, I have a useless left arm which I learned to live with. But at least I had a nice bust-line. Now, I have this ugly scar down my chest and scars across my breasts. I don't like to look at me and I don't like my husband to look at me. I'd like to punch whoever sewed me up. I'd like to punch him out. Didn't he know he was working on a woman? I can say it and feel it and I don't care who the fuck hears me. Because he did not consider me as a woman, because I have been in that hospital – I can't tell you how many times I've seen his other patients. I haven't seen one patient that has scars like mine or with staples on their chests except this schmuk sitting here. And why didn't I question it before? Where was my brain?

Counsellor: You were just saying to me how quickly everything was done, how quickly the surgery came about, how quickly you were feeling anger and you were in for tests and boom, you're on the operating table, just about. Um, I think maybe you're just feeling shock and I think. . . .

Patient: [Interrupts] Maybe. I – I remember telling him – I remember even saying to Dr Sloane when he first told me about it. He said there was no way to avoid it. I'm so mad at myself. How stupid, so stupid I am.

Counsellor: So what could you do now not to be so mad?

Patient: I think this is it. I am able to say it. I'm able to get it out and say it. I don't have to think about it and swallow it. And doing something about it. [She was also going to a plastic surgeon.] The surgeon said that he was very glad I came in when I did. He said if I had waited for a year, that he doesn't know if anything could have been done for me unless it was surgical. Now he is treating my scar and now I have hope. Uh, let me tell you. I undid a little last night. And looked for the first time and it's uh, it's flat like this [points to the table top] and it's not quite a week. It's already disappearing. But the lumps – and the discoloration will fade eventually. It will become flat and that's what I want. I don't care if it's a flat scar. I'm only concerned that it doesn't stick up. I'm not complaining that I have a scar here. What I complained about is that it's so ugly and raised. He injected it with silicone. And over it placed a rubber strip that I have to wear all day. He said it'll probably take about two to three months. It will be better.

Counsellor: Does it go all the way down from the neck?

Patient: Yes. I really – I really get excited about this part – and over here or somewhere, about this much is flat [takes finger to illustrate the measurement]. I have to go back a week from Friday and he'll look at how it's doing, he may have to inject it again but we'll go from there. Okay, he said, the chances of it working by itself were maybe 10 per cent. If I had waited a year like people say, wait a year and it will fade. So whereas now it's about 90 per cent that it will work because the incision is still new. I dread telling my cardiologist about the plastic surgeon but I have to handle it when the time comes.

Counsellor: Why would you dread telling the cardiologist?

Patient: Because he likes to be the one [laughs] who says do this or do that. And he's – I tell you he brushed it off [the scar] and I should be happy to be alive. Like it was all over my head. About needing this surgery. Even the plastic surgeon said that it was an ugly scar.

This example illustrates that patients and health care professionals can have different understandings of which issues are important to focus on or act upon for the patients' successful treatment and recovery from surgery.

Counsellors can help reduce stress in health care settings by providing patients, their families and professionals with a treatment model that uses many perspectives, as will be discussed in subsequent chapters. For example, health care teams can use every interaction or meaning system as a treatment resource for the noncompliant patient and family members. Counsellors can reframe stress or tension as a positive by pointing out, for example, that in health care relationships it is common for patients and sometimes doctors and nurses to experience stress, and that some tension is useful because it increases both personal and professional vigilance. Attentive counsellors can interrupt emotionally damaging cycles of reactions between patients, families and health care professionals at the beginning of health care. However, counselling is often offered in health care treatments only as a last resort after the traditional methods for treating patients' emotional cycles have been exhausted. Medication, expensive investigations, surgery, rehabilitation, diet, behaviour modification and so on are commonly prescribed first. Counselling as relief for emotional stress and tension is almost never offered, which is unfortunate because any illness affects not only patients and their family members but also the health care professionals involved.

EXPLORING BELIEFS IN COUNSELLING SESSIONS

The emphasis thus far in this chapter has been on the theoretical ideas which underpin illness meaning systems and their relevance to counselling. This section lists the ten most relevant beliefs about health, illness and treatment which are likely to arise in the course of counselling, and illustrates how to set about exploring them in sessions.

Beliefs may either be constraining or facilitative (Wright *et al.* 1996) and are at the heart of understanding how the patient and family cope with and adapt to illness. The counsellor can gain an understanding of these beliefs by asking directly about them. For example: 'What is your view about how this new treatment will help with these symptoms?' Meanings given to medical events, treatment and care are important because they can further or inhibit an understanding of disagreements between family members, between the patient and doctor, and between members of the health care staff. A lack of concurrence can cause or exacerbate psychological problems, or even prove hazardous in some situations. A patient may, for example, believe that his illness has been caused by some 'wrongdoing' earlier in his life and consequently seek out a traditional healer rather than a medically qualified doctor for assessment and treatment. Another patient may not be fully informed about recent advances in the treatment of a condition and erroneously believe that he is about to die. Disagreement over the diagnosis and views about the efficacy of treatment may lead to the patient not complying with the prescribed treatment regime. Below is a list of topics which help to address patients' views about the causation of illness, the prognosis, family relationships and what counselling can offer. Examples of questions to patients which may help to explore those beliefs are listed below.

Information from the medical system about the problem

It is important to understand what the patient has been told by doctors and nurses about his illness, its cause and possible outcome. Establish whether the patient agrees with what he has been told or whether he has alternative views. Finally, find out whether the patient has been given an opportunity to discuss some of his own views about the medical problem and how these ideas were received by others. Some examples of questions:

'What have you been told by the doctors?'
'What do you think they see as the problem?'
'Do you agree with them?'
'Do you have any ideas as to what might have caused this problem?'
'Have you been able to discuss these with the doctor? If not, what has prevented this from happening?'
'Is there anything you want to know more about that has not been discussed with you?'
'Is there anything you would prefer not to be told about?'

Information from the patient and family about the problem

In the same way as it is important to understand what the patient has been told by professionals, the views and beliefs of other family members should also be discussed. It is then helpful to explore whether there is agreement or some difference of opinion between the patient, family and health care professionals, as this may be the source of relationship and personal problems.

'What do family members think about the problem?'
'Do they all agree with one another or are there differences of view within the family?'
'Whose ideas do you agree with the most?'
'Have any family members discussed your condition with the doctor? What came of that?'
'How might you deal with disagreements that may arise between yourself, the family, and the doctor?'

Ideas about the source or cause of illness

It is incorrect to assume that only people treated outside modern, Western health care settings are likely to have non-medical views about the source or cause of illness. Lay beliefs are just as common among patients attending specialist and highly developed medical centres. Knowledge about how the patient believes he may have contracted the illness may also help to understand the patient's views about and attitude towards treatment, especially if an alternative and possibly conflicting view has been discussed with the patients by others, such as a relative or another professional. Some ideas about the cause of illness are socially created; for example, in the early 1980s some people believed that AIDS was caused by promiscuity. Others hold the view that infertility automatically results from a past sexually transmitted disease and is therefore just punishment for premarital sexual intercourse.

'How do you think you contracted this condition?'
'What do you think caused your illness?'
'Do you have any ideas about why this has happened now?'

Previous history and experience of health-related problems, and meaning of illness or disability

How a person reacts and subsequently adjusts to their illness is influenced by previous personal experience either of illness or of helping a relative or friend to cope with illness. Patients often fear that they will suffer in the same way as a relative who, for example, had cancer or another debilitating and potentially painful condition. Similarly, a person who has enjoyed several months free of symptoms while their illness was in remission may find it especially difficult to face up to the prospect of re-hospitalization and further treatment and may deny the fact that they have relapsed. It is therefore important to explore previous experience of illness and treatment.

> 'Have you previously had a serious illness?'
> 'What helped you to cope?'
> 'Has anyone else in your family or any close friends had a serious illness?'
> 'What effect did this have on you?'
> 'How does this affect how you see things now for yourself?'

Ideas about what medical investigations and treatment can offer

Although similar to the first point, this directly addresses the issues of prognosis and the likely endpoint of medical treatment and its consequences. Patients who suffer from a chronic or life-threatening condition are likely to reflect on the limits of modern Western medical treatment and to consider either alternatives (e.g. complementary therapies) or the cessation of the active treatment. Sometimes it may be difficult to discuss issues of this nature openly with the patient, particularly if the doctors continue to treat the patient when palliative or respite care may be more applicable. Patients, families and health care staff may each hold different views as to the limits of active treatment, and these may also change during the course of the illness and from patient to patient. Open discussion about these views can help to avoid unnecessary suffering and conflicting opinions about treatment.

> 'What are your views about how the treatment is helping?'
> 'Have you given any thought to how much more treatment you would want to undergo?'
> 'Who would be inclined to agree with you?'
> 'Have you been able to discuss this with anyone?'
> 'What have been/might be their views?'
> 'What might need to happen for your ideas to change?'

Ideas about information and its dissemination

Patients may present with problems that are medical but have psychological and social implications. Foremost among these are issues pertaining to confidentiality and secrecy (see Chapter 9). In an attempt to 'protect' others, patients may choose not to tell anyone else about the illness, denying themselves the benefit of social support. The effect of keeping a secret is seldom completely positive or negative. Confidentiality between members of a health care team can also give rise to problems, as some colleagues may feel excluded by virtue of their not having being told about a patient's condition. It is important to recognize that the patient's views about who should be told may change over time, not only because of the obvious signs of advancing disease or disability, but also in response to counselling or discussion with others.

'Is there anyone you would like to tell about the diagnosis you were given today?'
'How do you think this may affect them, and their relationships with you?'
'Is there anyone you would prefer not to tell?'
'What does this suggest about the relationship between them and you?'
'At what point do you think your views about this may change?'
'If your husband asks you about your prognosis, what do you think you will say to him?'
'How do you think keeping a secret from him about your diagnosis may affect your relationship with him?'

The person's position or role within the family

Life-cycle and developmental issues affect how people view the impact of illness. Views may be different depending whether, for example, it is a child dying before its parents, or an elderly relative who has already been unwell for several years. Similarly, the loss may have different implications if the person is a mother, a child, breadwinner, childbearer and childrearer, or single parent. Exploring the actual or anticipated loss associated with a person's position or role within the family can help them address the meaning and implications of different losses, and how they might cope and adapt.

'What position or role do you hold in the family?'
'What do you feel that others may think might be lost if you were unable to fulfil this role?'
'If you were unable to fulfil this role, who else do you think would be able to do so?'
'Who could provide additional help and support so that you could continue to fulfil this role?'
'Who is most likely to be able to take on some of your responsibilities?'

Ideas about the psychological resilience of the patient or family members

Perceptions of or assumptions about how people may cope (whether it is the patient or family) determine how people relate to one another and what is said between them. If, for example, the health care professional or family members believe that a person would not cope well with bad news, this will influence whether, how, what and when they are told. Some views may be derived from family myths about coping or actual events in the past when severe psychological problems were directly linked to news of illness or death in the family.

'How do you imagine your wife will cope with the news?'
'What makes you think that she would not cope well?'
'How would you know that she is not coping?'
'Has this happened in the past? What actually happened?'
'Just say your wife found out by accident, how do you think she would react?'

Ideas about the future

This is similar to views about treatment and prognosis (see above) but directly addresses the outcome at a psychological level and can help to open up discussion about the most feared outcome or fantasy (see Chapter 11). It is important to explore whether the future is feared or welcomed by different family members and not to make assumptions about how people might adapt and cope. Problems may arise if hopes or fears are unrealistic in the face of medical evidence, possibly creating an impasse in treatment or leading to potentially hazardous outcomes, such as the patient not attending regularly for follow-up.

'How do you see the future as things stand now?'
'Does it look any different from when we last spoke?'
'How do you think others see the future for you?'
'Is this openly discussed, or is this what you imagine they think?'
'What do you most look forward to?'
'What do you most fear?'

Ideas about what counselling can offer

The majority of patients seen by counsellors in health care settings are unlikely to have had previous experience of therapy and counselling. Some may be bewildered or frightened by a referral, expressing concern that others may feel they are not coping well or that it implies that they are psychologically disturbed. Others may welcome the contact and an opportunity to talk with a receptive professional, but have little understanding about how counselling may help. Previous experience of counselling which was perceived as unhelpful or harmful may result in the patient feeling resistant or behaving in an uncooperative manner. Open discussion with patients about the referral, their expectations and needs can help to avoid misunderstandings which could otherwise adversely affect the therapeutic process.

'Have you previously talked to a counsellor or therapist?'
'What first went through your mind when it was mentioned that it might be a good idea for us to meet?'
'Do you have any ideas about how this meeting could be of help, or how you would like it to be of help?'

CONCLUSION

An individual's understanding of what is meant by illness, health care experiences and health is situated within cultural, societal and universal meaning systems. These are publicly and privately held by patients, families, social groups and health care professionals. Meaning systems impact on each other through values and beliefs about illness, diagnosis, symptom recognition, treatment and the recovery process. Health care relationships are unique because they are formed at a specific time, for a specific purpose, and require degrees of intensity and involvement from all participants, e.g. patients, their families, social agencies and health care professionals.

Counsellors and health care professionals tend to agree that health care relationships are complex because of the social boundaries and rules that are found in any interpersonal relationship. Miscommunication can be due in part to different illness meaning systems coming together, which then combine and construct another illness meaning system for those involved in the current health care relationship. For example, fatigue is often misinterpreted by patients and family members as indicating that the patient's condition is worse than previously indicated by the health care professionals. However, this may not be the case at all if the fatigue indicates that the patient is feeling better and is naturally beginning to feel the increase of their level of activity. Counsellors can help to integrate different meaning aspects into the development of effective action and identification of communication patterns.

CHAPTER 4

Reframing and Creating Balance in Patient Beliefs

INTRODUCTION

Many psychological problems stemming from health-related concerns have their origins in personal beliefs about coping with adversity and disability. They may also arise where previous experiences, including one's upbringing, do not sufficiently prepare an individual, couple or family to cope with the changes brought about by illness or disability. These problems frequently relate to coping with uncertainty (about the course of the illness, the outcome, the effectiveness of treatment, and so on), feelings of hopelessness, a denial of the severity of the problem, fear of loss or abandonment, and resentment towards care-takers for having to depend on them. Family members may perceive patients as brooding, depressed, passive, confused or agitated, which in turn may lead patients and health care providers to perceive the patient's family members as demanding or hypervigilant on behalf of their ill family member. These complex dynamics may, in turn, affect relationships as people either avoid talking about their fears or anxieties, or appear to talk about nothing else. Resilience may be related to the extent to which others are involved in the patient's care.

THE THEORY BEHIND REFRAMING IN COUNSELLING

'Reframing' is a psychotherapeutic intervention which can address complex relationship dynamics, especially at times when it appears that coping and adjustment are being thwarted by reliance on unhelpful beliefs. Reframing as an intervention serves to introduce new views and possibilities. The approach, firmly embedded in systemic theory, directly reflects the concept of the relativity of people's views and feelings. It is closely connected to Bateson's (1979) idea of 'difference', which introduces the concept of balance or complementarity. 'Happiness', for example, can only be comprehended in the context of, say, 'unhappiness' or 'despondency'.

A range of therapeutic themes can be discussed with patients. There are many possible views of reality. *Counselling can introduce to the patient a different view of the problem, that is, reframe the problem.* Campbell and Draper (1985: 7) state that 'many families who are "struck" with a problem have lost contact with multiple views of problems or reality. The meaning they attach to symptomatic behaviour becomes lineal, that is, "it is mad or it is bad".' One task of the counsellor, in such cases, may be to identify the patient's beliefs about his problems and to offer alternative views where appropriate. This is done by addressing both sides, or the complement, of a particular theme. Some of the most common themes pertaining to patients' concerns that arise in the context of illness, presented as complements, are shown in Figure 4.1.

Life ◀──▶ Death

Openness ◀──▶ Secrets

Wanting to know ◀──▶ Not wanting to know

Hope ◀──▶ Hopelessness

Past ◀──▶ Present ◀──▶ Future (temporal issues)

Resentment of dependence ◀──▶ Fear of abandonment

Separateness ◀──▶ Involvement

Relationship with family of origin ◀──▶ Relationship with family of affiliation

Individual concerns ◀──▶ Family concerns

Change ◀──▶ Preservation

Figure 4.1 Counselling themes as complements

Addressing the complement of a problem is the beginning of a reframe. The counsellor may be able to reframe one side of the problem in the context of the other. The need for separateness, for example, may be viewed in relation to levels of involvement and dependence, and vice versa. Some counsellors only place emphasis on one side of the problem, such as fear of dying, hopelessness, depression, dysfunction and pathology. Neither the counsellor nor the patient considers other possible views of the same problem, mainly because the initial problem presented by the patient may also reflect this one-sided emphasis. By addressing the complement, the counsellor may be able to amplify, add complexity to, and ultimately reframe, the patient's view of his problems. This may not only influence or change the patient's view of his illness, but may have a ripple effect on other people's views, such as the family and health care providers.

By using circular questions and addressing hypothetical outcomes (see Chapter 7), new ideas, beliefs and connections may emerge. Discussing the complementary aspects of an idea can help to change the patient's perceptions of a problem, leading to emotional and behavioural change. This can be achieved where the patient comes to a different understanding of his situation by making new connections and recognizing alternative but plausible perspectives to a problem. In the seemingly hopeless situation of a fatal illness, a patient may, for example, recognize the extent of caring and closeness in his family for the first time.

The patient's sense of autonomy and capacity to cope may be enhanced by providing a context in which the patient can recognize that *he* is the resource for dealing effectively with difficulties and the potential for confusion which may threaten his psychological stability. This can be done, for example, by validating *all* the patient's perceptions and adopting a non-oppositional stance, whilst at the same time carefully introducing ideas about the complementary side of the problem. This therapeutic task of reframing is rarely used and yet it is especially relevant and helpful in a context where patients, their care-takers and professionals hold rigid views and beliefs. Reframing is a potentially powerful therapeutic intervention, but counsellors require training and supervision in order to prevent its misuse. The patient's view of the problem should not be invalidated.

EXAMPLES OF ADDRESSING THE COMPLEMENT IN PRACTICE

A number of complements may arise in the course of counselling. These are described below and the method of reframing is also illustrated with short examples.

Life and death

Many medical conditions are potentially (and sometimes inevitably) fatal. The theme of death, and associated fears, may be common in conversations with the patient. In thinking about death or dying and its implications for an individual, its complement, life or living, also has to be considered at some stage in the course of counselling. Thus, it is not possible to think about living with a serious illness unless one also thinks about the possibility of death. Thoughts about death and dying may need to be balanced by thoughts about life and living and the challenges they present. In this way, the counsellor switches the focus between the two in order to help the patient gain a different perspective and perhaps to live better with his illness. An extract from an interview illustrates this:

Patient: The doctors have told me that I have a very high viral load and that my immune system is weakening rapidly. I really feel nervous about the future.

Counsellor: What do you feel most nervous about?

Patient: Most about dying. It's often on my mind nowadays.

Counsellor: This may seem a strange question, but I was wondering: are there any aspects of living that you are concerned about?

Patient: Having to face my parents with this news.

Counsellor: If they knew that, do you think that they would agree that you need to be concerned about telling them?

Patient: That's a good question. Possibly not. It's probably on their minds and we're all getting along by not talking about 'what if . . . '.

Counsellor: And what are the worries or concerns about 'what if . . . '?

Patient: One of them is the way in which I might die. It may be unpleasant.

Counsellor: How do you think you might begin to discuss this with them?

Openness and secrecy

Some patients wish to protect others from so-called bad news. Others fear the ostracism, isolation and social stigma that may result from telling others about their illness. For these reasons, they may seek to keep it secret. In some circumstances, keeping secrets may prevent the patient from receiving adequate or desired social support or interfere with co-ordinated management and care. The tension between secrecy and openness can be discussed in counselling, as illustrated below.

Patient: I see no point in telling my mother that I will be having these tests. It would only worry her.

Counsellor: OK, but from where will you get support if you need it during the tests and while waiting for the results?

Patient: If I tell anyone, they will only worry. And that would add to my worries. I'd rather wait until the results come and then I'll decide what to do at that point.

Counsellor: I can understand your concerns about not worrying others. If, at a later point, you choose to tell your mother or others, do you think they would have wanted to be told sooner?

Patient: It cuts both ways. If I don't tell them, I'll be blamed for being secretive and uncaring. If I do tell them, they may add to *my* worries. It's still best to err on the side of hoping that it's 'good news' and that this was just a scare.

Wanting to know versus not wanting to know

Patients will sometimes say that they want to know the results of clinical tests and investigations or other procedures. In reality, however, they may not want to know or they may be ambivalent. This problem may never be entirely resolved and can cause frustration to doctors and nurses. Patients and health care workers may have different views about how much information should be made known. Counselling sessions can be used to explore the patient's views about information and its dissemination, so as to improve communication between the patient and the professionals caring for him. This theme is closely linked to the patient's view of himself and his ability to cope. The patient can be helped to regain a sense of control over his management by asking him (a) to clarify what he wants to be told; (b) what he specifically does not want to know; (c) at what stages he wants to be told; (d) whether anyone else should be present when he is given information; and (e) how he would indicate that his views have changed. For example:

Mother: I understand what the doctor was saying about my daughter having diabetes, but I wonder if she is really too young to be told. What do you think?

Counsellor: I can understand your reluctance to tell her too much at this stage, especially because it is not yet clear how this will affect her and whether she will be on insulin. Maybe you can tell her gradually. Perhaps just some of the main details at this stage, such as an explanation for why she has to see the doctor. Then, as you are told more by the doctor, you can think about whether and how you would share the information with Susie. If your husband was here, what do you think he would want to do?

| Mother: | Probably the same as your suggestion. Do it slowly, one step at a time. Use words and descriptions that she'll understand. When she gets older, maybe tell her more. |
| Counsellor: | Seems a very good approach to me. We know that children's reactions to illness and how they cope is directly influenced by how their parents cope. It's best to tell Susie only what you think she needs to know and in a time-frame that best suits the two of you. |

Hope and hopelessness

With any serious illness, there is likely to be tension between feelings of hope and hopelessness. These feelings are directly linked to the complements of certainty and uncertainty. The counsellor can seek to support the patient's hope in the face of his life-threatening illness without invalidating or dismissing his fear of dying. This is not easily done. The counsellor can offer hope in relation to small goals, and at the same time not deny the reality that the possibility of illness is ever-present. The course or outcome of an illness can never be predicted with precise accuracy. It could be said that as long as there is some uncertainty in relation to treatment and the outcome of the patient's illness, there is an element of hope. On the other hand, certainty can also give rise to feelings of hope. A patient who has been told that he is suffering from leukaemia may be relieved that some of his symptoms can be diagnosed and promptly treated. Clearly, the converse is also true and in other situations uncertainty may erode a patient's feelings of hope. The introduction of the complements of hope and hopelessness into counselling is illustrated in the example below.

Patient:	I feel really down . . . actually quite hopeless now that I've been told that in time I could become incontinent.
Counsellor:	It must be very difficult for you to have to cope with more and more symptoms. Are there any areas in which you see some possible hope?
Patient:	At least I can make some plans ahead of time and investigate what devices or contraptions I may need. Who knows, maybe things won't deteriorate too much, and becoming incontinent is just a worst-case scenario.
Counsellor:	That is possible. What could you hope for in more personal areas, for example, with family and friends?
Patient:	That they would continue to care for me, whatever the symptoms or problems.
Counsellor:	Is there anything you might think about doing to ensure this continues?
Patient:	I need to keep them up to date with developments. I need to share this news with some of them.

Temporal themes (past, present and future)

Perspectives on time can be used to help patients gain a new perspective on a problem by linking past experience with the present and even with anticipated situations. At any one moment in counselling a particular time period is being referred to. A patient may, for example, say that he currently feels depressed. The counsellor may then examine two other periods of time, asking the patient whether he has felt depressed in the past, his circumstances at that time, and how he coped. He may also ask him, in thinking about the future, what would happen if he continued to feel so depressed and these feelings did not seem to go away, or how things might look if his depression lifted. In this way, the counsellor can always introduce a new view of the problem with a temporal theme.

Patient:	I have felt so depressed for the past two weeks.
Counsellor:	When last did you feel so depressed?
Patient:	About two years ago.
Counsellor:	Do you remember for how long it lasted?
Patient:	No.
Counsellor:	What were the signs to you then that you were feeling less depressed?
Patient:	I enjoyed my work more and went out with my husband and friends.
Counsellor:	What helped you get over feeling depressed?
Patient:	Time. It just went away over time. It took about a month to go away.
Counsellor:	Do you remember what signs there were that it was beginning to lift?
Patient:	I don't remember. But I do remember that my husband said that my sexual interest had begun to return!
Counsellor:	What might be the signs this time that you were beginning to feel better in yourself?
Patient:	At this moment, I have no idea. It just seems like I'm in a long black tunnel.
Counsellor:	If these feelings carried on, what do you think would most help?
Patient:	My husband. And some anti-depressant pills.

Relationship with family of origin and affiliation

The patient's ideas about what his family of origin (biological family or blood relations) or social family (partner(s) and non-biological kin network) might think about a particular problem should also be discussed. He may already know their views or he may be asked to imagine what they might be. It is important to stress that in counselling it is the patient's perception of problems and beliefs that are important, rather than 'the truth'. An exploration of the patient's views about different family members helps to place a problem in the context of relationships. It gives a patient a reference point from which to look at difficulties, especially where there are different views within the family affecting the patient's beliefs. An excerpt from a counselling session illustrates this.

Patient:	My girlfriend feels that I am too ill to continue working.
Counsellor:	What does she think you should do when you've stopped?
Patient:	Just stay at home and rest.
Counsellor:	Who else agrees with her?
Patient:	I think my parents both disagree.
Counsellor:	What makes them think that you should continue working?
Patient:	They think it will take my mind off my troubles if I'm occupied or busy.
Counsellor:	And what does your girlfriend think will occupy your thoughts while you are resting at home?
Patient:	Perhaps how we can continue to have a good relationship and to cope with the difficult times that lie ahead.

Dependence and abandonment

The nature of chronic and acute illness is such that there may be times
are satisfactorily able to look after themselves out of hospital, and other times
they will need to be in hospital or rely on care-takers. This may present as a dilemma
in the context of counselling because some patients resent being dependent or even
coming to counselling sessions. On the other hand, the patient may simultaneously
express a fear of being on their own or being abandoned. Such a dilemma can be played
out through contradictory messages given by the patient to the counsellor or other
members of the health care team. There are times during counselling when it is
important to discuss the patient's fears of abandonment and dependence. For example:

Patient: I really don't think it's necessary for me to be here today.

Counsellor: How is that different from the last time you were here?

Patient: Then I felt really unwell and needed someone to talk to and answer questions for me.

Counsellor: What sort of things do you think you might want to talk about during well periods?

Patient: Perhaps if I could get more involved in my relationship while I was feeling better.

Counsellor: What do you think you would need to do in order to get more involved in your relationship?

Patient: I could see you less when I am feeling better and spend more time with my partner.

Separateness and involvement

These dilemmas are similar to those of dependence and abandonment. When a patient
becomes ill and understands the possible implications of his illness, he may wish to put
some emotional distance between himself and others. This may be, for example,
because he does not want to infect others, he feels too unwell physically to have close
relationships, he feels self-conscious or inadequate socially, or there is a fear that a
partner will desert him. On the other hand, at a time of crisis the patient may feel a real
need for a significant relationship and a close emotional involvement. A similar process
can occur in the course of counselling, with patients either not wanting to keep
appointments or asking for more frequent appointments. For example:

Counsellor: You mention that no-one has been to visit you the past two days. Is there any special reason for that?

Patient: I've told everyone I need some space to be on my own.

Counsellor: Can you say more about that?

Patient: I don't want to be a burden on my friends and family. If they visit me here in hospital, I think they're doing it out of a sense of duty.

Counsellor: Are there any benefits for you of them visiting even if it is out of a sense of duty?

Patient: I like the company, but get very tearful when it's time to say 'goodbye'. It's like I want them, and at the same time I don't want them.

Change and preservation

One goal of counselling is to address the balance between helping people to adapt and change and at the same time preserve a sense of stability and continuity in their lives. This goal addresses the therapeutic balance. The counsellor constantly thinks about psychological process in the session and may ask himself some of the following questions: 'What is the patient telling me? What is the problem? What does the patient want changed? What does he want to keep the same?' Sometimes the counsellor may try to generate too much change, which in turn can unbalance the therapeutic system. Through responding closely to the feedback, the counsellor can redress the balance by identifying whether the patient is becoming emotionally more stable or whether he has become 'stuck'. In the face of the latter, the counsellor might ask himself: 'Am I pushing for change when change is not wanted? Am I trying to change the patient or system in a way that is inappropriate or too rapid?' The problems of change are addressed in the example below.

Patient: I want to try to change some things in my life now the operation is over.
Counsellor: I realize that there are some things in your life that you would like to change. Are there any aspects that you would like to keep the same?
Patient: How my parents look after me.
Counsellor: What does your boyfriend think you'd like to change most?
Patient: The fact that I have so little energy to enjoy our relationship.
Counsellor: What would he most likely want to keep the same?
Patient: That I won't ever feel like leaving him.

CONCLUSION

Some of the more challenging problems in clinical practice stem from rigid beliefs and the management of views or feelings of hopelessness. These problems can affect communication between the patient and his family, and with health care staff. An approach has been described for counselling about patients' belief systems to enhance their perception of choice in how they view their relationships and what may be happening to them. This is not to suggest that, by creating balance in difficult clinical situations, patients will be completely relieved of their problems. Balancing techniques are a first step towards reframing a belief or problem. There may be some personal advantage, for example, in being in hospital because it may encourage the patient to be more open about his illness than he felt he could be while he was at home and managing to mask his problems. Complementarity can be introduced into counselling by asking hypothetical and future-orientated questions such as: 'You say that the doctors only seem to give you bad news. Given your situation, what might you consider "good" news for you? How do you think that good or bad news would affect how you see your illness and your relationship with your doctors?'

There are potential problems for the counsellor in reframing, using the ideas described in this chapter. It requires training, care and delicacy. Without training in this approach, the counsellor may use this technique as a means of avoiding confrontation of problems with patients. The counsellor could also inadvertently deny or disqualify the patient's negative feelings and become combative with him by insisting on the 'good' or psychologically 'healthy' side.

CHAPTER 5

Counselling Tasks in Health Care

INTRODUCTION

Patients may seek counselling because illness has intruded into their life and affected their view of themselves, their relationships with others, and how they see themselves coping and adjusting both in the short term and in the future. Others are referred to counsellors by professional colleagues, such as doctors and nurses. Irrespective of the route of referral to the counsellor or the theoretical framework used, there are several therapeutic tasks which guide the counsellor in therapy sessions. The main task of the counsellor is to co-create with the patient new beliefs and ideas about a situation or problem that will enable the patient and his family to adapt to changes brought by illness. The initial goal in counselling is to determine whether there are problems, to discuss the context of problems and to explore ideas about how illness may affect people's beliefs and ideas.

This chapter summarizes the theoretical ideas discussed in the preceding chapters, highlights the therapeutic tasks in counselling and places them in a health care context. Examples illustrate these tasks and how to explore issues in the context of counselling sessions. The examples used are not comprehensive case studies, but rather brief vignettes which link a theoretical idea with clinical practice.

TASKS

The following tasks help to achieve the aims of counselling with patients (see Chapter 8).

1. To determine whether any part, or which part, of the patient's caring system has defined a problem and to have a conversation about the problem (to elicit the patient's story).

   A patient came to see a counsellor and stated: 'Dr Simpson says that I must see a counsellor because I have diabetes. But I don't have mental problems.' The counsellor responded by saying: 'What do you think it was that made Dr Simpson refer you?' 'He said that I wasn't looking after myself properly; my diet is bad and I'm not injecting regularly enough', replied the patient. 'And what do you think he was concerned about?' asked the counsellor. The patient replied: 'That I could land up in hospital, or worse. And he wants you to prevent that by "shrinking" me,' replied the patient in a mildly challenging and sarcastic tone. The counsellor replied: 'I'm not sure whether I should be seeing you or Dr Simpson.' The patient then conceded: 'No, it's me. I'm not a "good" patient; I always buck authority. I don't like to be told what to do and diabetes is the worst kind of problem to have with that state of mind.'

2. To elicit all of the problems, as the patient sees them, and then to discuss with the patient which need to be worked on first; that is, to assign priorities and an order to problems for resolution.

Peter was recently diagnosed as HIV positive by his doctor. He was referred to the counsellor working in the practice as he felt overwhelmed by the news of his illness and its implications. In the first counselling session, Peter asked for advice about a wide range of issues. These included whether he should tell anyone else the result; who in the family he should tell; how he might tell them; what he should do about his job; whether he should take a holiday already postponed for a year; how he could start new relationships and whether he should inform sexual partners he was HIV positive; and how he could cope with symptoms of psychological distress, including insomnia, loss of appetite and being short-tempered with friends and colleagues. The counsellor felt overwhelmed by the large number of problems and, in addition, considered it an important therapeutic intervention for Peter to identify the most pressing problems. The counsellor asked Peter to identify one or two of the most pressing problems. It would then be possible to consider how best to resolve them, rather than to try to solve all his problems in the limited time. Peter decided to discuss the issue of disclosure of his HIV status in the session. Once he had gained confidence in considering who he might disclose it to and how he could go about doing this, he felt that he might have the support of a friend in his crisis.

3. To create a reality with the patient which fits with his current world–view and beliefs to help sustain him through periods of change brought about by illness and loss. (See Chapter 3.)

In the case of a married man with advanced liver disease, one reality may be how he sees his role as a husband and a father and how this will continue in view of his medical diagnosis, both while he is alive and after his death. Questions for consideration that help to reveal personal and family beliefs include: How will he continue in his role? Who else may take some of the role? What ideas or beliefs does he want to preserve? What will help him to cope with and adapt to the changes confronting him and his family?

4. To understand how the patient views his problem and help him to consider other perspectives about the problem.

Patient: I am depressed. I find that having cancer of the prostate is getting me down.
Counsellor: Who else has noticed that you feel depressed?

Patient: Sometimes my wife does, but then she tries to cheer me up.

Counsellor: What impact does it have on you when she tries to cheer you up when you are feeling depressed?

Patient: It can make me feel even worse. And angry too. I just want to talk about what's going on with me, and us.

Counsellor: What most would you like to talk about with your wife?

Patient: Believe it or not, not the prostate cancer. Or not that directly. But the treatment and the effects. I'm practically impotent now. I feel a sense of failure as her sexual partner. It's an awful thing after so many years of having an active sex life.

Counsellor: What would it take to have a conversation with your wife about these concerns?

Patient: It's embarrassing, but maybe if I were to explain to her why I sometimes feel depressed, rather than to snap at her.

Counsellor: Yes, and maybe to do so at a time when you're not feeling as depressed, so you can talk to her without becoming too defensive or angry.

5. To help patients feel that they have choices. As a consequence of being unwell patients may feel that choices are being taken away from them. By reducing choices, one simultaneously takes away a level of autonomy.

Patient: The doctors tell me that the lymphoma is not responding to treatment.

Counsellor: What else was said?

Patient: Nothing really. I know I'm going to die soon.

Counsellor: If you were given the choice to be at home or in hospital, and you were very unwell, where would you want to be?

Patient: At home. I want to be able to look at the garden and have the dogs around.

Counsellor: What decisions do you think you will need to make over the coming weeks?

6. To retain a degree of neutrality in relation to the patient's lifestyle and decisions made about how he will cope with and adjust to his illness. This serves to enhance patient autonomy and self-confidence.

Patient: What's the use of taking these pills? They won't cure me. In fact the side effects are as bad as the illness.

Counsellor: What might happen if you chose not to take them?

Patient: Probably the same as if I take them: I'm going to die and the pills may keep me going a bit longer, but for what?

Counsellor: What has helped you to keep taking the pills thus far?

Patient: 'Help' is the wrong word. More like 'bullied'. The doctors say I have to take them. No 'ifs' or 'buts', just take them. I'm ready to die.

Counsellor: Have you thought how you might persuade the doctors to see your point of view?

7. To help the patient to continue to adapt and change (i.e. to give hope where appropriate).

A young man was seriously injured in a road traffic accident and sought counselling after it became clear that he would suffer a permanent disability, possibly confining him to a wheelchair. He wanted to discuss whether to give up the offer of a place at university, among other issues.

Counsellor: If I were to ask you what the most important implication is for you on receiving this news from the doctor, what might you say?

Patient: Going to university. I'm not going to university in a wheelchair. I might as well go for something different. Maybe weave baskets at home for the rest of my life.

Counsellor: I can understand how difficult it must be for you now to think about going to university and not being able to walk around freely as you once imagined you would do. How might it be for you, say in five years from now, looking back, if you had decided not to go to university?

Patient: Sometimes I can't even think five minutes ahead, let alone five years. Maybe there would be some regret though. I've still got my mind and that's as sharp as ever.

Counsellor: Yes, you do have that. How far ahead do you think you need to plan for?

Patient: Sometimes I have no idea. It depends on what a situation is like. If I was at university and it all worked out, then I could think about a future there. Maybe I need to try it out first.

Counsellor: Perhaps. And maybe that's something we could look at and also talk about what it might be like in a wheelchair on campus.

Patient: Yeah. And some days when I'm feeling down I just don't even want to think about all these hassles.

8. To place responsibility for problem-solving with those who define the problem.

Patient: This is the worst decision I've ever had to make. The one doctor says there's a one in five chance that the baby will be born with a deformity. The other says the scan is 'inconclusive'. And now I've got only a week to decide whether to terminate the pregnancy.

Counsellor: That's an incredibly difficulty decision for anyone. Is there anything that would help you in reaching a decision?

Patient: If you made it for me! I don't want the responsibility either way.

Counsellor: I can understand that it might feel easier if someone else takes the responsibility. Is there anyone else you can discuss this with?

Patient: My boyfriend. But he's impossible. Doesn't care and would simply say 'do as you like'. Great source of support he's likely to be even as a father! Actually, I'm not prepared to take that sort of shit from him. He'll have to talk it through with me! It's about time he took some responsibility.

9. To examine with the patient the implications of the problem for other relationships.

Patient: I can't possibly tell my parents about the breast lump, they're old; it'll kill them.

Counsellor: If you weren't to tell them and something happened to you, how do you think it would affect them?

Patient: They would be equally as devastated. You see, I'm the youngest of the children. I've always had a special caring role in the family. Had it been my brother or sister, it would have been less of a problem. They're married. I'm not. The

> expectation is that one day I will take care of my parents. Not the other way around.

Counsellor: If your brother and sister were here today and had heard what you had just said, what do you think would go through their minds?

Patient: My sister would disagree because she's also very close to our parents. She would probably tell me I should tell our parents. She would say that they are stronger than we all imagine them to be. After all, my mom lost a sister during the war and my father's first wife died in a car accident. I just hate it when everyone at home is emotional and cries. Perhaps telling them that it's a lump is not the same as saying 'it's cancer and I'm dying'.

Counsellor: Maybe it's easier to take it one step at a time and to tell them about the lump and say that tests are being carried out to find out more about the lump.

Patient: I'll think about it.

10. To help a psychologically vulnerable person to cope with additional stresses, thereby possibly preventing the development of major psychological problems. This may engender addressing fears of death and dying.

A patient became very depressed after being told by his doctor that he would need to undergo heart by-pass surgery. He was withdrawn, stopped going to work, said little to his family and friends and could not make up his mind whether to have the operation even though he would probably die if he did not have it. He was referred to a counsellor and it appeared that his fear of dying had metaphorically immobilized him, preventing him from making any decisions. While the doctors and his family had understandably tried to discourage him, no-one, it seems, discussed with him what might happen if he were not to recover or he were to die. Once he had been able to talk about his fear of dying and his worries about loss and how others in the family might cope, he resumed his medical appointments. He soon reported that the atmosphere at home had improved. Although he did not return to work, he agreed to have the operation. He decided to spend the three weeks before the operation with the family, 'in case things don't work out'. The operation was a success and, in retrospect, he mentioned to the counsellor that he was pleased that he tried to prepare himself and the family for the worst.

11. To help patients deal with unpredictability. A patient's concern about unpredictability may be reflected in questions such as: 'Why should I carry on?' 'How should I carry on?' 'How will the illness progress?'

(This example is based on an excerpt from a counselling session with the patient with cardiac problems described above.)

Patient: What happens if the operation is not successful?

Counsellor: What worries you most about what could happen?

Patient: Maybe that I'd die.

Counsellor: What would you most want to do if you knew that you might die, for whatever reason?

Patient: Spend some time with my wife and children.

Counsellor: I know that you have discussed these concerns with the doctor and that he told you that, although the risks are small, there is some risk. Is there anything that prevents you from spending time with them now?

Patient: Not really, other than I get a bit morose and they always try to cheer me up. It cuts both ways; if I don't spend time with them I'm not preparing for the worst; if I do, they can annoy me with their cheeriness!

Counsellor: Difficult decisions, I agree.

Patient: I don't like uncertainty in my life. But it looks as if I should spend time with them. At least I would have done what they most would want me to do.

12. To view medical problems as the entrée to other problems, such as relationship difficulties. Health care problems need not necessarily be the main or the most enduring difficulty for patients. How people cope with and adjust to medical problems may sometimes be viewed as a symptom of other problems.

A young man treated for a brain tumour found that he had become dependent on his family for support and care. He had always been strong-willed to the extent of sometimes defying his parents' wishes in order to assert his need for separateness from them. His illness and period of convalescence resulted in his becoming dependent on them. The family sought counselling to help address past patterns in relationships and the new circumstances. His parents felt uncertain as to how to care for their son, and the patient in turn resented having to depend on his parents.

13. To help the patient maintain realistic hope and to affirm his or her coping abilities. This may entail examining whether there have been any positive changes in the patient's life resulting from misfortune or illness. (See Chapter 4.)

Counsellor: We have spent a lot of time looking at the difficulties you have experienced in many different areas of your life since the road traffic accident. This may seem a strange or insensitive question, but I was also wondering whether anything good has come of this?

Patient: Definitely. Yes. I now live life from day-to-day. I don't let little things get me down. I've got my priorities sorted out.

14. To normalize the views, feelings and experience of the patient, as this can help reduce a sense of isolation, exclusion and difference.

Patient: It feels so empty without my wife. Some nights I cry myself to sleep. I also think she could have been treated sooner had she told me about the lump.

Counsellor: It must be very hard for you after all these years. I am not surprised to hear that you feel lonely without your wife and that you miss her. That is normal. Sometimes it's easier to think how things could have been different when looking back afterwards.

15. To help the patient to engage with his care-takers (family, friends, and others), if this is what he desires, and at the same time to prevent health care professionals, who may feel compelled to 'mother' patients, from crossing professional boundaries. Failure to address this can lead to over-dependence on staff and

feelings of burnout. Supervision can help recognize these boundaries, thereby increasing professional competence.

Patient: It feels so good when I come here for counselling. I feel safe and can save up all my feelings to talk about them here.
Counsellor: Apart from our sessions, where else do you feel supported and safe?
Patient: With a few good friends, but we don't talk about my illness.
Counsellor: To whom do you feel closest?
Patient: My mother. But I wouldn't want to burden her with some of the 'heavy' feelings, like when I'm down.
Counsellor: If you were to share these feelings, do you think the two of you might get closer or become more distant?
Patient: Closer. Definitely. But then I wouldn't need to come here as much!

CONCLUSION

The tasks described in this chapter consolidate a number of possible leads that counsellors can follow in order to identify and resolve patients' problems. Ill health can put severe stress on relationships as people face having to make significant choices and may simultaneously experience a sense of diminished options. Throughout our lives, we are confronted with numerous situations where communication is difficult, and the process of communicating with a person who is unwell or dying may be the most difficult of all. The barriers to effective communication affect not only the patient, but also the family, partner, friends and health care providers, each of whom may experience problems in communicating with the patient and with one another.

The complexity and unpredictability of different illnesses do not always allow for permanent solutions to be provided. Therefore, the counsellor may attempt, wherever possible, to introduce and create alternative views of the problem. The tasks of the counsellor are to bring forth and define the problem and become aware of the sub-systems to be addressed in attempting to resolve the problems. Although it may be tempting to see the patient at regular intervals and throughout the duration of ill health, sometimes the patient's needs are best served by having contact as the need arises and by maintaining an 'open door' in the counselling relationship.

Many different themes and beliefs emerge and recur when working with patients within health care settings. These include secrecy, uncertainty, dealing with threatened or actual loss, coping with reduced choices, having to make many important decisions, fear of not coping and diminished autonomy, among others. It is probable that at some stage in the counselling process, one or more of these problems will arise. The main task and challenge to the counsellor is to help the patient and others to find an alternative view of the problem and generate new solutions, in what may be a brief or focused period of counselling.

CHAPTER 6

Exploring and Defining Problems in Counselling

INTRODUCTION

We have already seen the circular and interactive relationship between health-related problems and their impact on patients, couples and family relationships, and vice versa. Health-related problems, however, do not necessarily lead to psychological problems. Furthermore, there is a distinction between a psychological problem (anxiety, depression) and symptoms of that problem (insomnia, flat affect, loss of appetite, inability to concentrate). Medical problems sometimes reveal related psychological problems, such as a fear of loss or dying, or feeling anxious when one is dependent on others for care. The medical problem experienced by the patient should not be dismissed in the quest to identify a more pervading or underlying psychological problem, and psychological problems do not preclude patients from having genuine medical problems.

A number of points should be considered before assuming that a patient requires counselling. The experience of illness affects people in different ways. The counsellor's task is (a) to identify the psychological implications of illness for the patient and any problems that may result from this, and (b) to assist doctors and nurses, as well as the patient's care-takers, in providing support and psychological care to the patient. Counsellors should also reflect on the possible assumptions being made about how people should be cared for, their relationships and their adjustment to illness.

GOALS OF SYSTEMIC MEDICAL COUNSELLING

There are three main goals of systemic medical counselling. First, to avoid situations in which patients may feel pushed to see things in the way we see them, or in which we may inadvertently disqualify their ideas or feelings. Second, to maintain a focus on the patient's and family's psychological condition without necessarily making this the dominant issue. Third, to be available to professional colleagues and take referrals or consult as appropriate. There is a danger of an over-emphasis on psychological issues when in fact other problems are pre-eminent, such as the patient's social or medical condition. To avoid making assumptions about the patient's problem and to keep these three main concerns in mind, the counsellor should consider from the start:

- What is the psychological problem, if any, and what is the context in which this problem occurs? Who is most affected by the problem and, therefore, who is it best to work with – the patient, or relatives? Is a consultation with a professional colleague also likely to be of benefit? Is this a problem that can possibly be solved through counselling? Are there any contra-indications to seeing the patient for counselling? Counselling often implies treatment of psychological problems. There is also a role for the counsellor in preventive interventions (see Chapter 17), consultation (see Chapter 15) and assessment even when no intervention or treatment takes place.
- What 'form' or approach to counselling should be taken in the light of how the problem is described and the setting in which the counsellor works. The approach may need to be adapted as the problem changes during the course of counselling. The counsellor must also decide whether a one-off assessment or consultation session is preferable to ongoing contact with the patient.
- Whether the patient has already been asked about how this problem or medical condition affects him and his family. If so, is further counselling needed? If it is, who is the best person to provide this – the doctor, nurse, myself as a counsellor or another person outside the team? If the patient has not been asked how this problem affects him, what effect might it have if I were to explore this with him? Would it increase his level of anxiety? Would the nurses feel that their role had been taken over? When would be the best time to approach the patient? Have I the time to spend with this urgent referral now?

It is important to emphasize that the nature and extent of the patient's psychological problems may be influenced by several factors. Some patients may be reluctant to talk about their concerns and counsellors should be familiar with the range of possible defences employed to avoid doing so. These include:

- *Fatalism*: 'I've had a good innings; this is what happens at my age. What can I do?'
- *Denial*: 'So, they tell me I've got diabetes. I'll change my diet a bit. Pills? No way! Injections? Never! You'll see; I've always been a survivor. This is not going to get the better of me.'
- *Avoidance*: 'I'm doing fine, thank you. I don't know why the doctor said you should come to see me. There must be many other people in the hospital for you to go and visit who have more serious problems. Anyway, my husband is about to come to visit.'
- *Humour*: 'So the doc said to me, "Mr Ellis, we had to do a colostomy – we will need to help you to learn to use the bag." And I said to him "You know, doc, my ex-wife used to call me a shit-bag. Maybe she knew something all those years ago." As the saying goes, "shit happens".'

In spite of the occasional use of defences by patients, it is important to make at least a preliminary assessment within one session as to the nature and extent of counselling that may be needed, to devise a treatment plan and to discuss this with other colleagues.

By the very nature of health-related problems, feelings of fear and anxiety are often at the surface and sometimes openly displayed. They may stem from fear of pain, loss of control, being incapacitated or disabled, dying, existential loneliness, concern about how others may cope, and the long-term effects of illness.

Counselling should address the patient's defined concerns from the start of counselling sessions in order to respond to and empathize with the patient. Indeed, failure to address the main concerns early in the contact with the patient may inhibit the development of a therapeutic relationship. Counselling should initially cover a wide range of issues and concerns because: (a) the patient may recover, be discharged, deteriorate or die before the cause of his concerns has been addressed; (b) opportunities to cope with problems or adjust to new circumstances may be lost and prove detrimental to the well-being of the patient and his family; and (c) the patient may wonder whether counselling can be of any benefit. A situation may arise in the counselling relationship in which the patient's main concerns and fears are never discussed. This may be the result of counsellor–patient 'collusion' which can take the following forms:

1. The patient is referred to a counsellor but is frightened to talk about fears.
2. The counsellor 'respects' the patient's pace in counselling and senses that the patient 'is not yet ready' to talk about his fears.
3. The patient interprets the counsellor's reluctance to discuss fears as a signal that the counsellor has concerns about this. The patient does not want to 'upset' the counsellor, who seems friendly and kind.
4. The counsellor believes that avoidance of the issue of concerns and fears is a measure or sign of the patient's defences which should be respected.

The importance of identifying and clarifying the patient's problems has been stressed. Exploring the patient's problems is an acquired skill. This task is made more complex when the problem relates to the patient's physical health. The following section describes how to explore, define and address the patient's problems.

FRAMEWORK FOR DEFINING PROBLEMS

The counsellor requires answers to certain key questions in order to understand the definition of the problem. These questions relate to three frames which help to conceptualize problems within a psychological or psychotherapeutic framework including knowledge about

- *The medical condition*, its consequences and likely outcome.
- *The psychological effects* of the condition on the individual, couple or family.
- *The context or setting* in which treatment, care and counselling are provided.

The problem is often initially defined by a medical term or a diagnostic label (coronary heart disease, multiple sclerosis, a fracture). The counsellor needs also to consider the psychological implications of illness and contextual issues; combined, these create a definition of the problem. We can illustrate the frames as follows:

The medical definition of the problem

TYPOLOGY OF ILLNESS

- Acute versus chronic
- Life-threatening versus non-life-threatening
- Stable versus degenerative, progressive, remitting
- Contagious versus non-contagious
- Inherited versus acquired

KNOWLEDGE ABOUT TREATMENT

- Is there an effective treatment?
- What does the treatment entail?
- Is it curative, palliative symptomatically, short-term, long-term?
- Is much known about this condition?
- Is there much uncertainty?

PROVISION OF CARE

- Is treatment and/or care provided within a primary, secondary or tertiary health facility?
- Will care require liaison between different doctors or carers?
- Will treatment require frequent visits to the doctor or will it be home-based care?

The psychological definition of the problem

DEVELOPMENTAL ISSUES

- What developmental stage has the person reached (e.g. infant, child, adolescent, adult)?
- At what stage of development is the person in relation to their family (e.g. at home and dependent, left home, divorced, children left home)?
- What effect does this illness have on this person in the context of their lifestyle and developmental issues?

PSYCHOLOGICAL ISSUES

- What is the patient's emotional and mental state?
- What are the main concerns?
- What dynamics are driving these concerns (too much uncertainty, too little information about the diagnosis and prognosis, fear of loss)?
- What losses are the patient and family facing?
- How are they coping with loss or anticipatory loss?
- How have they coped before with similar challenges?
- What relationship and attachment issues are relevant?

The context of the problem

The problem presented is related to *the family system or cultural background of the patient*; for example:

- A doctor refers a 'noncompliant' patient to a counsellor because the patient's family are against him taking prescribed medication.

The problem presented is related to *other systems with which the patient has contact*; for example:

- A patient is required to undergo a pre-employment medical examination but is concerned that they will discover that he has had hepatitis B and suspect that he may be an intravenous drug user or have acquired the infection through sexual contact. He seeks advice from a counsellor in a GP practice.

The problem presented is related to *other therapeutic systems with which the patient maintains contact*; for example:

- A nurse on the oncology ward with an interest in psychology thinks that a depressed patient 'is denying his illness and needs to work through his unresolved feelings towards his mother in order to come to terms with dying'.

The problem presented is related to the *system within which the counsellor works*; for example:

- A doctor refers a patient to a counsellor 'to help the patient with his feelings'. In the course of counselling, it becomes evident that the patient feels confused about his care. He is being given treatment for his cancer, but no-one discusses the prognosis with him. It seems that the medical team find it difficult to say to him that his condition is becoming untreatable.

These frames for exploring and defining the problem are useful for understanding the nature of the patient's problem. This can be further clarified by the counsellor asking some of the following questions of himself:

- What is the problem?
- For whom is this problem most a problem?
- How does this problem present?
- Is this a problem that can be dealt with by a counsellor, or should the patient be referred to another specialist?
- How long has the patient had the problem?
- When did it start?
- Why is the patient talking about it now?
- How does this problem affect the patient emotionally and physically?
- Who else should be involved in the patient's psychological treatment and care?

Patients will sometimes describe a catalogue of problems to the counsellor in a single session. This is understandable because the effects of illness may be complex and multifaceted. Some problems may stem from inadequate information about the medical condition, the reason for specific laboratory tests being carried out and uncertainty about the prognosis. Concerns about how family and friends may cope during the period of illness or disability often present as practical issues such as loss of income or inadequate housing.

The counsellor's choice of words and use of language is important (see Chapter 18), and complex issues may need to be simplified in order to be meaningful to patients. Using language that fits with that of the patient and checking that the meanings of words used are understood may prevent misunderstandings or assumptions being made. Anxiety, for example, is frequently expressed by patients in general and non-specific terms. Counsellors may find it useful to help the patient convey how he feels by asking him to describe behaviours. It is easier to consider therapeutic approaches for dealing with behaviours rather than categories of feelings such as 'depression' and 'despair' and diagnostic labels such as 'borderline personality disorder'. The following example illustrates how this can be done:

Counsellor: Can you say something about what it felt like when you went home from the hospital after you were given the test results?

Patient: I felt really depressed.

Counsellor: When you were depressed, how did that show?

Patient: I went quiet. I slowed down . . . like I switched off and curled up inside. I also sighed a lot.

Counsellor: Judy, what ideas come to mind when you're slowing down, switching off, curling up and sighing?

Patient: I suppose I wanted to be alone. I'm not sure that there are any ideas in particular.

Counsellor: OK. What effect did that have on people around you when you needed to be alone?

Patient: That's when things get even more difficult. My husband can't deal with my need to be alone. He's very kind and wants to help, but he keeps asking if there is anything he can do. That drives me mad.

Counsellor: If you were to tell him that you needed some space, how might he react?

Patient: You mean over-react! The last time I told him that, he started thinking that I didn't love him anymore. The tension that followed for weeks just wasn't worth it. So now I just don't tell him I need space.

Counsellor: Can you think of a way of saying it to him without him over-reacting?

Patient: I could start the conversation by assuring him that there is nothing wrong with the relationship. Then I could explain to him what I mean by 'space' and how long I may need, to give him some idea of what's going on in my head.

Counsellor: That sounds a good way to start the conversation. Perhaps you could try that the next time. Let's go back to the day of the test results . . .

It is useful for the counsellor to keep in mind a number of levels of problem definition which can be explored with the patient. The counsellor can explore the recursive link between ideas or statements, behaviours, relationships and beliefs in any order.

Figure 6.1 illustrates these different levels and the recursive link between them.

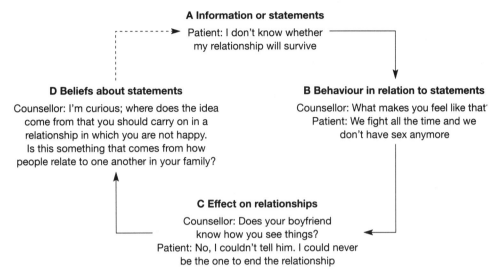

Figure 6.1 Establishing links between ideas, statements, relationships and beliefs

SHOWING UNDERSTANDING OF THE PATIENT'S PROBLEMS

Patients seeking help want to feel they are being understood by the professionals who counsel them. To do this, the counsellor may nod from time to time or reflect on what has been said. A strong confirmation to the patient that he has been heard is to use the patient's own words to form the next question or intervention, as in the example above. We can use the following framework for exploring the problem therapeutically:

SHOW EMPATHY

- Respect the patient's views and ideas.
- Do not invalidate or disqualify what the patient says.
- Use the patient's words and language in your conversation with him.

VALIDATE

- Use co-operative and non-confrontational language.
- Try to convey that you are trying to understand his story from his point of view.

AMPLIFY

- Talk about the problem that the patient brings to counselling.

- Take care not to digress from this until that particular problem has either been solved or a new problem becomes more pressing.

ADD COMPLEXITY

- Adopt a stance of curiosity (i.e. not knowing) and ask questions of the patient. The answers to questions should lead to further questions.
- Complexity can be added by asking questions which either expand or narrow the field, or both.

SIMPLIFY

- Complex ideas should be simplified. This intervention helps to give a new frame or perspective to the problem.

REFRAME

- Give new meaning to ideas and problems without disqualifying the patient's distress.
- Tentatively offer another perspective on a problem.
- Help the patient to view the problem differently.

UNDERSTAND SLOWLY

- Although you may be required to work briefly or quickly with a patient, do not jump to conclusions about what is the problem.
- Avoid making any assumptions.

ELICIT FEEDBACK

- Check with the patient whether you have understood him.
- Ask whether you are addressing his concerns.
- Maintain an overview of the counselling process and a clear definition of the problem but avoid making the patient's problem fit perfectly into some previously conceived theory about psychopathology.

OTHER CONTEXTS WHICH AFFECT THE PATIENT'S PROBLEMS

The counsellor should not presume either the presence or the nature of a problem until it is defined or confirmed by the patient or a context of which he is a part. These systems may include his own personal and social milieu, beliefs about illness, treatment and disability, the professional health and social care systems, or the wider social and political system. Personal or psychological problems resulting from ill health or disability may also change from time to time. New problems may arise or old ones may cease to be problems for a number of reasons.

The following is a list of some of the sources of psychological problems resulting from changes in the health care system. They include:

- the advent of new illnesses, such as HIV disease in the 1980s;
- advances in medicine leading to different and/or more effective tests and treatments, with some conditions no longer being life-threatening;
- the outbreak of a transmissible infection exacerbated by social conditions, such as viral haemorrhagic fever, resulting in the rapid spread of infection;
- changes in the treatment of certain conditions, including greater use of day surgery;
- more widespread early detection (genetic screening) for some conditions;
- limitations (rationing) being placed on the provision of health care.

Problems for the patient change during the course of illness. At the pre-diagnosis phase there may be anticipatory anxiety. During an asymptomatic phase, the patient may have to cope with uncertainty as to when or if symptoms may occur. Later, the patient may have to adjust to new and unwelcome circumstances when symptoms of disease prevent him from working or engaging in family life as he used to.

The definition of the problem may reflect not only the stages of illness the patient has reached but also the professional background of the counsellor. A psychodynamic counsellor may be more interested in the patient's attachments and family relationships when he was a child, while a cognitive therapist may wish to focus on ideas or beliefs about illness, disability and coping. Although a range of therapies are used in health care settings, they differ in terms of how psychological problems are conceptualized in the course and nature of treatment.

The way in which patients view their illness or disability as a problem will in part be a response to how others view it. A person who has suffered a brain injury may find that the stigma attached to this is as severe as the problem itself. In other words, there may be times when the social implications are as pressing, or even more so, than the medical ones. There is a reciprocal and circular relationship between the problem and its context. One or both may change at any moment in relation to the other. The problem may therefore change from session to session, sometimes even within the counselling session. In health care, there are sometimes rapid changes and advances in approaches to treatment and care. The counsellor needs to be flexible in his working practice to accommodate these changes and the ripple effect they may have on the patient and family. In one session, the counsellor may be discussing the patient's fear of undergoing an MRI (magnetic resonance imaging) scan. At the next session, they may be talking about the possibility of the patient having to undergo major surgery.

With whose problem is the counsellor dealing?

The patient is but one part of the system with which the counsellor works. Invariably there are other systems, including members of the health care team and the support network of the patient. The immediate task is to obtain a definition of the specific problem and to try to identify for whom it is a problem. The patient's partner, a member of his family or someone in the health care team could all be affected, although each may have a different view of the problem and what should be done about it. The redefinition of the problem can start at the beginning of the session by exploring different people's views. For example:

Counsellor: Mrs Davis, what do you think is your husband's main concern?

Mrs Davis: I'm not sure, but I think that it may be that Tanya could die.

Counsellor: Mr Davis, do you agree with what your wife said?

Mr Davis: I do worry about that, but my main worry now is how we will cope as a family during her illness. We're all very stressed and upset.

Counsellor: Mrs Davis, were you aware that this was your husband's main worry?

Mrs Davis: Yes, but surprisingly I find it easier to think about Tanya dying than her being ill for a long time.

When the apparent solution becomes part of the problem

It is important to examine other sources of problems in counselling. In some cases, the referring person may create a new view of the problem in the light of his professional opinion, which could even exacerbate the problem. A man being treated for leukaemia may, for example, be referred by a nurse on the ward who is concerned about the patient because he keeps checking his body for signs of skin problems – a possible side effect of his having to take immunosuppressive drugs. In addressing the problem, one task of the counsellor is to consider and discuss the nurse's concerns and beliefs about the patient and his 'obsessional' behaviour.

For any problem to exist, it must first be defined by someone as a problem. If others do not agree with the definition of the problem, the lack of consensus over problem definition becomes a further problem. In a counsellor's conversations with a patient, he has the opportunity to confirm or refute problems. This is illustrated by two statements of professional opinion: 'From what I have heard, I do not feel that this is an issue for which counselling is indicated and I'm not sure that there is any further need for meetings.' This conveys an entirely different message from 'This seems a very serious problem and we should meet on a regular basis for several months.'

A professional makes explicit or implies something about the *nature* of the problem when he makes a referral. The referrer may, for example, mention that the patient is 'depressed'. At the same time, a view is conveyed about *the person for whom this is a problem*, be it the patient, a family member or a member of the health care team. The referrer may also indicate *what should be done about the problem*. If the referrer suggests, for example, that a patient sees a psychiatrist, the message may be conveyed that there is an organic or biochemical basis to the behaviour; whereas if the referral is made to a psychotherapist, there could be a belief that there were problems in the early development of that person or extreme anxiety about the illness. No referral is therefore a completely neutral gesture. Some consensus about the problem between referrers and counsellors is needed in order to ensure that patients are satisfactorily managed. The case example below illustrates how lack of consensus was a problem with a patient in a clinic and how similar problems can be resolved. In this example, the attempted solution becomes a problem.

Stephen, a 52-year-old man, recently had a heart attack. He did not have a history of heart disease and had had a reasonably healthy lifestyle. He was transferred from a cardiac intensive care unit to a general medical ward before being sent home to convalesce. The counsellor had seen Stephen's wife soon after he was admitted because she was worried about what things would be like when he was back at home. She was concerned that he would want to go back to work too soon and that she would constantly worry that he might suffer another heart attack and die. The couple were seen together by the counsellor on the medical ward shortly before Stephen was discharged from hospital. They were also given an out-patient follow-up counselling appointment.

After they had seen the doctor in the out-patient department, Stephen asked to see the counsellor on his own. Stephen walked in, sat down and said to the counsellor: 'Doctor Mundy says that I should see a psychiatrist.' Apparently Stephen had told the doctor that he had become impotent and felt depressed. Although he wanted help, Stephen now felt that his problem was very serious. He had never seen a psychiatrist before and became very anxious at the suggestion, made without any explanation as to how a psychiatric assessment and treatment could be of help. Furthermore, he had read that these were common symptoms in men recovering from a heart attack and was somewhat reassured by this.

This situation presented the counsellor with a dilemma. On the one hand, the counsellor agreed that the patient's symptoms of depression and impotence were probably related to his medical condition and treatment. On the other hand, the patient agreed that he was depressed but did not want to take up a referral to a psychiatrist as he believed that this would compound his problems.

This case illustrates that it can be helpful to ask patients how they think some of their problems might best be solved before offering what may seem the right or best solution. There are several options for the counsellor in the above example. The counsellor might agree with the view of the doctor and suggest that it is a good idea for the patient to be referred to a psychiatrist. A second option might be to delay offering treatment until the patient has been assessed by a psychiatrist, and then to do so in collaboration with the psychiatrist. A third option might be for the counsellor to disagree with the doctor about the need for a referral to a psychiatrist. However, this might put the counsellor in conflict with his medical colleagues, which could also have serious consequences for the patient.

The counsellor might ask the doctor: 'Having spoken to Stephen today, there seem to be some issues that we need to discuss. How do you think the patient's psychological problems should best be managed? If the patient were to see a psychiatrist, how do you think this might affect his view of himself at this stage? What problems or advantages do you see arising from having a psychiatrist involved in this case? How do you see the work of a counsellor in relation to that of a psychiatrist with such a patient?' By asking questions such as these, it is possible to begin to examine the options open to the professionals and the potential consequences.

The counsellor may feel that the patient is coping despite his unhappiness. The doctor may want the patient attended to by someone else because of his busy clinic and suggest that the patient see a psychiatrist in order to pass on the responsibility for assessing and managing the patient's anxiety and depression. On the other hand, the patient may express feelings of unhappiness but be content not to do anything significant to change this. The psychiatrist in turn may be faced with a 'resistant' patient rather than one who is depressed. It may be that the lack of consensus over the nature of problems and how they should be dealt with can lead to unforeseen difficulties in the management of the patient. These differences between professionals must be resolved first.

Problems arising from not properly defining problems

Lack of agreement over the definition of a patient's problem, or about not consulting the patient about the referral, or, indeed, over the purpose of referring a patient for counselling, can lead to additional problems for the counsellor, the patient and the referrer. Experience shows that additional problems which can occur include the patient not keeping appointments; the patient resisting counselling; the patient's problem becoming worse than it already is; conflict between the referrer and counsellor; and referrals being made at a time when little counselling can be done with the patient.

Whenever problems like these arise in the course of counselling, the counsellor should look beyond the counsellor–patient interaction to the wider system for some understanding of what is happening. He may also look to the wider caring system, including the family and other professional care-takers, to determine whether different views or beliefs about treatment and care are at the root of the problem.

Problems in counselling relating to the competence of the counsellor

The practice of skilled professional counselling requires many years of supervised training and experience. All counsellors are expected to seek supervision or to refer cases which are beyond their competence, irrespective of their level of experience. Supervision provides an opportunity for support and professional growth. In some cases, barriers within the counsellor may stand in the way of progress in the course of counselling (see Chapter 16). This may stem from inadequate theoretical ideas or a lack of therapeutic skills. A personal difficulty with particular issues or processes in counselling can impede the exploration or resolution of problems. A drive or mission to make people feel better, for example, may result in repetitive cycles of emotional 'first aid' which may not help patients deal with anxieties about illness or death. Where the counsellor feels that the problem has become too difficult to deal with, there is a danger that he may become 'infected' with the same emotional problems as the patient unless more experienced help is sought.

CONCLUSION

The counsellor's task in exploring the patient's problems includes providing the physical and emotional setting and information which will help patients to make their own decisions. The patient can be helped to make decisions and sustain emotional growth even in the face of serious psychological and medical problems. Patients can also be helped to examine difficulties before they become major problems, placing medical counselling in the domain of preventive medicine.

By enabling patients to clarify their concerns, it is possible to begin to reframe them by asking questions which seek to place problems in context. Effective counselling depends on a clear definition of the problem. This guides the counsellor in his task and helps to determine when the problem has been solved or become more manageable. There is a dynamic and interactive relationship in systemic medical counselling between the questions asked, the therapeutic interventions and the tasks, some of which are described in the following chapters.

CHAPTER 7

Principles and Aims of Counselling, and the Structure of the Session

INTRODUCTION

This chapter focuses on translating some of the theoretical ideas described in the previous chapters into counselling practice. Effective counselling about medical problems needs clarity of purpose. To help achieve clarity, a framework is described which includes the principles and aims of counselling. In addition, having a 'map' or structure for the session can make it easier to achieve the tasks. This map can lead to:

- better use of counselling sessions;
- fewer misunderstandings about how counselling can help;
- increased patient satisfaction with counselling;
- a clearer set of criteria against which the efficacy of counselling can be evaluated.

THEORETICAL CONCEPTS

The approach to counselling described here has been adapted from the techniques of the Milan Associates (Selvini Palazzoli *et al.* 1980a and b) which enables the counsellors to develop a map of therapeutic practice. A salient feature of this approach is the *structure* to the counselling session, which helps to ensure that important issues are addressed in the context of busy medical settings (Miller and Bor 1988).

USE OF QUESTIONS

As the session develops, the exact order of the steps depends on the flow of conversation, which is guided by questions. They facilitate the process between patient and counsellor and help to achieve a structure to the session.

These questions

- help to keep a focus;
- explore ideas or hypotheses;
- avoid making assumptions;
- identify knowledge, concerns and wishes;
- rank concerns and wishes;
- help people to be specific by clarifying the meaning of what is said; for example:

    'You say you are depressed. Can you say more about that? How does it show?'

- link people with ideas and other people they had not previously considered;
- address and inform about unfamiliar and sensitive issues, for example:

    'When you say you are frightened of death, what exactly about death frightens you most?'

Different types of questions are the cornerstone of the systemic approach.

- *Linear questions* usually lead to 'yes' or 'no' answers. Under some circumstances their use is appropriate, but they do not readily open up ideas for discussion. For example:

    'Do you agree with the doctor that you should have this test?'

- Those that show a *difference* between the present, past and future help people to make connections over time. For example:

    'How have you coped with difficult news in the past? How do you think you might manage in the future, and how might you cope right now?'

- *Hypothetical, future-orientated* questions address future concerns and help to explore perceptions of others by linking ideas that might not otherwise have been considered. They are useful in helping people to address difficulties and prepare for the future, whilst the reality of these situations is some distance away. For example:

    'If you were to become ill what might be your main concern? Who would help most, or who or what might make it more difficult?'

- *Circular questions* link ideas, beliefs and relationships in a way that helps people to view problems from different perspectives or reference points. For example:

    'What do you think your husband might most want to discuss today? Would it be the same or different to what you would choose?'
    'Where do you get the idea that you always have to take the opposite stance to your husband?'

- *Reflective questions* help to reframe problems, allow the counsellor to gain time and allow the patient to glimpse another perspective. For example:

    'So you might see yourself as protecting your wife by not telling her that you are here today.'

GUIDING PRINCIPLES FOR FOCUSED COUNSELLING

Guiding principles form a theoretical background to practice and help to focus on the tasks. They include:

- Recognizing that there are different theoretical approaches. None are necessarily right or wrong, but some will be more relevant and applicable in health care than others.
- Avoiding making assumptions about a patient's knowledge, concerns, possible reactions or views about treatment and care.
- Having small, achievable goals, overall and for each session. This increases the likelihood of the counsellor and the patient agreeing about which issues are being dealt with and whether progress is being made.
- Using language carefully, as everything said during a session and in interactions with patients has an impact and may alter perceptions and responses.
- Accepting that patients cannot be completely reassured about a large number of issues, even though certainty and reassurance may be sought from the counsellor.
- Being realistic about the patient's medical condition, what can be achieved from a medical and counselling point of view, and the counsellor's availability.
- Seeking regular consultation and supervision to enhance skills, avoid 'burnout', audit practice and determine effectiveness.

AIMS OF COUNSELLING

The *aims* of counselling are sometimes confused with its *tasks*. The aims give a broad, as well as defined, purpose to the counselling tasks. The tasks (described in Chapter 5) are the steps taken to achieve the aims, and may involve the use of various techniques (reframing, creating balance, reducing anxiety to manageable proportions). The aims of counselling can be specific to a particular setting or task (genetic counselling, termination of pregnancy counselling, pre-HIV antibody or other testing), but also encompass the more general aims of counselling in health care (psychosocial assessment, support to patient and family). Clarity about the aims of counselling helps to:

- develop a relationship with the patient by not raising false expectations about what counselling can achieve;
- dispel misunderstandings (such as that counselling is a friendship relationship);
- reduce myths about what may happen in the sessions.

The aims must always be appropriate for the particular medical context. Inappropriate, vague, all-encompassing or diffuse aims are less likely to lead to a satisfactory outcome for the patient, and the counsellor is more likely to feel that the goals for the session have not been achieved. The main aims for the counsellor include:

- Establishing rapport with patients through a dialogue (talk, listen and note what is *not* said).

- Leading the session by:
  - starting the conversation
  - keeping a focus when confronted by difficult or challenging situations
  - closing the session when it seems appropriate.

- Eliciting and giving information by establishing:
  - what patients *want* to know (tests, diagnosis, prognosis, treatment)
  - what aspects of their health situation they *do not want* to know about (details of tests and results, side effects of treatments)
  - their views and wishes in relation to treatment and care (beliefs in alternative medicine, life and death preferences)
  - *who else*, from the patient's health care point of view, should be included in the patient's care (partners, family)
  - *when* patients want to discuss concerns or receive information, and when it is considered appropriate from a health care perspective (prior to testing, on diagnosis, transmittable disease).

- Defining the problem, exploring its implications and considering how counselling can help address the issues that emerge.
- Identifying concerns and issues of importance to the patient by helping patients talk about their concerns.
- Considering relationships with family, friends, employers and other health care professionals (family doctor, dentist):
  - who else knows about the problem
  - who might be most affected, and in what way
  - who they least want to be involved.

- Assessing the severity of the patient's concerns, and his medical, social and psychological state by reviewing:
  - what the patient has said, how he has reacted
  - to what extent the medical condition impacts on the patient's daily living activities.

- Helping to manage the concerns by enabling informed decision-making, and helping patients to view their situation from different perspectives, thereby increasing their perceived options.

PRACTICE GUIDELINES

Having a check-list with a limited agenda for the first counselling session can help keep a focus, especially in work settings where patients:

- are likely to have high levels of emotional intensity;
- are unfamiliar with counselling and therapeutic processes;
- have a diminished capacity to participate in counselling due to the effects of illness, treatment or the constraints of the setting;

- are likely to have multiple or complex issues that may need to be discussed;
- may have only a single, one-off session or may be unwilling or unable to be followed up.

The counsellor's check-list

1. *Discuss the referral*, including:

   - ideas about being seen by a counsellor;
   - issues about confidentiality;
   - special issues pertaining to the setting (will the patient be in bed, in an open ward, can the patient talk easily, is the patient in pain, is the patient likely to have visitors or other interruptions?).

2. *Aim to obtain sufficient information* to understand how the patient is affected by the condition and treatment, by:

   - focusing initially on the story of the illness, the medical problems it presents and its consequences;
   - considering where the patient is in their 'life cycle' and the natural history of the illness;
   - identifying any critical events;
   - refraining from passing any opinion, giving a diagnosis or suggesting any treatment.

3. *Address the impact of the illness* on the patient and family, and how different relationships are affected. Use a genogram to:

   - obtain a map of family composition and relationships;
   - note life-cycle, developmental and medical issues that may be relevant to the patient and those close to him. (See Chapter 8.)

4. *Explore the patient's beliefs* about the illness, treatment, care and coping strategies.

5. *Address the patient's main fears and concerns.*

6. *Examine past strategies* for coping with adversity and ideas for managing current problems; discuss a treatment plan if appropriate.

7. *Facilitate discussion about the patient's relationships* with members of the health care team and identify potential problems. Discuss what should be fed back to other members of the team.

8. *Invite the patient to give feedback* about the session by finding out what was helpful, anything that was painful and what ideas he has for further discussion.

9. *Provide a summary* of what was covered in the session, and highlight what can and cannot be done in areas where problems have been identified.

10. *Arrange for future follow-up* and realistic contact numbers, should the patient require help.

The counselling session

The following steps construct the 'map' that guides the interview. Although the illustration below is an example of a first session with the patient, many of the steps are equally applicable to follow-up contacts with patients. They can also be adapted in style when sessions are held with more than the index patient (couples or families). The 'map' includes the principles, aims, skills and techniques which are woven into the steps.

1. *Think first* before the start of each session, in order to anticipate issues and problems for each patient. Traditional approaches to counselling define the start of the counselling process as the first meeting between the counsellor and the patient. The systemic approach recognizes that this process begins when a referral is being considered or discussed (Selvini Palazzoli *et al.* 1980b). An *hypothesis* is made about the impact of health problems and other related issues on the patient and his relationships, taking into account the stage of the medical condition, the stage of life of the patient, the patient's social, cultural and medical context, and the referral.

2. *Introduce the session* by clarifying:

   • who you are;
   • where you work;
   • your task in relation to the patient;
   • the purpose of the meeting;
   • the time available.
   (The same procedure should be followed, apart from introductions, in subsequent sessions.)

3. *Engage the patient* (build rapport) by asking questions to gain information rapidly about expectations, who is the patient's support and what type of difficulties might arise. This helps to focus the discussion on:

   • what the patient understands about the meeting;
   • what he wants to achieve and his expectations for the session;
   • who else knows about the illness or that the patient is having counselling;
   • whether there is anyone he might want to be made aware of his illness or problems.

4. Give a focus to the session by setting *small, achievable goals*, for example:

   'If there was one thing you wanted to achieve from our meeting today, what might it be?'

5. *Elicit and give information* throughout the session, in different ways, by exploring the extent of the patient's knowledge about his condition. Sometimes it is the patient who wants information (about symptoms and prognosis). At other times it is the doctor and/or counsellor who consider that there is information to impart. If the patient's knowledge is first explored through questioning, misinformation can be corrected and the gaps in knowledge can be filled at the patient's pace. It is useful to check what the patient has understood at the end of a period of information-giving (see Chapter 10).

Counsellor: What do you know about diabetes?
Patient: Only a little.
Counsellor: What is the little that you do know?

6. *Identify beliefs* about the illness through questions, for example:

   'What information do you want to be given about the laboratory tests that are being done?'
   'Is there anything that you do not want to know?'
   'What is your view about treatment for diabetes?'

   (This last question can reveal the patient's beliefs and rapidly gives information about the likelihood of compliance.)

7. *Identify the patient's main concerns early* in sessions to enable the most pressing issues to be addressed in the time available.

   'If the doctors were to find that you are infected with hepatitis C, what might be your greatest concern?'

8. *Rank concerns* in order of importance or severity; this

   • reduces anxiety to manageable proportions;
   • helps people to be specific;
   • helps to set small achievable goals, giving individuals a sense of control.

   It is recognized that if problem-solving is successfully applied to one issue it often highlights and gives experience about how to tackle other difficulties. For example:

   'Of all the worries about an uncertain diagnosis, who to tell, whether your wife could be infected and your financial troubles – which worries you most, and what is of the least worry today?'

9. *Use language* carefully to avoid or reduce misunderstandings. Using people's own words is a technique which:

   • Helps the counsellor, when he feels stuck, to gain time and to enter the patient's world-view (see Chapter 16):

   'You say you are depressed all the time. How much of the time is all the time? Is there ever a time when you are not depressed?'

   • Builds rapport with the patient, because it confirms that he has been heard, and helps the counsellor to move at the patient's pace:

   'You say that you feel depressed. How does that affect you?'

   • Facilitates the discussion of sensitive or unfamiliar issues, for example:

   'You say that you fear death. What about death do you fear most?'

10. *Help patients to manage concerns* by:

    • Reframing problems, enabling them to consider their predicament differently. This may ultimately help them to cope better on a day-to-day basis, while at the same time being realistic about the nature of the illness, the limitations it imposes on activities and its effect on relationships. For example:

    'In choosing not to tell your mother it seems that you are protecting her from hurt and disappointment.'

- Exploring resources available to patients (how they have coped with past difficulties, how they might cope in the future, who is around to help).
- Engaging the wider health care team whenever possible (team discussions, and including other team members in interviews with patients and families). This also helps to relieve stress on staff, avoid 'burnout', and increase the range of useful interventions (see Chapters 15 and 16).

11. *Maintain clear boundaries* between a professional and a friendship relationship. Enable the session to be therapeutic (the essence of the counselling relationship) by:

- Always being thoughtful about the impact of what is said and what happens during the session.
- Maintaining a neutral stance (showing no surprise, asking questions). For example:

'You say that you feel like giving up all efforts to take your pills. How do you think that will affect your health?'

- Sharing responsibilities with patients (concerns about them, diagnoses) and with colleagues (case discussion and specific consultations). For example:

'If you do decide to stop the medication, how do you think it might affect your diabetes? Who else do you think knows about your feelings? Is there anyone you think should know?'

12. *Make an assessment* towards the end of the session, based on what has been seen and heard, from emotional, social and medical points of view. Those hypothetical, future-orientated questions which explore how patients might cope, and who else is around, are especially useful if suicide is an issue.

13. *End the session* by summarizing the issues discussed. Ending the session well is as important as the beginning, and includes:

- *Decision-making* for the patient and the counsellor. The patient may have to decide whether or not to come back to the counsellor; whether to undergo tests or talk again to the doctor; and may have issues to share with his family. The counsellor has to decide whether he is the right person to deal with the counselling; who to discuss the problem with in the future; and the intervals between sessions with the patient.
- *Summarizing* what has been seen and heard, focusing both on identified strengths and weaknesses. If emphasis is only placed on the positive aspects of the situation, it will not be realistic and the patient will not be effectively supported. For example:

'From what I've heard and seen today you have many worries, but seem to have people who you could turn to for help. However, something is stopping you. Maybe you are protecting them. Maybe you are also protecting yourself from feeling dependent or facing up to your changed state of health. It seems that you will know when the time is right to take a move towards getting the support you want.'

- Indicate what *follow-up* there will be, as this reduces the likelihood of unexpected phone calls or visits. If there is to be an ending and no follow-up, this should also be clarified. Details include:
  - Who can be contacted between sessions and how this can be done.
  - Careful consideration of the time between sessions. If patients are seen too frequently they could be given a message that they cannot manage alone. If the time between sessions is too long the threads of help may be weakened.

BRIEF, FOCUSED COUNSELLING

Focused counselling skills are valued in busy medical settings because of pressure on time and because of the nature of many illnesses where symptoms and problems may change rapidly. The briefer the time available, the greater the focus required to achieve an effective outcome. A case example illustrates the main aims and how they can be addressed.

A 60-year-old man was being investigated for the cause of extensive bruising. He was seen by the haematology team on a ward round. Prior to the ward round the junior doctor told the team that the patient was extremely anxious. The counsellor recognized that it was important to clarify his main concern and to develop an optimal relationship with the patient in the shortest time. In the following conversation the counsellor was able to establish a rapid rapport and allow the patient to express his real concern in a few minutes. Doing this in the presence of the whole medical and nursing team was a way of demonstrating effectiveness and passing on skills to other colleagues.

Counsellor: I understand from Dr Black that you are very anxious and tearful. Is that correct?
Patient: Yes. Very.
Counsellor: Can you tell us what you are most anxious about?
Patient: I want to be well. All this waiting for the results of the investigations is intolerable.
Counsellor: What is it you are most worried about?
Patient: Cancer. Actually I already feel a little better just having said it.

Eliciting and giving information concisely and effectively is also important in brief sessions.

Exploring and addressing main concerns and issues for the patient and their contacts helps to get the underlying problems into the open and thus creates more understanding of the patient's behaviour.

Counsellor: What is your main concern about cancer?
Patient: Everything.
Counsellor: What most?
Patient: Well, my wife and family.
Counsellor: Have you told them about your worry?
Patient: Not really, but my wife guesses. I find it hard to speak about it.

Developing, with the patient, an appropriate plan and identifying achievable goals helps to lead to some solutions and reduction of anxieties.

Counsellor: As you will not get these results until next week, how do you think you will manage during this time?

Patient: It will be hard, but I shall have television and my wife visits. That is not necessarily a help, as I try and not show all my worries.

Counsellor: Would it be a help if I came up and saw you either alone or with your wife?

Patient: If you could I would like you to meet my wife, as maybe she has some worries also.

The patient was more settled after this discussion and the medical team felt more at ease as his behaviour was better understood.

CONCLUSION

Clarity about the principles and aims of counselling can give counsellors the confidence to focus on the tasks when dealing with illness and its complex repercussions for patients and their relationships. Having a structure for the session enables the maximum to be achieved in a relatively short period of time. This can help both those who are trained counsellors and those who use counselling skills as part of their role.

CHAPTER 8

Genograms

INTRODUCTION

Most counsellors are trained to work with individuals and consequently focus in counselling sessions on intrapsychic processes, self-beliefs and the patient's feelings. When working in health care settings, issues pertaining to disclosure of illness, access to emotional, social and practical support, and the impact of illness on other family members are also highly relevant. A genogram, also known as a family tree, pedigree or genealogical chart, is a clinical tool used for acquiring, storing and processing information about family history, composition and relationships. A genogram can be used to develop a map of family relationships with the patient, identify sources of support within the family, and explore transgenerational illness meanings. Genograms have been used in psychotherapy for years and are a natural fit for medical settings.

This chapter is for counsellors with little or no experience of using genograms with patients and their families, or for counsellors and health care professionals who want to use genograms more effectively. A brief survey of the basic use of the genogram will show how it incorporates a patient's family medical history. The family medical genogram can be used as a collaborative tool to incorporate patients' illness narratives and meanings of illness. These highly efficient diagrams share relevant information with other health care professionals in a way that can optimize diagnosis, care and recovery of patients.

THEORETICAL BACKGROUND

The information contained in a genogram may include medical, behavioural, genetic, cultural and social aspects of the family system. This information can provide a rich source of hypotheses with regard to how a clinical problem may be linked to family history and relationships, and how a problem may evolve through time. Genograms help to reveal patterns and events which may have recurring significance within a family system. McGoldrick and Gerson (1985) explain that the act of constructing a family diagram with a patient or family, to map relationships and functioning patterns, acts in a way similar to language – to potentiate and organize thought processes. To this end, genograms can be conceptualized as both a therapeutic intervention *and* a part of the process of counselling.

Knowledge of a patient's family history is important in a health care setting for several reasons. Information about a patient's family background helps in:

- making a diagnosis of familial, biological and psychiatric disorders (e.g. cystic fibrosis, heart disease, haemophilia, asthma, schizophrenia);
- genetic counselling and the prediction of illness and disability;
- evaluating somatic complaints;
- understanding the family's role in the aetiology of illness (e.g. in the case of diabetic ketoacidosis);
- helping patients to make informed choices;
- identifying psychological problems in different family constellations such as step-families;
- devising health promotion and treatment plans.

A genogram provides an immediate picture of the family and its medical history. It is a useful alternative to having to search through thick files of patient notes for biographical and background information. Critical medical information can be highlighted and current medical and psychosocial problems considered.

A family genogram going back at least two generations will provide specialized information to act as a quick reference and to highlight choices so that health care teams can begin to construct a treatment plan (e.g. smoking cessation, dietary changes, exercise) that will fit the patient's lifestyle. This can be done by:

- discovering patient and family attitudes, beliefs and understanding of illness;
- highlighting the emotional pay-off for different members when the patient is either ill or well;
- finding examples of the positive problem-solving skills of patients and their families in their historical accounts;
- revealing the resources needed for patients to negotiate the challenges of current illnesses (serious, chronic, terminal) or disabilities;
- providing a reference map that facilitates easy movement back and forth between the family's emotional and physical resources;
- discovering strengths and locating vulnerabilities that will affect medical situations, for example, the family's structure, life cycle, generationally repetitive emotional and illness patterns, life experiences of families, and the family's relationships with each other.

From a systemic perspective, the family life cycle is an important variable to consider when counselling, since it will have implications not only for the patient and his illness but for the family as a whole. In order for an individual to move on to the next stage in the family life cycle (e.g. a parent facing the empty nest after children have left home), the family must reorganize itself at each pivotal point that it enters in the life cycle. These transitions can be difficult for some families, especially where there is a medical illness (Rolland 1984). The listing of ages, dates and significant family events (i.e. births, deaths, divorce) on a genogram enables the counsellor to examine whether or not life-cycle events occurred within expected parameters (McDaniel *et al.* 1992). The genogram also allows for important anniversaries to be considered, especially those relating to change and loss within the family. This may be particularly relevant in the case of a death or a suicide within the family or illness relating to distress, even though no conscious connection is made between these events and illness. Josse (1993) describes the case of a man whose dyspepsia coincided with the anniversary of his uncle's death from stomach cancer. The man had not realized the extent to which his uncle's death had affected him until he began to discuss it while working on his genogram in counselling. The following example highlights the relevance of a genogram in patient care:

> Sally was a 13-year-old girl in fairly good health with recurring sore throats all winter. Her physician explained to the girl's parents that removing her tonsils would greatly reduce her susceptibility to sore throats, colds and flu. Sally's parents decided on the surgery, which they understood would require two days and an overnight stay at the hospital. Sally would then be able to recuperate at home and in ten days or so be able to return to school. After routine surgery for the removal of her tonsils and adenoids the physician told Sally's parents that it might take two full weeks for Sally's recovery because she was a bit older than the average tonsillectomy patient. Sally's surgery was scheduled over a break from school and in between her recurring sore throats. However, during Sally's surgery her respiration, blood pressure, and heart rate dropped and she had to be revived. As the surgery team stabilized her and intubated Sally again, they lost her vital signs. Once Sally was stable and perceived to be out of danger, she left the recovery room for her hospital bed and was scheduled for release the next day. Some time during the night Sally began haemorrhaging and again her vital signs became unstable. She remained in the hospital for several days. Sally eventually recovered and it was not until years later that she learned that her mother, grandmother and her mother's sisters all experienced the same problems that she had had during surgery. A simple medical genogram tracking the illnesses, surgeries and recoveries of this family's female members would have been useful. The physician could have taken steps to help prevent Sally's surgical trauma and the psychological distress to Sally and the family.

Genograms provide more than a quantitative measure through which clinical predictions can be made; they can be employed as a means of subjectively interpreting information about relationships and forming tentative hypotheses for further investigation. By obtaining an 'image' of the current family context, the counsellor can assess the family's strengths, as well as the possible links between the presenting problem and family relationships. Individual symptoms can therefore be recast in interpersonal terms. For example, a genogram might help to reveal that the onset of a child's enurisis – possibly as a result of his feeling anxious and insecure – coincided with his mother starting an extra-marital relationship; this could lead to bringing the couple together to work with a counsellor to help their son to overcome his problem.

Although the origins of the genogram lie in family therapy, this tool can also be used effectively in individual and couple medical counselling. Indeed, it is especially useful in cases where:

- a psychological problem has implications for other family members, but they are not present in counselling;
- the presenting problem appears to stem from family relationships;
- illness and issues of loss need to be addressed in counselling;
- other care-givers seem to have inadvertently maintained or exacerbated the problem, and a sociogram (genogram which also includes significant non-biologically linked relationships) together with a genogram can help to map out all the relevant players and relationships;
- the 'family' is typically overlooked in counselling, e.g. with gay men, lesbians and people in individual counselling or therapy.

Genograms provide a means of engaging the whole family in the counselling process. The procedure of gathering information and mapping it onto the genogram helps the counsellor to develop a rapport with the patient. They can also be used to free the therapeutic process from an impasse. The index patient or symptom-bearer (the person with presenting psychological and/or health problem) is often viewed as the person with the problem, and therefore the person who needs to be helped or needs to change. Viewing the presenting problem within the context of family relationships and within a multigenerational framework is a powerful way of reframing the problem and removing blame from any one individual (see Chapter 4). The effect is to normalize the family's understanding of the problem, and perhaps also the reactions of different family members to it. Indeed, once the family patterns which underlie problematic behaviour are identified, it is possible that the behaviour will change without the need for further psychotherapeutic intervention. Genograms can also help to focus questioning on significant family experiences such as births, marriages, leaving home transitions and deaths, all of which may have some significance in the context surrounding family beliefs about illness.

CONSTRUCTING A GENOGRAM IN COUNSELLING

A carefully gathered and constructed genogram will provide clues to clarify the biological and legal relationships of the patient and other family members. The comprehensive medical and psychological information includes: who lives with the patient or who the patient lives with; the family's past and current experience with illness; and who copes best with anticipated or surprise changes. A medical genogram can provide clarity about the biological and stepfamily members on both the maternal and paternal side of the patient's family, in addition to marriages, divorces, births, deaths, illness, and the current health of members and siblings.

The patient is usually given the option of choosing where to start the genogram but the counsellor can suggest the immediate household if this appears to be a problem. The counsellor should be sincere, open-minded, interested and non-judgemental when constructing a genogram. Starting with straightforward questions is also a useful way of setting the patient or family at ease. Direct, linear questions are useful at the beginning, e.g. 'Who lives in your household?', but the interview may later progress to questions concerning views about relationships, such as: 'Who in your family has the closest relationship to your father? How does this show?' The counsellor should not only identify the composition of the family or household, but also look out for unusual family configurations and significant developmental stages and how these are or have been managed. A transitional delay or a premature occurrence, for example, will be of interest. Major illnesses are also recorded next to the relevant family member. All this information may help to identify structural patterns and relationship similarities, such as divorce or overly close relationships, and the frequent occurrence of a particular illness, which may have a functional as well as a medical significance.

Constructing a medical genogram is not as unmanageable as may first appear, if counsellors use it as part of the joining process with patients and families by asking respectful and well-constructed questions. It is useful to include at the initial mapping session three generations on the patient's maternal and paternal sides. Information should include first a list of parents, siblings and children, then grandparents, aunts, uncles and cousins from both sides. Patients may only provide medical information from one family side or the other, and what health information is provided may be incomplete. However, a medical genogram is a document that can continually be added to as patients and family members are more forthcoming with information. The medical genogram is constructed from the bottom row up, starting with the patient, the significant other and children. The second row includes the patient's mother, father and siblings and the patient's placement in the family. The third row lists the patient's grandparents, aunts, uncles and cousins. All rows indicate marriages, separations, divorces and remarriages, highlighting key persons interacting in the patient's life. The symbols used in genograms to denote gender, family structure and emotional relationships are shown in Figure 8.1.

For each relative, the medical genogram records date of birth, date of death, cause of death, known illnesses, major medical events (e.g. coronary by-pass, tuberculosis), ages when these conditions occurred, and lifestyle or occupational factors that may contribute to ill health. This information may also provide counsellors and health care professionals with relevant ideas about the onset of, and susceptibility to, genetically linked diseases. A medical genogram with such information will help health care professionals with diagnosis and help patients and family members to make informed treatment choices.

The counsellor fills in the medical genogram with psychosocial issues, typical emotional reactions, coping skills, problem-solving abilities, family interactions, and social and religious beliefs. All of these affect the patient's diagnosis and ways of dealing with illness, treatment, rehabilitation and lifestyle changes. For example, McGoldrick and Gerson (1985) outlined interpretative psychosocial categories based on family-systems theory:

- family structures
- life cycle
- repetitive patterns
- life experiences
- relationships, marriages, separations, divorces, estrangements
- attempted solutions
- current problems.

Relevant information about these areas of concern make a genogram a valuable collaborative map for discerning:

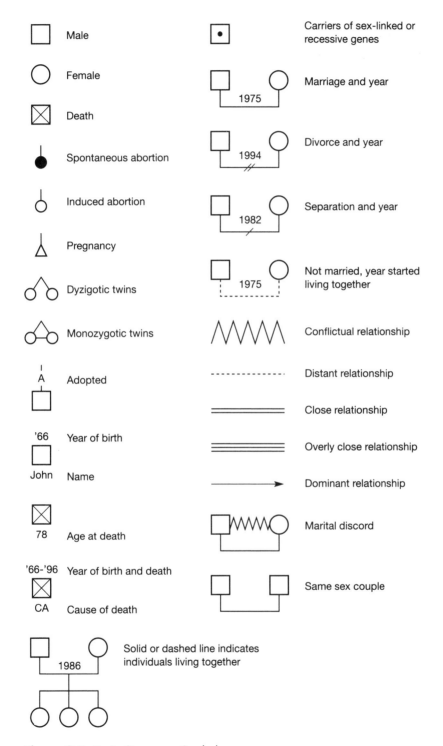

	Male		Carriers of sex-linked or recessive genes
	Female		Marriage and year
	Death	1975	
	Spontaneous abortion	1994	Divorce and year
	Induced abortion	1982	Separation and year
	Pregnancy	1975	Not married, year started living together
	Dyzigotic twins		Conflictual relationship
	Monozygotic twins		Distant relationship
A	Adopted		Close relationship
'66	Year of birth		Overly close relationship
John	Name		Dominant relationship
78	Age at death		Marital discord
'66-'96	Year of birth and death		Same sex couple
CA	Cause of death		
1986	Solid or dashed line indicates individuals living together		

Figure 8.1 Basic Genogram Symbols

- the impact of a patient's illness on the family;
- which family members contribute to the illness cycle;
- who are supportive or nonsupportive;
- which relationships are stable;
- economic influences;
- communication patterns;
- appropriate referrals.

Questions should be asked concerning developmental stages and transitional life events, particularly where these coincide with the onset of or changes in medical conditions. Counsellors can use questions about the family's medical history to help patients and their families regain a sense of control in a situation they had perceived as out of control. Sharp (1994) suggests that counsellors and health care professionals encounter the most resistance while constructing medical genograms when patients and family members think the questions are too personal and prying, e.g. those about sex, miscarriages and abortions. The best way for counsellors and health care professionals to avoid this perception when delicate questions are asked is to use extreme tact and sensitivity, clearly stating that highly personal information is confidential and will not be disclosed for any reason without the patient's permission. It is important for patients and family members to know and feel confident that medical genograms are not constructed 'to pry into your private lives [and there is] no need to be afraid to answer any question' (Sharp 1994). Finally, counsellors need to assure patients and family members often during the process that all information is confidential between the counsellor and physician.

Patients and their families may view genograms as too personal, or as airing dirty linen (Papazian 1994). Counsellors need considerable skill with some patients and family members because they may not wish to talk about sad, secretive or stressful events. A useful approach for the counsellor with the reluctant talker or family could be to say simply, 'Because of your condition and the risks involved, any and all information that you or your family provide will be useful in diagnosis, treatment choices or chronic medical conditions.' Counsellors and health care professionals can gather answers to medical questions by enquiring about familial medical conditions, physical characteristics, susceptibility to disease, hereditary diseases, chronic lifestyle conditions and illness patterns.

Counsellors can establish patient confidence in the value of the medical genogram by placing present health care issues in a context of how the family normally responds to illness and crises, by asking, for example, 'Who do you think has been most supportive at this difficult time?' or 'Who in the family was most surprised by your daughter's response to her grandfather's illness?' Patients and family members can be helped to understand the different ways they can address anxiety about illness. Counsellors can do this by reframing the current situation, normalizing the emotionally charged medical situation, and organizing a broad spectrum of information about the patient's illness, care and prognosis.

Basic genograms have expanded to track multigenerational health, illness and emotional patterns found in families. The household depicted below is identifiable from the rest of the family by the solid line drawn around it. James and Clare are a young couple living together, aged 29 and 25 years respectively, with two young children, Stephen (5) and Gail (3) and a baby *in utero* (8 months). The couple were referred by Clare's obstetrician because Clare had become increasingly depressed and distant over the past two months, and James was also concerned in view of the impending birth. At first, her mood changes were put down to 'hormonal changes in pregnancy', but the couple were not reassured by this because Clare's previous pregnancies had gone smoothly and had even brought the couple closer together.

Following an initial interview with the couple, the counsellor drew up a family genogram with them (see below).

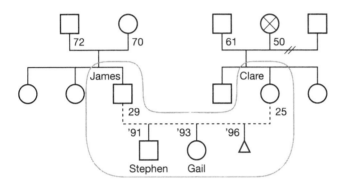

The counsellor observed from the genogram that Clare's mother was deceased and on further enquiry was able to add to the genogram that she had died in 1993, soon after Gail was born. The discussion opened up after this and the psychosocial importance of this death in relation to the new birth three years later became very apparent. The use of the genogram enabled the counsellor to discuss a bereavement which, having taken place three years before, had not been mentioned by the couple but was evidently painful for Clare to talk about.

Combining a patient's basic genogram with their medical history becomes an effective tool to locate significant generational illness patterns and attitudes. This can provide counsellors with a clearer context for a systemic evaluation of how patient families interact in problem-solving, communicate, and respond to crises and emotionally saturated situations, and how the patient's family is likely to react to medical crises which impact patient recovery. Discovering the lack or presence of coping skills for problem-solving will increase the counsellor's ability to bring to the forefront which-ever skills will be needed to alleviate difficulties and interrupt anticipated behaviours that may hinder the patient's recovery in the current medical situation. Charting the evolution of a problem while discussing the genogram also invites the patient and family to relate the family narrative and to participate in the domain of storytelling.

Constructing and exploring a genogram can be a very emotional experience for a patient or family and may reveal issues which need to be addressed further either in additional sessions or through referral. In order for this tool to be effective in clinical practice, it needs to be regularly updated during subsequent visits to the counsellor. As it is an unfamiliar tool to most counsellors, and also an emotional process, counsellors should first do their own medical genogram with a counsellor or colleague in order to gain experience in its use and experience at first hand the impact of talking about family relationships using this method.

CONCLUSION

The medical genogram offers counsellors a process tool for the construction and reconstruction of treatment plans and disease progression. It can also boost patient and family morale by highlighting each member's coping skills. The genogram can integrate a wealth of physical and psychological information into an inclusive diagnostic presentation, linking relationships with the medical and psychological problems in a more inclusive way that becomes a biopsychosocial cycle.

The standardized symbols (Figure 8.1) used in the construction of genograms may be expanded or amended according to the specific need of a particular patient's medical situation, e.g. for illness tracking in a health care setting. These amended symbols would offer quick tracking at a glance that highlights the unique patient population or health care setting. When eliciting the medical history of a family, therefore, counsellors clearly need to make a distinction between social and therapeutic information because this type of genogram breaks with the social rules of conversation. The medical genogram is an exercise in the counsellor's curiosity about the patient's family and social relationships. The information gathered is useful in so far as the counsellor learns about the patient's social context. But genograms become an even more useful therapeutic tool when combined with commentary about the patient's affect when talking about different relationships, discussion about taboo or sensitive issues (e.g. substance abuse or incest within the family), and previous experience with other health care professionals and settings. Useful as well are the patient's and family's social and cultural history, because this element promotes awareness of other issues connected to patient and family meanings in the current medical context. Tracking the family's social and cultural history will point out particular strengths and weaknesses that may otherwise be missed within the family system – factors that may be a resource for the patient's recovery.

CHAPTER 9

Confidentiality and Secrets

INTRODUCTION

Psychotherapeutic relationships are bound by confidentiality parameters. This is fundamental to the aims and principles of good counselling practice and the therapeutic relationship and process. The rules governing confidentiality in health care settings are no different to those which apply in other settings. However, the issues are sometimes more complex, given the need for collaborative working relationships with colleagues and the effects of secrets on the patient's overall care and on relationships when working within multidisciplinary health care teams. The British Association of Counselling (1990) *Code of Ethics and Practice* sets out to define and operationalize confidentiality; for example:

> A counsellor should take all responsible steps to communicate clearly the extent of confidentiality they are offering to patients. This should normally be made clear in the pre-counselling information or in the initial contracting. (B.4.6)

> If counsellors include consultation with colleagues and others in the confidential relationship, this should be stated to the patient at the beginning of counselling. (B.4.7)

The breaking of confidentiality is likewise subject to rules and guidelines. There are a number of circumstances where confidentiality can be broken. These are as follows:

- When the patient gives consent to the counsellor to break confidentiality.
- When the information to be disclosed is already public knowledge (and as such is no longer secret or a breach of confidence).
- When it is in the public interest to do so, that is, the public interest outweighs the individual interest (e.g. the patient is a risk to the public).

Each situation has to be taken on its own merits, and the counsellor can use supervision and consultation to reach a shared decision about the need to disclose. But even the parameters of confidentiality within supervision and consultative relationships may be open to interpretation:

> Care must be taken to ensure that personally identifiable information is not transmitted through overlapping networks of confidential relationships. For this reason it is good practice to avoid identifying specific patients during counselling supervision/consultative support and other consultations, unless there are sound reasons for doing so. (British Association for Counselling, 1990, B.4.8)

How do colleagues who are seeing the same patient, but are not aware that other colleagues are involved, come to share information and generate group ideas, if the person discussed is 'unidentifiable'? Does this really happen? An example from a health care setting illustrates this problem:

> A patient with hypochondriasis kept phoning numerous health professionals within the same team in a hospital to discuss her symptoms and seek advice in a bid to allay her anxieties, albeit temporarily. Without discussion in the team or other affiliated health professionals, this individual continued to make regular telephone contact with different team members. This only served to sustain her health anxiety problem rather than treat it and she felt she was being given slightly different information each time she spoke to someone. Her calls (and worry) went on for several months before a member of staff eventually recognized what was happening and started to compare details with other members of the team. It was only when her name and clinical details were shared that a more appropriate way of managing this patient's problems could begin. Instead of offering limitless and differing reassurances, firm boundaries were set as to who and when she could call, with the same information and intervention being used. This served to contain and reduce her anxieties so that problems underlying her health worry could be addressed and treated.

WHAT IS CONFIDENTIALITY?

Central to the concept of confidentiality is the sharing or withholding of personal information according to a set of rules or guidelines. Where rules are implicit, however, there is scope for ambiguity, assumption and idiosyncratic approaches to maintaining and breaking confidentiality.

Secrets and power games

Confidentiality is sometimes understood to imply secrecy, which is not altogether correct. Secrets, like confidential information, may be withheld or selectively shared between individuals or groups. It is the withholding and sharing of secrets which creates alliances and boundaries between individuals and systems. A shift in the power dynamics and relationship between 'those who know' and 'those who don't know' can emerge, creating a context for power relationships (Campbell *et al.* 1994). There are three main forms of secrets.

- *Individual secrets* are those in which a person withholds information from others in a system (e.g. colleagues, family). An individual belongs to many systems which may interrelate or function independently. For example:

  Mr Jones decided not to tell anyone about his biopsy until after the results. He thought he might tell his wife if it were positive, but at this stage, no relatives or friends were told that he was having the biopsy.

- *Internal secrets* require at least one person in the system to be privy to the secret. Different levels of knowledge (about the secret) create two sub-systems, those who know and those who do not know. For example:

  A counsellor who promises that everything the patient says to him or her is entirely confidential – 'no-one will ever know' – and therefore the information is shared between the two of them, has an internal secret.

- *Shared secrets* are secrets which belong to the system organization and are withheld from external groups (e.g. colleagues, GP). They differ from internal secrets where the information is shared with only one other person. For example:

  Mary told her mother, father and sister that she had cancer of the cervix, but asked her mother not to tell anyone else for the time being.

In order to ensure effective procedures for managing issues and problems stemming from confidentiality, the rules need to be made explicit and disseminated to the target or affected audience. This may include patients as well as health care professionals, in order that everyone has the same knowledge of what is meant by confidentiality within a given context or setting. This balances out the power dynamics and creates a uniting context where 'everybody knows' (replacing the 'those who know' and 'those who don't' context and perceived difference and power dynamic). Counsellors can help patients to reach decisions about disclosure of information by addressing the reasons for someone needing to be informed, as well as the possible consequences of sharing personal and sensitive information.

The consequences of secrets

The effect of keeping a secret may be both positive and negative. On the positive side, it might protect someone from something, such as a parent from upsetting news about his or her child. On the negative side, it can lead to feelings of anxiety, dishonesty, suspicion and exclusion. It is not uncommon for people diagnosed with a serious illness to keep this information as an individual or internal secret, at least for a time while they consider the implications or wait until symptoms show and they are no longer in a position to conceal it. Although significant others may be protected, keeping this secret may produce anxiety and isolation in the individual. Also, late disclosure could create further anxiety and complications because the significant other may construe the withholding of information as a sign of a lack of closeness, fear of the significant other, or being lied to.

Another unforeseen problem may arise when the information withheld needs to be shared for ethical and safety reasons. For example, when a person tells the counsellor not to tell her doctor she is saving up her tranquillizers to take her own life, the counsellor is colluding with the patient's suicide attempt and is in fact obliged to disclose the threat to the doctor for the patient's safety. Likewise, if a patient tells his counsellor that he is not going to tell his sexual partner he is HIV positive and will continue to have unprotected intercourse with him or her, the safety of the partner is in question and raises ethical dilemmas for those holding this information. Counselling can help individuals find more constructive ways of addressing the dilemmas and complications of sharing and withholding information. It can provide a method for opening up communication and looking at the underlying issues. Within the wider clinical system, it may be helpful to promote team confidentiality and more comprehensive care, with health care workers working together rather than in opposition or ignorance of others' involvement.

CONFIDENTIALITY IN HEALTH CARE PRACTICE

A two-tier approach

Confidentiality is an absolute term. Something is either confidential or it is not. In lay language, however, it has become common to refer to confidentiality in a graded format:

- top-secret information
- very confidential information
- not so confidential information
- common knowledge.

In health care practice it is not uncommon to observe a two-tier approach to confidentiality (Salt *et al.* 1992): the 'top secret' or 'very confidential' information is only disclosed under the strictest procedure and the 'not so confidential' information can become common knowledge amongst health care staff and anyone listening or glancing at available records and forms. Examples of the 'top secret' or 'very confidential' information include diagnosis of terminal illness, HIV status, sexual abuse history, alcohol abuse history, depression and suicide attempt. Examples of the 'not so confidential information' or 'common knowledge' include the patient's blood group, tonsillectomy, marital status, number of children, profession, blood pressure recordings and extraction of wisdom teeth. Whether patient information is deemed very confidential or not so confidential often depends on the degree to which the information is considered by the health care professional to be private or associated with stigma.

If the absolute definition of confidentiality is adopted, then all the above examples are technically as confidential as each other. Value judgements abound in clinical practice, however, and staff may base their 'confidential' conversations on these values. Consequently, disclosure of patient information is open to individual interpretation, ambiguity and conflict between staff and discriminatory practices.

Differences can occur between health care professionals, particularly between the medical and nursing team and allied paramedical groups. This is especially apparent for psychosocial health care workers, who see the confidential relationship as a therapeutic relationship based on trust. Only in the exception would these health professionals disclose patient information. This is juxtaposed to the medical team approach, which relies on 'shared confidentiality' and open discussion about patient details, including name, age, relationship status, etc., as well as their physical and mental health state.

The above differences in perspective may be at the root of many battles in a health care setting, where communication between health care professionals becomes impeded by different notions of confidentiality parameters. Counsellors need to be aware of this potential source of ambiguity and seek to clarify team confidentiality boundaries so that everyone involved can develop a common view of what is meant by confidentiality for each client and set of circumstances. The open flow of information within a team is essential in order to provide consistent medical care. Other professionals within the health care team will feel more secure in the knowledge that important issues will be brought to the attention of colleagues. The issue of trust, on which all counselling relationships are based, is central to effective practice. Confidentiality helps to regulate relationships between counsellors and their patients, and between counsellors and their colleagues. It may fall to the counsellor to highlight any potential impasse and to strive to maintain open communication between different parties. Failure to do so could compromise the patient's care and jeopardize trust in complex relationship systems.

Management of secrets

The following suggestions provide a practical approach to managing secrets in clinical practice.

- Identify whether there is a secret.
- Identify whether there is a problem related to the secret and for whom.
- Clarify dilemmas and problems associated with maintaining this secret, e.g. consider the advantages and disadvantages and the implications (using future-orientated and hypothetical question – see Chapter 7).
- Reflect on your involvement in the process, i.e. are you *colluding* with the individual by agreeing to keep the secret, or *challenging* the individual by not agreeing to keep the secret? The patient should be advised at the outset that it may be necessary to break confidentiality for legal/ethical reasons. Or should you *opt out/refer* – for problems which do not have legal implications but rather create an impasse in therapy that might require treatment to stop or for the patient to be referred?

Secrets, families and children

Secrets in families are common and may involve outside agencies in the maintenance and disclosure of these secrets. The counsellor can play a role in helping families and professionals to acknowledge secrets in families, particularly transgenerational secrets between parent and child, which may involve professionals working on behalf of the child or the parent and result in 'conflicts of interest' and dilemmas.

Example 1

A parent wants to be told everything about her 16-year-old daughter's visit to a doctor, but the doctor refuses to discuss the consultation because of 'patient confidentiality'. The counsellor can help them overcome the impasse by addressing the key dilemmas of parental versus medical responsibility for the girl's welfare. Mutual concern for her welfare and the wish to respect the girl's independence whilst acknowledging her need for professional and parental help can be introduced as a theme which unites both parental and medical interests, and collaborative working.

Example 2

At the outset of counselling, the counsellor had explained to his patient that 'confidentiality' meant some discussion with the family doctor. The patient agreed to this. When she disclosed that she had given her daughter her sleeping tablets, it was possible to discuss her reasons for doing this and the consequences, and to remind her that her family doctor needed this information in order to care for her daughter. Mrs Jones was unhappy about this, and concerned that her daughter would be taken into care. However, since she had consented to the family doctor knowing, she was resigned to the outcome rather than feeling let down by the counsellor.

The following excerpt from another counselling session further illustrates how a counsellor can explore dilemmas associated with how information is disseminated between family members.

Counsellor:	You say that you can't tell your children about your motor neurone disease. What do you think they have noticed about your health?
Patient:	Well they must see me hesitate and have difficulty walking. I also slur my words. Jack even joked about my being drunk . . .
Counsellor:	What do you think *they* think is going on?
Patient:	I know Pat is concerned, she keeps telling me to go back to the doctors . . . I think she is worried.
Counsellor:	What do you think she is most worried about?
Patient:	. . . that I have something serious, something incurable . . . that I'm not doing anything about it . . . but what she doesn't know is that there is no cure for my disease . . .
Counsellor:	Do you think it would help her to know this?
Patient:	Yes I guess so . . . and Jack, I don't want him getting the wrong idea . . . but I don't know how to tell them.
Counsellor:	You know them very well; how would they suggest you tell someone some difficult news?
Patient:	They would say just do it straight . . . no frills, to the point . . .
Counsellor:	How could you do it in a way that they would appreciate?
Patient:	. . . just say it . . . say I've got a disease which affects the nervous system and that it is incurable and take it from there . . .

Secrets in families may present as a communication impasse, in which a professional feels immobilized and unable to help the family break entrenched communication and behaviour patterns. Unpacking the secret can remove an obstacle to change for the family, the health worker and the counsellor.

Preventive methods

The counsellor can play a key role in preventing problems and improving patient care by facilitating communication between agencies and individuals. In particular the counsellor can identify situations in which themes of 'impasse' or 'over-protection' occur. Examples would be (a) when a doctor informs the relatives of an individual's terminal diagnosis before discussing it with the patient, and (b) where a health adviser does not involve other multidisciplinary workers for fear of breaking the confidentiality of a therapeutic relationship.

To avoid ambiguity and enhance patient care, it is also helpful to develop a confidentiality policy which details who needs to know what, when, why, and how. Where there is an explicit confidentiality policy made available to health care workers and patients, open communication is more likely to take place. This is because people can know in advance what are likely to be the implications of disclosure. They are also less likely to withhold information based on fears, assumptions and fantasy. If patients feel more able to be open and honest about their problems, health care workers are in a better position to address their needs and generate appropriate solutions. A sample confidentiality policy is outlined below to suggest ways in which an agency could develop guidelines to govern communication within health care teams and between groups (teams, departments and organizations). Such a policy is different from a professional code of conduct. Codes of practice and ethics are often drawn up with a particular professional discipline in mind. A confidentiality policy should take account of how information should be *shared across* disciplines and between departments and external agencies.

A sample confidentiality policy

1. The organization needs to have a set of written rules which are accessible to all members of staff, governing the way in which personal information about patients is obtained, stored and used.
2. It is necessary to specify how information is to be passed between agencies (computer network, paper, etc.), how letters should be posted and received, who should read them and what discussion is necessary and with whom.
3. Rules need to be identified for storing information on computer disk (in accordance with the Data Protection Act), in paper files, etc. Accessing and storing of information should be limited to those who really need to know.
4. Who needs to know and who does not need to know should be made explicit. Procedures need to be installed to ensure that access to information is limited only to those who need to know (this will include security procedures).
5. Strict guidelines need to be set out about how information is to be used. This includes how it should not be used, in order to protect patients from discriminatory practices.
6. Information which needs to be shared with other agencies should be detailed in the document. This would include how, when and why information might be shared with other health care workers, family, employers, occupational health, human resources, GP, etc.

CONCLUSION

Confidentiality is a much used and misunderstood concept because it is ambiguous and open to interpretation. It always relates to the passing (and withholding) of information between people and has to be construed in terms of its context. In health care settings, confidentiality is such an important and integral aspect of patient care that it is often 'taken as said', without due care and attention being paid to its meaning within a given context. Consequently, patients, families, health care workers, employers and others may have different views about what is meant by confidentiality, and this can create difficult and confusing situations. Breaches in confidentiality often arise from lack of clarity about policies and practices, and lack of openness between individuals. Counsellors are well placed to consider, with the patients, the advantages and disadvantages of secrets, how they differ from confidentiality and how to share information in the interest of optimal patient care.

CHAPTER 10

Giving Information

INTRODUCTION

This chapter highlights relevant issues for counsellors when they give information to patients. Consideration is given to the different emphases placed on *who* gives information; *to* whom it is given; and *how* information should best be given.

Giving information (imparting knowledge; telling about facts or circumstances) is an integral part of the role of doctors and others involved in health care, including counsellors. Counselling implies the exchange of ideas about information and thus is by implication integral to this aspect of health care. The impact of information about illness on patients and relatives may precipitate referrals to a counsellor or requests for counselling from patients.

There is a difference between giving information (imparting knowledge and facts), and giving advice (an opinion and recommendation about future action). This chapter concentrates on giving information and responding to situations where the patient seeks the counsellor's professional opinion. The counselling approach described encourages patients to reach their own decisions about treatment and care, but recognizes the important role a counsellor may have in helping patients to make such decisions.

Information-giving is but one component of the communication between the counsellor and patient in health care. The information imparted may encompass a range of issues about specific illnesses, tests, diagnoses, prognoses, treatment options and the impact of all these on patients and their significant relationships. Information-giving counselling has been well established in infertility clinics, genetic screening, sexually transmitted diseases clinics, pre- and post-HIV antibody testing and cancer care. Counselling interventions in prevention of illness and health promotion in the 'healthy' population are discussed in Chapter 17.

Aspects of communication in information-giving which need to be considered include the following:

- Information-giving in the medical context can imply a monologue (the patient being lectured to); for counsellors it is a dialogue.

- One cannot *not* communicate in a counselling relationship, even if no information is given.
- Information-giving implies *content* (what is said) and *process* (how it is said, or what is being conveyed/implied).
- Information-giving has a context which conveys meaning. Each context implies different relationships with patients; for example:
  - a patient returning for test results;
  - telling a relative that someone has died;
  - a lecture or teaching students in front of a patient;
  - informing a patient that the session time has ended.

SPECIFIC ISSUES ABOUT INFORMATION-GIVING FOR COUNSELLORS

Some counsellors may be uncomfortable with information-giving as part of their task because:

- It can be at variance with counselling approaches which focus on responding to the patient's emotional state and avoid giving information and advice.
- There may be confusion between giving information and advising patients.
- There can be dilemmas about how much specialist medical knowledge counsellors may require for the task.
- There may be lack of clarity about the role of the counsellor in giving information where the doctor has ultimate responsibility for the patient.
- There may be legal implications if counsellors give incorrect information.

Despite these potential difficulties, counselling training usually includes acquiring knowledge of human growth and development, loss and bereavement, interpersonal relationships, illness processes and how people cope with adversity. Core counselling skills of listening, engaging with patients and assessing problems are well suited to information-giving in health care, not only in those specialist settings where it is well developed, but in almost every health care encounter and every setting.

RATIONALE FOR EFFECTIVE INFORMATION-GIVING

The main rationale for enhancing the practice of giving information is to achieve a better outcome for patients and facilitate the process for the person giving information, be it doctor or counsellor. A sense of frustration, anger or withdrawal can be experienced by both the giver and receiver of information if it is given without due concern for a person's wishes or ability to understand. The reason or requirement for giving information may seem obvious, but a lack of clarity about the main goal can cloud how it should be given. The following are some reasons for giving information:

- Patients may request information and wish to be actively involved in decision-making about treatment and care. This is especially the case in the current climate of increased patient participation in decision-making.

- Understanding the implications of a particular medical condition can help patients adjust to and make decisions about a range of issues, including:
  - behaviour and life style restrictions (infectious transmittable diseases such as HIV, hepatitis and tuberculosis, or diabetic, cardiac and neurological conditions);
  - legal and financial considerations such as declaring inherited conditions to a partner in the context of having children, or taking out insurance.

- The patient's family may request or require information about the medical condition to help them plan care.

THE COUNSELLOR'S ROLE IN INFORMATION-GIVING IN HEALTH CARE SETTINGS

There is a hierarchical structure in most medical settings about who gives what information to whom, and who receives what from whom. It is most frequently the doctor who considers what information needs to be passed on to the patient and also determines when and how to do this. When giving information in health care settings, the legal implications of the doctor's responsibilities must be taken into account. In most circumstances doctors give information to the patient alone. It is helpful to encourage medical colleagues to invite the counsellor to be present from the outset, as this can help to deal with any repercussions for the patient and in turn assist the doctor in time-limited situations.

Consideration needs to be given to some aspects of the counsellor's place in the process of giving, re-inforcing and confirming information. *Accountability* can vary from setting to setting; some counsellors may be a part of a multidisciplinary team with the doctor delegating responsibility for certain aspects of information-giving to patients. In this case, the counsellor is giving information on behalf of the doctor. In other situations, the patient may request information from a counsellor who is either not a part of the wider team or does not know the answer. In such a case, the counsellor should mention to the patient the limits of his competence, be tentative in his answers and direct the patient to the appropriate person, agency or team. For example, a patient who has been referred to a counsellor by an orthopaedic surgeon for exploration of an apparent anxiety state prior to a decision about a knee replacement may ask technical questions about the artificial joint to be used. The counsellor should refer the patient back to get this information from the surgeon and also check if the patient has difficulty in speaking to the doctor (Miller *et al.* 1997).

A counsellor working in a health care setting may be strategically placed to:

- Reinforce information given by other members of the health care team.
- Clarify aspects that were not understood or where information has been misinterpreted.
- Offer some support to the patient through difficult periods of time.
- Help patients formulate questions to doctors and nurses to obtain the information they require, which may also help in decision-making. In the above example of the patient requiring knee surgery, he was unable to formulate the questions he needed to ask until he had time to discuss his fears with the counsellor. He wanted to know

how long the replacement joint would last and whether he would be able to resume his favourite occupation of hill-walking. The counsellor was able to help him consider these questions and raise them in a brief consultation with the surgeon in a busy out-patient clinic.

When relatives request information about patients it is good practice to clarify with the index patient, wherever possible, who he or she wishes to be kept informed or to be part of decision-making. This avoids breaches of confidentiality and misunderstandings that can arise in the information-giving process. In the terminal stages of illness this balance may change, with relatives being the main focus (see Chapter 12). For example, the mother of a 40-year-old man with cirrhosis of the liver requested to be given his diagnosis; she assumed he had liver disease because of his history of heavy drinking. In this case the counsellor or doctor talked generally about liver problems but avoided linking a diagnosis to the actual patient.

Counsellors may also be able to supplement the information about patients' social and psychological situations for the doctor and other members of the health care team. This can take place through ward rounds, writing letters, making entries in medical records or giving verbal feedback to the doctor. Information about the patient's situation which can affect medical care sometimes emerges during counselling sessions. In other circumstances doctors may require a psychosocial assessment before making decisions about a patient's care. The following example illustrates this.

A 38-year-old married woman, Mrs Grey, was referred by her general practitioner to the counsellor for a psychosocial assessment. He wanted this information prior to further investigations for chronic fatigue and vague abdominal discomfort which she had experienced for two years. During this time she had undergone a number of routine tests and consulted a number of specialists but nothing abnormal was found.

The counsellor's objective was to elicit Mrs Grey's views about what she considered could be done to help her, and her main concerns and expectations; and to consider the general practitioner's underlying uncertainty about the aetiology of her symptoms.

It emerged that she had been married for ten years and that she and her husband disagreed about having children. She had a successful career in advertising and, until recently, did not want to forgo her job to have children. The dilemmas about keeping her career and giving in to her husband's wishes to start a family had become more acute since they both recognized that she could soon be too old to bear children. She had not been able to talk about this to her husband or the general practitioner, and she had become increasingly anxious that she might not be able to conceive if she later decided to have children. The counsellor gained Mrs Grey's agreement that her general practitioner needed to know this in order to understand her situation better. This in turn helped the doctor to raise the subject with Mrs Grey and consider what steps should be taken. Mrs Grey was relieved to be able to talk about her dilemmas and agreed to see the counsellor again before any further tests were carried out for her abdominal pain. The counsellor was able to suggest that if her tests were normal there might be a symbolic link between the abdominal pain and the dilemma about having a child which was causing emotional pain for her and her husband.

SOME THEORETICAL CONSIDERATIONS ABOUT GIVING INFORMATION

The way that information is given has a major impact on patient care (Lloyd and Bor 1996). The patient's level of stress and anxiety can be reduced in most cases by giving adequate information prior to investigations, surgery and entry into drug trials. False hopes and unreasonable expectations may be reduced if, for example, patients are given the opportunity to discuss their concerns, such as the side effects of prescribed drugs, and are informed about what may happen to them in the course of their illness and care (Miller and Telfer 1996). There is even evidence to suggest that if patients are fully informed before undergoing surgery, they have a shorter recovery period and may require fewer pain-relieving drugs. Patients are found to be more satisfied with their care, and more likely to comply with advice, if they have received clear explanations about their problem and its management.

The traditional method of giving information is to lecture – in other words to resort to a monologue rather than a dialogue. For example, 'You have diabetes and will need to have daily insulin. The nurse will show you how to do the injections.' This is done without checking whether the information is understood or has relevance to the person receiving it. This approach in health care comes from a traditional, hierarchical doctor–patient relationship, with the doctor in a powerful, knowledgeable position. The patient is neither invited nor expected to participate in decision-making. Anxiety can be created if patients do not understand or absorb the information given to them, or if it is misinterpreted. Effective counselling skills are also necessary for obtaining informed consent from patients for treatment and care. Counsellors have an important role in furthering this in practice, as well as teaching specific counselling skills to other professionals.

Some difficulties encountered in giving information may arise where counselling training is insufficient and there is pressure on time in busy clinics. In some health care settings, these difficulties are overcome by counsellors working alongside doctors as an integral part of specialist teams (such as haemophilia, nephrology, bone marrow transplantation). The counsellor can consult the patient together with the doctor, ensure that information is understood, and encourage the patient to seek clarification where necessary.

Giving information, as with any other aspect of counselling, is likely to be more easily and effectively accomplished if due thought is given to the principles, aims and tasks of counselling.

The following are the *main principles* for counsellors in giving information.

- Clarify *what* should be communicated *to whom* and *by whom*, and *when* to communicate information.
- *Avoid making assumptions* about the patient's knowledge, concerns, beliefs, wishes, expectations, need or desire for information. Failure to do so may result in important information being omitted or inadequately explained.
- *Choose words carefully*, being mindful that everything said can have an emotional impact and consequences. This occurs particularly when patients have to be given unsought or complicated information.
- *Share responsibility* for decisions with patients by eliciting their views about what

they want to be told, by whom, and if there is anything they do not want to be told.

- *Record* in medical notes a summary of the information given to the patient, what patients wish to be passed on to relatives, and what is important to pass on to other doctors.
- *Maintain clarity about the role of the counsellor* in any information-giving session with the patient. Sometimes the counsellor is part of a team, acting as a consultant for the patient and/or the medical team; or the counsellor may sometimes be the first person to give information. This affects how information is given and how the counsellor relates to the medical team.
- *Discuss with the patient the potential for an impasse* between the patient and the medical team, such as a patient not wanting to be told a diagnosis but then being unable to benefit from certain treatments or enter clinical trials which require their consent. For example:
  - A patient with hepatitis may not wish to know the results of regular liver-function tests. If these are at a level that indicates the need for treatment and the patient does not want to be informed, the doctor is left with the responsibility unless it is challenged.

Counsellor: I understand that you do not want to know the results of your latest liver tests, as you fear what might happen to your liver in the future.

Patient: That is right. My philosophy is just to live day-by-day. I don't think of the future.

Counsellor: If the tests indicated that it might be important to offer you some treatment now, what should the doctor do with this information?

Patient: I'm not sure right now. I hadn't thought of it like that.

GUIDELINES FOR GIVING INFORMATION

Prerequisites for giving information

Giving information requires knowledge on the part of the person giving the details and a willingness by the patient to be informed (Lloyd and Bor 1996). Thus it is essential to determine who wants the information, and the use to which it will be put.

The *counsellor* must:

- Start by enquiring what information is sought. This helps to avoid making assumptions; gives an indication about the patient's ability to understand issues; and helps to ascertain what language and style are best suited to the discussion.
- Ascertain the extent of prior knowledge about the issue being discussed.
- Be knowledgeable about the information and understand it sufficiently to be able to convey it accurately and simply.
- Give information gradually, in small amounts, avoiding jargon and technical words.
- Allow sufficient time for discussion.
- Respond to the patient's questions as far as possible, and with honesty if answers are not known.

- Be sensitive to, and prepared for, the possible impact the information will have on the patient and close relatives.
- Have resources for dealing with different situations that might occur (colleagues to consult for disturbed, suicidal patients).
- Check out the patient's available support systems to deal with the impact of the information. Often this is not possible prior to the first information-giving session.

The *patient receiving the information* must be:

- In a fit state of physical and psychological health to receive the information (conscious, not too critically ill).
- Able to listen to what is said and not be distracted by other overriding anxieties or physical symptoms.
- In a situation where they are either seeking information or are willing to be the recipient of unwelcome but necessary information.
- Wanting and able to communicate. Some patients are withdrawn, anxious, angry and aggressive. Others have hearing and speech defects, including the elderly.
- Able to understand the information (there may be problems with children, the elderly, individuals who have learning difficulties, cultural and language barriers).

Issues covered in information-giving

A range of practical and technical issues are covered when doctors or other health care colleagues give information to patients. When the implications of the information have consequences for others (infectious and sexually transmitted diseases and genetic conditions), it is especially important to be proactive and explain to patients the relevance of the discussion and information. Knowledge about some of the following can help reduce patient fears and misunderstandings:

- The nature of the tests (invasive or not and the degree of discomfort likely to result from them).
- The time required for procedures, the length of the possible wait for the results, the possible duration of in-patient treatment and so on.
- Advantages and disadvantages of keeping secrets if patients are not planning to tell anyone else.
- Availability of the counsellor or other health care worker to answer further questions if necessary.

Example of an information-giving session

The following case demonstrates the steps taken during a counselling session where information-giving was important.

Mrs Green, aged 45, had experienced chest pains and discomfort for some months. She finally consulted her general practitioner and he sent her to a cardiac specialist. The specialist planned to investigate whether her arteries were blocked by doing blood tests and performing an angiography (an invasive procedure). Following the first appointment, he referred Mrs

Green to the counsellor on the team as he was concerned about her level of anxiety and wanted this explored before carrying out invasive tests. He found it difficult to get her to respond to his questions during consultation and she appeared withdrawn.

1. *Think first* about who made the referral and for what reason, what information it is planned to give, and the age, gender and medical context of the patient. These all have an influence on the start of the session and help to focus the discussion.

2. Find out *what the patient perceives as the problem* and what he wants to know.

    Counsellor: Following your meeting with Dr Brown, what is your view of your situation now?
    Mrs Green: I just feel trapped.
    Counsellor: Trapped in what way?
    Mrs Green: Trapped because I have this pain and it worries me, but I also fear being told that I've got a heart condition.

3. *Explore concerns, beliefs and wishes.*

    Counsellor: What is it that you fear most about the possibility of having a heart problem?
    Mrs Green: That there really is nothing that can be done and that I may not be able to do all the things I do now.
    Counsellor: Where do you get the belief that there is nothing that can be done to help you?
    Mrs Green: I'm not sure. Perhaps because my father died of a heart attack.

4. *Outline the information to be given.*

    Counsellor: What did you understand about the tests Dr Brown suggested?
    Mrs Green: Not too much except I'd have an anaesthetic and have to be in hospital. But he didn't say much. You know what doctors are like: rushed, looking at his notes, and his bleep going off.
    Counsellor: Do you know why he wants to do these tests?
    Mrs Green: He said something about calligraphy. At that point I just 'shut off', I was so scared.

5. *Use understandable language* devoid of jargon and present the information in clear short parts, being specific. Vague information can raise anxieties.

    Counsellor: I think he means angiography? Do you understand what Dr Brown means by angiography?
    Mrs Green: Not really.
    Counsellor: Tell me what you do know.
    Mrs Green: It means a tube is put in so they can look to see if the veins are blocked.
    Counsellor: That is correct.

6. *Give important information first.*

    Counsellor: Dr Brown says he can't help you or make any decisions until he has done some tests. The most important is to insert a tube through a leg vein to your heart to see what is happening. This usually means a day and night in hospital and an anaesthetic. He will also need your consent to do this.

7. Use *diagrams* or drawings to clarify information if appropriate. It might be easier to explain some things diagrammatically than in words.

8. *Use genograms* (see Chapter 8) to obtain a family history; this is important in some conditions to reach a diagnosis or calculate the risks of transmission (heart disease, rheumatoid arthritis, diabetes), and can help in establishing current relationships.

> Counsellor: Is there anyone else in your family who has had heart problems apart from your father?
> Mrs Green: My mother has angina.
> Counsellor: Who else knows that you have had this pain?
> Mrs Green: No one except my doctor.
> Counsellor: What might your husband say or do if he knew you were here?
> Mrs Green: He'd be more worried than me and that would be too much for me.

9. *Negotiate how the next steps are to be managed* and share responsibility for decisions with the patient.

> Counsellor: For Dr Brown this is an important first step and will help him to confirm whether or not there is a problem with your heart. He said that he would also feel happier if you told your husband, or someone else close to you knew about what is to happen.
> Mrs Green: I'll have to tell my husband if I'm to stay in hospital. I suppose that I'll have to do what Dr Brown says!

10. Check the patient's understanding of what has been said.

> Counsellor: Before we go any further I would like to hear from you what you understand about what we have discussed so far.

11. *Acknowledge the patient's ambivalence and 'reframe'* the patient's viewpoint. Both are important techniques for giving advice and information in a way that is consonant with the patient's viewpoint. 'Reframing' may mean taking time to understand the patient's situation, whilst keeping the balance of imparting those aspects of the diagnosis, treatment and prognosis that are important for the patient's health and maintaining hope (see Chapter 4).

> Counsellor: I can hear that it is very hard for you to decide what to do right now. It seems that you are protecting your husband from the worry and at the same time also protecting yourself from a certain diagnosis, fearing it is your heart. This means that although you want to ask advice you are stopped right now from doing so.
> Mrs Green: You are right. I think I want to know and at the same time I don't want to know. Dr Brown thinks it is my heart, I am sure.
> Counsellor: Yes, he did not deny that there might be a problem because of your symptoms and the family history. However, do you think it might give you more discomfort to continue with the pains and uncertainty and no diagnosis? Or would you think it would be easier to know for sure one way or the other?
> Mrs Green: I had not thought about it like that.
> Counsellor: If the doctor found out that you had a problem with your heart, what might be the advantage of knowing? How might it be different to your father, who had no idea that he had a problem?
> Mrs Green: I had not thought about that either.

12. *Obtaining informed consent* is the responsibility of the doctor performing the procedure, and includes the nature and purpose of what is to be done, as well as the benefits and any risks there might be. A dilemma for many doctors, especially if the patient is anxious or appears not to fully understand medical issues, is how much information about risks should be given and how much a patient needs to know in order to give informed consent. To overcome such problems, patients should be encouraged to ask questions and discuss fears. Counsellors can check perceptions and correct any misunderstandings prior to consent being given. Patients should also be given written information and, whenever possible, not be rushed into making a decision. They should also have the opportunity of discussing issues with another person such as a relative, friend or counsellor.

13. *Summarize* what has been said and the next steps. Asking the patient to do this is also a useful way of correcting misinformation and misunderstandings before ending the session. In some circumstances it can be equally effective for the patient to hear the summary in order to confirm information. Summarizing the points made during the discussion can help to slow down events that seem to be going too fast for the patient; clarify the medical terms and procedures; and address anxieties.

> Counsellor: From what I have heard in our session it seems that you have suffered for some time from this pain and now worry that you may have some heart trouble. This is a special worry because of what happened to your father. It seems that you are afraid to ask Dr Brown his views about your heart and so you feel trapped. You will know when you are ready to remove the uncertainty by asking questions and facing what has to be done. It just might be different to what you fear and expect.

CONCLUSION

Counsellors can use their particular skills and knowledge about illness and its effects on individuals and relationships to enhance effective, satisfactory information-giving to patients. There are dilemmas about whether or not counsellors need to have specialist knowledge about particular conditions in order to give information. It seems that having skills in dealing with one disease can usually be transferred to other situations. Counsellors may feel that it would be an advantage for them to be present when patients are given information by another health care worker. However, it may be helpful to be able, in the course of counselling sessions, to check the patient's understanding of what he has been told.

The consequences of how information is given to patients can have a profound effect on the way they subsequently react to illness. In some situations there might be less need for counsellors if more thought, time and skills were devoted to the way patients are given information about their condition. Unfortunately, pressure on time and underdeveloped counselling skills may mitigate against this.

CHAPTER 11

Giving 'Bad News'

INTRODUCTION

This chapter describes how to give so-called 'bad news' to patients and relatives. Consideration is given to:

- What may be considered bad news in general, and in particular conditions.
- What may inhibit health care providers from communicating openly and effectively with patients about their condition.
- What information should be disclosed and when.
- Who should be given the news.
- Who should be involved in giving the news.

Imparting bad news is an inevitable part of information-giving in health care (Hoy 1985). Counsellors may have a role either in giving bad news or, more frequently, in helping the patient and others to deal with the consequences of bad news. The problems associated with giving bad news and the potential difficulties and barriers this can create in the doctor–patient relationship are not new to medicine (Buckman 1984). The skills required in giving bad news are similar to the basic counselling skills of listening, observation and reflection, all of which are used in giving information. Additional skills focus on dealing with specific problems in communicating bad news of any kind, such as techniques for maintaining hope and creating balance in adjusting to illness; obtaining compliance with treatment; or dealing with extreme situations (accidents) or emotional reactions (anger or crying). The focus of this chapter is on those additional skills and techniques needed for imparting information that constitutes bad news and dealing with the reactions of patients and their relatives to this news.

Traditionally, bad news about health is given to patients by doctors who have medico-legal responsibility. Ideally, a multidisciplinary care team connected with patients (nurses, physiotherapists, counsellors) can provide back-up, but often this is not the case. A counsellor may be the designated person in the team to deal with the impact of the bad news given to the patient, although other members, such as nurses, can also contribute to patient support in this regard. The ideas and suggestions described in this chapter can be applied in different degrees by all health care workers. Counsellors' appreciation of the issues associated with giving bad news can enhance their contribution. Even if they do not have to give the news themselves they may be required to deal with its consequences.

THEORETICAL BACKGROUND

The meaning of 'bad news'

Conventionally, the concept of bad news is perceived in situations where there is

- a message which conveys to the individual there are fewer choices in his life;
- a threat to an individual's mental or physical well-being;
- a risk of upsetting an established lifestyle;
- no hope.

It is tempting to make assumptions about whether news is *good* or *bad* for an individual. However, news of whatever kind is only information, whereas the idea that it is either good or bad is a belief, value-judgement or affective response from either the provider or the receiver of the information in a given context.

It is personal perceptions that define whether news is good or bad. There are also degrees of bad news from very bad to not so bad. There are many situations when health care providers might preface giving bad news with 'I am sorry to tell you that . . .' or good news with 'I am pleased to tell you . . .', illustrating how value and meaning are attached to information from the outset by the conveyer of the information. Such preconceptions about what is good or bad news associated with any medical condition may influence or constrain the patient's range of responses to the information. A patient, for example, who is given so-called good news in the form of a negative HIV antibody test by a relieved doctor may feel ashamed to cry or to discuss new problems for himself. For that person there may also be an element of bad news; the patient may now feel that there are no excuses for failing in a new sexual relationship, whereas his fear of HIV had previously protected him from meeting new partners. Similarly, a patient who feels some relief and is more settled in his mind about a cancer diagnosis may be concerned that the doctor will misconstrue this as denial, emotional blunting, or suggestive of a psychiatric disorder.

Clinical experience highlights the value of eliciting from the patient what would be bad news, or waiting until the patient attaches meaning to the information before defining it as either good or bad news. This does not mean that health care providers are unaffected by the patient's feelings and responses, but that they should neither make assumptions about what these may be, nor inhibit the patient's spontaneous reactions by responding in a manner it is assumed the patient wants, without assessing this beforehand.

'Dreaded issues', or what do patients fear the most?

It is important to have an understanding of patients' fears about their health. Bad news is closely related to loss, whether it be physical, emotional, or social. The responses to loss are similar to a bereavement (see Chapter 13). Clinical experience has shown that common fears include:

* Loss of physical well-being and its impact on relationships, work, finance and social life.
* Loss of mental ability and ultimately being unable to make decisions for oneself.
* Lack of control and increasing dependence on others.
* Loss of a sense of future.
* Living with uncertainty.
* Disfigurement and pain in the course of illness.
* Social stigma resulting from disfiguring or infectious conditions.
* Life-sustaining measures, such as mechanical ventilation and resuscitation.
* Living with a reduced quality of life.
* Death and dying.

Other fears which patients have are related to the development of symptoms, how they will manifest themselves and how they will be recognized. Patients may especially fear symptoms visible to others, such as a disability or disfigurement, which affect self-image and others' perceptions of them. There are also invisible manifestations of symptoms as revealed through tests and internal examinations, such as some gynaecological symptoms. Infectious or transmissible diseases (tuberculosis, herpes, hepatitis B and HIV infection) raise fears about disclosure and effect on relationships. Symptoms of neurological impairment, such as epilepsy, may be especially frightening to patients because this may be equated with loss of self-control and 'madness'.

Patients' psychological responses to such fears are mediated by a number of personal, social and cultural factors which may determine the extent to which they are distressed by their changing physical condition and appearance. For example, actors, models and those in the media who depend on their physical appearance, may exhibit greater anxiety in relation to the effect of their condition on their work. Some patients find that psychological problems become more pressing after they have been discharged from hospital to convalesce, because the hospital provided a protective social environment. Similarly, the signs and symptoms of neurological disease can impair patients' functions in a number of ways and therefore have different implications for them. These range from apathy, social withdrawal, impaired handwriting and headaches, to memory loss, seizures, dysphasia, hemiparesis and even coma. The individual's life-stage and relationships to family and others all contribute to how individuals manage bad news and illness.

What inhibits health care providers from giving bad news?

There are a number of factors which might make it difficult for health care providers to give bad news to their patients.

* Some health care providers may be concerned that they will distress patients if they either tell them the bad news or talk to them about any fears they may have in

relation to their health. This may stem from the myth that to talk about the potential for bad news is to 'tempt fate' or destroy any feelings of hope the patient may have.

- Uncertainty about how to respond to the reactions of patients who openly display their emotions (showing anger, crying) or seem to display no feelings at all may make health care providers unsure whether their own responses should be personal or professional. Should they be clinical and aloof, or more engaged by showing that they are upset?
- Some may identify strongly with some patients and their problems, especially if their ages and lifestyles are similar.
- Not knowing all the answers to questions patients may ask and having insufficient counselling skills may arouse anxiety, resulting in some health care providers delegating to colleagues the task of giving bad news.
- Working alone can also increase stress and tension.
- Giving bad news can also lead to time-consuming conversations with patients and this may deter some doctors from being more open with their patients in busy clinical settings. This inevitably leads to more dependence on other health care workers such as nurses and counsellors.
- Conflicting information and differing responses to the diagnosis or treatment proposals, due to a lack of communication between the different health care workers, can create problems for the patient.
- If the patient's self-confidence and hopes for the future are eroded by bad news, the health care worker may feel guilty and fear being blamed for this.
- Giving bad news may also involve discussion with patients about sensitive topics, including sex and sexuality, procreation, chronic ill health, dying and death, all of which are difficult issues to discuss and require advanced training in communication skills.
- If patients are young, an implication of a serious diagnosis is that they are being told that they may have a shortened life-span.

Approaches to giving bad news

Various approaches can be taken by doctors to giving bad news. These include:

- *Non-disclosure*, where the physician decides what should be told to the patient.
- *Full disclosure*, where everything is told to the patient, whether or not the patient has been consulted.
- *Individualized disclosure* where each patient is considered separately.

Non-disclosure was a model used particularly in the case of cancer, because of the unique fears and anxiety generated by this disease. Its use has lessened over time. Often the diagnosis was given to a 'responsible' relative rather than the patient. This approach is based on assumptions that patients need to be protected from bad news; that they invariably do not want to know bad news about themselves; and that it is appropriate for the doctor to decide 'what is best' for the patient without reference to the patient. This model is untenable in times of increased consumer pressure for information, and can be seen as a violation of the right of human beings to have information about themselves. It denies the patient and relatives the opportunity to work through their grief and resolve issues related to loss. It creates barriers between who is informed and not informed and so obstructs mutual support, and there is a likelihood of noncompliance with treatment. All responsibility is left with the doctor who is keeping the information to himself and not enabling the patient to have wishes and participate in the process. Counsellors would rarely be involved with these patients.

Full disclosure is when all available or known information is given to every patient. It is based on the assumptions that the patient has a right to full information and the doctor has an obligation to give it; all patients want to know bad news about themselves and are better off knowing; and it is appropriate for patients to determine what treatment is best for them, since they have to live with the consequences and thus must have full information. This is not a tenable model, because to discuss all options with a patient who is already frightened and confused is neither helpful nor appropriate. Such patients could well end up being referred or referring themselves to counsellors.

Individualized disclosure is a model where the amount of information and its rate of disclosure are tailored to the desires of the individual patient through patient–doctor negotiation. This model is based on assumptions that people are different in the amount of information they want and in methods of coping; most people need time to absorb and adjust to bad news, so disclosure should be given over time; and a partnership relationship between doctor and patient is a basis for decision-making that is founded on mutual trust and respect and is in that patient's best interests. This model can take time and skills that individual doctors may feel they do not have. Therefore whenever possible the supporting health care team should be involved. Counsellors in multidisciplinary teams are particularly well placed to add their contribution. However, offering psychological help to patients which is isolated from their medical care can exacerbate problems by compartmentalizing their difficulties. This can lead to less than optimal solutions.

OPTIONS FOR THE COUNSELLOR WHEN GIVING BAD NEWS

There are three options for when to give bad news and how to manage patients' concerns.

1 Reassure the patient, potentially colluding with denial

The counsellor can reassure the patient that his fears are probably worse than the reality. This option may be difficult to resist because it can result in the immediate reduction of the patient's anxiety and emotional distress. It is a form of supportive emotional 'first aid'. It may be indicated when patients appear to be vulnerable, isolated and under extreme distress. Sometimes there are areas of information where there is much uncertainty and where the outcome of either the disease process or medication is not known. Reassuring patients may serve to 'sweep the fear under the carpet', only for it to resurface at another time. If patients are repeatedly reassured, the counsellor or doctor takes on some of the anxiety of the patient by assuming responsibility for some decisions that could be shared with the patient. This is more likely to result in feelings of stress for the doctor and dissatisfaction on the part of the patient. The counsellor might also be colluding with the patient's denial of the severity of the problem, or potential problem, if false hope is offered.

2 Impose views on patients when it is too late and possibly face resistance

A second option is to wait until a crisis occurs before discussing bad news. The patient may be seriously ill before his concerns are elicited. This has certain limitations. Patients may be unprepared for bad news; they are not only anxious about their physical condition, but will inevitably have fewer ideas about how they might cope. They may present as anxious, depressed and withdrawn, and some will express suicidal thoughts. Counselling is less likely to be successful if the referral and intervention are made when patients are already seriously ill. If referrals for specialist counselling are made at a time of crisis, patients may then seem to be resistant to any intervention by the counsellor. Referrals made when patients are still well tend, on the whole, to have a better outcome. In some cases, however, giving bad news at times of crisis may be the only option.

3 Use hypothetical and future-orientated questions; avoid denial and resistance

The third option is to address the potential for bad news and concerns about the future with patients, using hypothetical and future-orientated questions, at appropriate times while patients are still relatively well. There are several advantages to this approach. Patients are some distance from potentially serious conditions or situations that concern them. If issues are raised and addressed at this stage, patients can plan ahead of crises; they can be helped to view their situation more objectively; and it may help to increase their future options. The ideas can be put across in a non-confrontational way, through the use of questions. Nevertheless denial can be a vital coping strategy with some patients, and should therefore not always be viewed as dysfunctional. Thus patients who indicate that they experience it as too unsettling to talk about their fears for the future should not be pushed to do so. However, finding out what patients know, what they want to know, what they do not want to know and what might be their main concerns are central to this approach, rather than challenging or laying bare a patient's psychological defence.

The task of helping patients to deal with uncertainty can be made easier by the use of hypothetical questions such as 'If you were to get ill what might be most difficult for you?' Such questions can inoculate patients against extreme stress in the future by having them think about possible problems, and how they might cope with them, before they actually occur. The main concerns of the patients are thereby addressed and this can also lead to the more efficient use of clinical time. Hearing the questions may be as important in changing perspectives for the patient as the answers given at the time. All questions convey an idea or imply a statement. Questions are also a way of giving back to the patient some responsibility for finding solutions to concerns at a stage when they can be realistically acted upon. This use of questions may prevent the staff from becoming overburdened with the patient's needs and worries. The approach emphasizes helping patients to cope on their own, which may lead to the need for less patient contact.

GIVING BAD NEWS

When to give the bad news

The medical model of diagnosis, treatment and care contains the potential for bad or good news at every stage. The stage at which a patient seeks medical help is often prompted by their real or perceived ideas or fears about bad news. Thus every consultation holds within it some aspect of the giving of news, which can either be 'good' or 'bad'. All tests have an outcome which has to be interpreted by the doctor and the patient. Communicating results of tests, radiographs or invasive procedures are clearly defined times when news has to be given. Confirming a diagnosis is a well-understood moment of giving news for patient and doctor. Less emphasis perhaps is given to patients' apprehensions connected with first consultations and routine follow-up appointments to monitor conditions or the effectiveness of medication. Every drug has a side effect and conversations about medication include weighing up the risks and benefits for that particular patient and his condition. The side effects of medication are included in fears that are often expressed. What is less often discussed is what is available if medications are not suitable, especially where there is no substitute or alternative treatment.

Where there is chronic illness, with the possibility of acute illness superimposed, there are many situations in which bad news may have to be given to patients. In other situations, as new tests become available, dilemmas arise about when, how and if to inform patients about conditions for which there are no treatments and little knowledge about prognosis. Such patients may have to live with unremitting anxiety about what may happen in the future. Counselling can help some of these more acutely worried patients to gain different perspectives. It is the ultimate responsibility of the doctor to impart information to patients and share the uncertainties. The uncertainties may change as time passes, and it is important that patients are informed so that they can consider diagnostic and treatment advances as they become available. There are many examples of this scenario, including HIV in the mid-1980s, hepatitis C (HCV) in the early 1990s and the emerging issues surrounding testing and treatment. Any condition can give rise to anxiety and distress, and for this reason psychological morbidity may be associated both with a fear of a medical condition or infection, and with having to cope with it.

Who should give the bad news?

It is important from the outset that there is clarity about who has medico-legal responsibility for giving news. If this is not agreed and understood, the process can become confused and messages to the patient may be unclear. Thus a first step in preparing patients for news is to clarify who will give them the news. If this is not clarified there are inevitable problems, many of which relate to the difficulties of the referring person.

To whom should the bad news be given?

It is generally considered that patients above the age of 16 have rights as well as responsibilities. This includes the right to 'informed consent'. However, even if the index patient is considered able to give informed consent and receive information, there are usually relatives involved as well. Good communication with patients has to come first, but in various situations and at different stages of illness, communication with those closest to the patient is also important and they can become vital members of the caring team (McLaughlan 1990). An early part of any preparation should thus be to clarify whether patients have shared their illness concerns with any relative, who that is and to what degree they wish them to be involved. An opening question is: 'Who else knows that you are here today, or about your problem?'

When dealing with children, consideration has to be given to:

- The views of the parents about how much information should be given to the child.
- Any conflicts that might arise between a child's right to know and be involved in decisions about their health care and that of the parents. For example, a child might have the ability to understand about an illness such as leukaemia at an age of 8 or 9, but the parents may want to shield him from the knowledge of the severity of the condition and the prognosis. The child may ask questions that cannot be answered unless some facts are given about his condition.

Preparing patients for bad news

Preparing patients for bad news can be a discrete activity, nevertheless all information-giving embodies aspects of preparing to give news. Unlike accident victims or those with unexpected medical crises, patients with chronic illness can be helped to make practical changes and prepare themselves emotionally for bad news. Talking to patients about their fears, which often relate to the future, is one of the most important psycho-therapeutic interventions. It provides an opportunity to help patients cope with any anxiety and uncertainty about what may happen to them through the course of their illness. If this is done satisfactorily, the counsellor may even have helped to prevent some psychiatric symptoms in those patients who seem very anxious about addressing their fears. A deterioration in a patient's clinical condition affects his relationships, his feelings of hope and his view of himself in the context of his illness. For some patients it may mean being open with people about the diagnosis. For patients who are neuro-logically impaired, an important additional issue may be dealing with loss of control in relationships and an increasing dependence on others for support and care.

Preparing patients for bad news can be seen as an opportunity to open up communication between health care workers, the patient and his family members by enabling views about care and treatment to be expressed. Identifying the patient's views provides an opportunity to challenge beliefs and enables the meaning of bad news to be viewed from a different perspective.

GUIDELINES FOR GIVING BAD NEWS: THE STRUCTURE OF THE COUNSELLING SESSION

Although there is no right or wrong way of giving bad news, some principles, tasks and techniques may make it easier for the health care provider to prepare patients and family more effectively for bad news.

Guiding principles

The guiding principles are similar to those of any counselling situation, but some should be re-emphasized. These include:

* Make *no assumptions* about what might be particular concerns or bad news for an individual, and recognize that these concerns can change over time. For example:

  'When I last saw you your greatest worry was how you would cope if you began to get ill. Now that you have started medication, is this still a worry or is there anything else of more concern today?'

* *Consider the timing* of how and when to impart 'bad news'. Assessment of the patient's physical, psychological and social circumstances, available resources, and the clinician's readiness to discuss the news with the patient provide guidelines for resolving this key counselling dilemma.

* *Maintain some neutrality* by responding thoughtfully and professionally to a patient's reactions, and not making value-laden judgements such as: 'There's no need to be upset; it's not the end of the world.' Neutrality enables patients to respond more freely, without the feeling that certain responses are expected of them. For example:

  Patient: I can't believe that I have breast cancer. It's the end. (Patient sobs)
  Counsellor: What is the hardest for you to believe right now?
  Patient: (Continues to sob loudly)
  Counsellor: (Pause, passes patient a box of tissues). What would help you the most right now?
  Patient: Nothing. Though I wish I could think straight.
  Counsellor: Let's talk about the things that you can't think straight about and are in your mind.
  Patient: I'll be alright in a minute . . . (pause) . . . This is the day I've feared the most. Actually things look a bit clearer now. Could the lump just be eradicated without cutting off my breast?

* *Share responsibilities* with patients whenever appropriate. This may mean helping patients to talk about and live with the uncertainties, and often the certainty, of their condition and even death, by showing them that the health care provider is not afraid to discuss their concerns.

Guidelines for the session

The following guidelines can act as a check-list to ensure that important aspects are covered when imparting bad news.

* Firstly, *attend to some practical details* which can make it easier for the health care provider and the patient. These include ensuring that there is privacy, a reasonably comfortable ambience, sufficient time available and established links with other colleagues who can support the patient afterwards if necessary.
* If the patient has been well prepared, *give the news* immediately in order to leave the maximum time for discussion.

- On hearing bad news many people are unable to absorb anything further and do not hear what is being said. Take care not flood patients with 'helpful' information. Rather, *check what they have remembered and understood* about the investigations and laboratory tests that have led to the diagnosis. Also check again what they want to know about the subsequent test results.
- *Identify* who else may be available to *support* the patient. This helps patients to look to their natural support network outside the health care setting and reduces dependence on professional staff.
- *End the session* by asking patients to summarize what they remember, particularly about the options for treatment and care. It is easy to assume that patients have retained and understood what they have been told. If this is not done, the patient may leave only having heard the bad news, which increases the risk of depression, anxiety and even suicide.
- Make an agreed *plan for future contact or referral.* Give patients realistic contact numbers in case they want further information or help before the next appointment; this provides a 'safety net'. Avoid giving home telephone numbers as this draws the patient into a one-to-one relationship which may exclude other social and professional support.
- *Discuss with colleagues* the essential components of the patient session. This can make the task of giving bad news easier by increasing professional support and sharing the care of the patient.

Counselling tasks

The main counselling tasks in preparing patients for bad news include:

- Helping the patient and their close contacts to maintain hope in the face of life-threatening illness by introducing ideas that balance feelings of hope and hopelessness. These may include information about treatments and follow-up medical and psychosocial care.
- Enabling the patient and those important contacts, if they wish, to discuss issues they find difficult or need to be settled, so that they do not part with unfinished business between them.
- Helping patients make informed decisions for themselves which can give them the feeling of some control over a debilitating illness. For example:

  'What information would you need to help you decide what to do about taking these anti-inflammatory drugs for your arthritis?'

Techniques for giving bad news

The particular techniques that are used in the scenario of bad news include:

- *Facilitating communication* (establishing rapport and trust) by introducing yourself, defining the purpose of the meeting, maintaining eye contact and being aware of body postures (leaning forward). Convey information without disguising it in language that is either vague or ambiguous – for example, by not using coded words like 'immunosuppressed' for a condition like HIV infection, or a 'breast lump' for cancer of the breast. Be clear that there are treatments for many of the associated infections, but no cure for HIV; and in the case of breast cancer, that there are different options but it is malignant and needs radical treatment.

• *Showing empathy* by introducing the topic of bad news sensitively and demon-strating respect and care. This will influence, to some degree, how the patient responds. It is sometimes helpful to embroider a little and use prefaces such as 'I was wondering whether you had ever thought about how things might be if this infection does not clear up as quickly as last time?' Taking a 'one-down' position also encourages the patient to talk more freely. For example, 'You may think that some of my questions seem a bit odd, but I can't help wondering whether . . . '. Showing patients that the counsellor is not afraid to discuss their concerns, no matter what these might be, is a way of showing empathy and closely tracking the thoughts of the patient.

• *Using future-orientated and hypothetical questions* which can help patients to think about situations, and even solutions, while they are some distance from the real problems. Such questions also link people with ideas and other people whom they might not otherwise have considered in relation to the problem or concern. For example:

'What if you did become ill, who might you turn to for help?'
'What might be the effect on your wife if you decided to tell her about your heart problems?'

• *Placing emphasis on how the patients have coped* with difficulties in the *past*, and helping them to consider how they might cope *now* and in the *future*. This stimulates people to consider how they might manage if the news turned out to be bad for them. For example:

'Have you ever had news in the past that made you feel very frightened and unsure how to respond? How did you manage to overcome it?'
'How might this experience help you right now?'
'Is there anything from the way you managed then that might help you if you had a problem in the future?'

CONCLUSION

Having to give bad news and helping people to cope with it is an important aspect of health care. How bad news is conveyed may determine, or at least influence, how the patient copes and adapts. The approach to giving bad news described in this chapter needs to be used with thought and sensitivity. Asking the patient questions should serve as an invitation to a conversation about difficult issues. The use of hypothetical questions is an approach that requires a high level of training, because it focuses on the most painful aspects of living and coping with disease. It may be damaging to patients to ask hypothetical and future-orientated questions which raise their anxiety, without addressing the patients' feelings and how they might cope.

In order to retain a sense of balance over feelings of hope and hopelessness about the future, the positive aspects of the patient's coping should always be discussed.

The counsellor can help to normalize the views of the patient by conveying an understanding that these may be uncomfortable conversations to have and that there may be difficult decisions to be made. It is inappropriate to push patients to talk about their fears for the future when the feedback from them indicates that they are not ready or willing to do this. However, addressing concerns about the potential for bad news with patients can help them to feel that they can talk about their worries and show their emotions. Most of the associated worries are probably already in the mind of the patient, and an experienced counsellor will find an appropriate moment to talk to the patient about them.

CHAPTER 12

Counselling for Loss and Terminal Care

INTRODUCTION

Physical illness and lack of the 'healthy state' lead to various losses for individuals and their close contacts. The loss of health and accompanying decreased physical or mental ability is central to counselling sessions in health care settings. An understanding of human growth and development and of specific illnesses and their impact at different stages of life is essential.

Loss is most usually followed by a period of bereavement and mourning. Bereavement counselling is addressed in Chapter 13. Death is part of the life cycle and the most obvious, and often the most feared loss associated with a period of serious illness, although long-term disability and diminished health status are equally feared. While there may be a special emphasis on counselling the dying patient and the bereaved, this is but one aspect of the counsellor's task in relation to loss.

Clinical practice has shown that ideas about, and feelings of loss may start from the moment a person receives a diagnosis of illness. Others may perceive themselves as ill or vulnerable to illness when they have not sought medical advice or disbelieve that which has been given (see Chapter 14). Both groups of patients can experience anticipatory loss and this may be the initial focus in counselling sessions. This chapter presents some ideas and approaches relevant to counselling about loss, especially in relation to terminal illness and dying.

THEORETICAL IDEAS ABOUT LOSS

Clinical approaches to loss and bereavement are based on theories about the psychological aspects of death and dying (Kubler-Ross 1969). Views about bereavement and approaches to counselling the bereaved are usually related to a theoretical understanding of change and loss in relationships (Carter and McGoldrick 1980). As a function of emotional growth and development, individuals are required to process change in their relationships with others. Death and dying are but one point on the arc of the wider life cycle which, in the context of the family, social relationships, and belief systems, continues after the death of an individual.

Terminally ill patients, their family and other close contacts are faced with life-cycle changes brought about by dying and death; these can be made more difficult if there are unresolved relationship problems. Terminal illness can also evoke reactions from health care professionals about their own mortality, making it especially important to understand the implications of loss for the individual and family relationships.

Ideas about loss and dying may be introduced at an early stage of counselling. Even if they are not expressed openly in sessions, people may have fears, anxieties and misconceptions about a range of losses, and these are accentuated by illness. Addressing them is one way of preparing patients for loss and also helping the bereaved deal with actual loss when it occurs. The focus of counselling initially may be about the loss of health, changes in lifestyle brought about by illness, and the consequent changes to relationships. As illness and debilitation progress, patients may experience additional losses, including the ability to participate in decision-making and loss of body image and function. Counselling can lay the groundwork for further discussions about the impact of these changes on others and help the patient to retain a sense of control in different areas of his life for as long as reasonably possible.

Illness can lead to physical, psychological, economic and social losses. To a large extent these are idiosyncratic, and may change in the same individual over time. The losses brought about by acute, sudden illness or trauma are different to those that come from chronic conditions, where some adjustment over time is possible. Beliefs and perceptions about certain illnesses, as well as personal and family responses, may influence adjustment, and for this reason the typology of illness is relevant when counselling patients about illness and loss (Rolland 1994). Where illness has periods of remission (arthritis, leukaemia), adjustments to this fluctuating pattern of health and illness may be difficult but anticipated. Acute loss, which is usually unforeseen, can result from sports injuries and accidents, abruptly preventing an individual from pursuing his chosen career or hobby.

Some of the more common losses and fears experienced over a range of illnesses and diseases include:

- loss of the healthy state;
- loss of independence and fear of dependency;
- social isolation resulting from an inability to keep up daily living activities and contacts;
- relationship changes between patients and their family, social and work contacts;
- fear of perceived or real stigma attached to some infections and illnesses (cancer, epilepsy, AIDS);
- disability and disfigurement;
- loss of a previous lifestyle due to incapacity or a medical condition that restricts activity;
- loss of memory, concentration and ability to make decisions;
- loss of employment and finance;
- diminution or lack of sexual life.

All these losses can be of concern to patients in different ways over time. There are losses connected with chronic illness and with acute illness, and some patients may suffer acutely from anticipatory loss, a reaction which can be as complex and emotionally painful as having to cope with actual loss.

COUNSELLING ISSUES IN TERMINAL CARE

During the terminal-care phase of illness, some management and psychological issues can arise which may need to be addressed with patients and their close contacts.

- *Confidentiality and secrets.* Although issues of confidentiality – who should know about the patient's condition – require attention at all stages of disease, they become more complex and pressing in the terminal-care phase of illness. Foremost among these is the question of who should know about the diagnosis, especially in diseases such as HIV infection which carry stigma, or in inherited conditions such as Huntington's Disease. Problems are less likely to occur if confidentiality issues have been discussed before the patient's health deteriorates. Patients' views about who should be kept informed of their condition should be recorded in the medical and nursing notes and must be reviewed from time to time, as decisions may change.
- *Resolution of past relationship conflicts and difficulties.* It is sometimes assumed that it is imperative for the family and other close contacts to resolve past conflicts, or settle 'unfinished business' between them, before someone in the family dies. While it may be appropriate to facilitate this process, it is equally important to assess when *not* to pursue 'tying up' loose ends and, if necessary, help people to adjust to, and cope with, 'unfinished business'. The following dialogue illustrates how the counsellor can help family to leave some business unsettled.

Sister:	I read a book once which said that secrets between people are harmful. But my brother and I worry that if he is open about his drug problem, it would upset my parents so much that they would reproach themselves and might even reject David.
Counsellor:	Are you both happy to keep this secret from them?
Sister:	As happy as one can be in keeping a secret from one's parents.
Counsellor:	Do you have other secrets from your parents?
Sister:	No. We are open about everything else. They know he's ill, they know it's hepatitis but they do not know he has septicaemia. It would be awful for all of us if my parents got very upset now about drugs when there is nothing we can do.
Counsellor:	What will help you to keep this secret?
Sister:	It won't be easy not to just let it slip out, but we will have to watch out not to. Maybe I will tell them after David dies.

- *Pre-existing conflict between family members and partners or spouses.* This can emerge in the terminal-care phase of illness. Counsellors may find that they have to deal with conflicts about keeping the diagnosis secret or taking responsibility for important decisions. Ideally, such difficulties should be pre-empted much earlier, in discussions with the patient about how professional carers should best respond to these situations. An extract from an interview with a patient about his boyfriend illustrates how this may be approached.

Counsellor: What does your mother know about your relationship with Tim?
Patient: She thinks that he is just a friend. I've never told her more.
Counsellor: Would you now like her to know more?
Patient: Yes, because they may meet.
Counsellor: If your mother meets Tim and she asks him about your diagnosis, do you think he would tell her?
Patient: If he is stressed he might just 'blow it'. I think he feels angry that I won't tell her about us.
Counsellor: How do you think your mother would react if she did know about your relationship with Tim?
Patient: I don't know, but I think it may be better for all of us.
Counsellor: Does Tim know this?
Patient: No.
Counsellor: What stops you from talking to Tim about this?
Patient: Once I talk to him I may not be able to avoid telling her and I am afraid that she may reject him.

- *Next-of-kin and decision-making.* In the terminal stage of illness the focus of attention in counselling may broaden to include joint sessions with the family and close friends. As the time of death approaches, they may seek information, re-assurance, comfort or simply contact at a time when their own social support system may be taxed or withdrawn. In some cases, relatives may seek ways of engaging support by clear messages of distress, such as avoiding visiting the patient. In other instances they may complain about the patient's care as a way of venting feelings that may be difficult to express elsewhere, particularly within the family. Some under-standing of what is happening for the relatives and what prompts their behaviour can make the terminal phase less painful psychologically for all concerned. The extent of the next-of-kin or relatives' knowledge must be clarified between the counsellor and patient before any relatives are seen. Not infrequently, relatives and close contacts seek help from the patient's counsellor without the knowledge of the patient. In such instances, the discussion should be limited to concerns or difficulties that relatives may have in relation to the patient's illness, rather than revealing personal details about the patient, unless the patient's permission is obtained. For example:

Counsellor: Does your brother know that you have asked to see me?
Brother: No. I wouldn't want him to know.
Counsellor: If he did know, how do you think he might react?
Brother: I'm not sure, he might be pleased.
Counsellor: What might he be pleased about?
Brother: Well, it might be of some relief to him that I have someone to talk to about my worries.
Counsellor: I am happy to talk to you about your worries, but as with any other patient, I cannot give you any information about his condition as we do not have his permission.

- *Organizing and settling legal and financial matters.* Making a will is a practical step that acknowledges the possibility of death. Experience suggests that a will is better made when people are well. However, the task of making a will is neither routine nor familiar for many people, and they may need help to discuss the pros and cons for them. Opportunities should be made, either as part of their medical care or within counselling sessions, for patients to consider the benefits of making a will while they are still mentally competent to do so. Of course, it is not the counsellor's responsibility to help the patient to draw up a will or to act as a witness to it, because professional boundaries could be crossed which could lead to difficulties in the future and even legal problems.

Whilst the act of contemplating a will or indeed writing it may prompt some people to think more about dying, the psychological benefits of 'getting one's affairs in order' should not be overlooked. An extract from a conversation between a counsellor and a 40-year-old single man with acute leukaemia illustrates this.

Counsellor: Paul, you mention that you feel that you need to make a will, but that it is difficult to do so because it would make things seem 'final'. Is there anything that might be made easier for you and others if you were to decide to make a will?

Patient: I'm not sure. I might feel a bit more settled.

Counsellor: More settled in what way?

Patient: Well, I'd know my girlfriend would be taken care of, and I could also say exactly what things I would want my mother to have. Then sometimes I think what might happen if I didn't leave a will. The worst thing I could think of would be relatives fighting with one another if there was no will. I know I'll do one, but not until just before my next treatment.

By neglecting to make a will, some patients may indirectly communicate that they prefer others to make decisions for them about their estate. The effect may be to give rise to tensions and feelings of ambiguity in relationships, and this may be either the patient's deliberate choice, or an unforeseen consequence of not having made a will. The counsellor's task in such situations could be to anticipate these outcomes with the patient in the course of counselling sessions. Thereafter it should be left for patients to decide what to do in their own time. Examples of some questions that could be asked of patients in such sessions include:

'What would happen to your partner if you were to die without making a will?'
'What message would it convey to your girlfriend about your relationship with her if you do not make a will?'

- *Other practical issues that might be raised in counselling*. These include the provision of financial and social support; availability of home care; and who should make important decisions if patients are unable to do so for themselves. Counsellors can also help patients to obtain advice from legal or financial advisors.

Counsellor: Mr Bull, you say that you have so many worries about the future. Which do you think about the most?

Steven: We have talked about the stress of my wife if I become ill, and I have decided to see a lawyer about making a will. I am also worried about what happens if I get too ill to work. How would I manage without money? It is all very well to talk about wills!

Counsellor: What ways have you thought about? Do you know about state benefits? Have you anyone who could advise you?

Steven: I do have a good accountant and I think I should talk to him.

- *Dependency*. Patients who are very ill or dying can feel a loss of dignity, especially from the inevitable dependence on others for basic activities (going to the toilet, bathing and brushing teeth). Nurses usually take on some of these intimate tasks in hospital and sometimes in the community. Reassuring statements to the patient, which do not ignore the embarrassment or annoyance at being dependent, may help to put them more at ease. Offering some choices to the patient can help to maintain hope and restore a measure of dignity. The counsellor might respond to a patient's expressed embarrassment about nursing care as follows:

Counsellor: I know that this may be hard for you, but remember that it is part of the nursing role to help people who are ill. If it was not a nurse, who would you prefer to help you?

- *Talking to people about dying*. This, or telling people the fact that no more can be done to alter the course of an illness, is possibly the most challenging aspect of health care, especially when talking to patients who seek hope and reassurance. For some doctors it is hard to shift from curative to palliative care. For other members of the health care team, including counsellors, it is easier to respond to patient's questions about their prognosis when doctors have clarified treatment plans about terminal care. It is then possible to explore the patient's concerns and wishes against a more realistic background. It is common for patients at this stage to seek support for their relatives in the form of counselling. They perceive this help as relieving them of the strain of having to provide emotional support themselves by 'putting on a brave face'. Some relatives and friends may show their reluctance to 'allow' patients to die by encouraging them to fight on and keep eating, and by willing them to live. They may also inflict 'cheeriness' on them. This can be stressful and upsetting for some patients who, after an extended period of failing health, may welcome the relief from pain and suffering. Other patients are ambivalent about wanting to know the 'real' answers to their questions. They may ask questions of nurses or counsellors that they do not put to doctors. This may be because they seem to be more approachable members of the health care team. Sometimes patients do not really want the answer, so they avoid asking the doctor. An extract from a conversation illustrates the point.

Patient: When will I die?

Counsellor: That is not something that I would know, Craig. Have you asked the doctors? How might it help you if they were to tell you?

Patient: It wouldn't really, but I don't want to go on like this. I don't really want to talk to the doctors because it is easier to talk to you, and I suppose I don't really want to know the truth quite yet.

Counsellor: So what is your main concern right now?

Patient: Just keep me out of pain and make sure that I am not alone.

Counsellor: If the doctors and nurses know your wishes they will do all they can to keep you comfortable. You will have to let them know when you are in pain. You say you don't want to be alone. Who would you most want to be with you?

Patient: My mother.

Counsellor: Does she know this?

Patient: Not really. I haven't spoken to her in that way.

Counsellor: Do you think you could talk to her more easily now?

Patient: I might today if I feel like it when she comes.

• *Coming to terms with death.* Health care providers and family members may assume that 'coming to terms with illness and death' is necessary and desirable for the patient's psychological well-being. This notion emanates from theories that view the denial of problems as being detrimental to psychological health. This quest or belief may inadvertently cause more psychological problems for those patients who resist discussion about painful issues. Dying patients may connect the process of 'coming to terms with dying' with an attempt to come to terms with how they have lived. The following are examples of some ideas that can be used in counselling if patients want to talk about death or dying.

'What aspects of how you lived might make dying easier?'
'In whose life did you play a significant role?'
'Whose beliefs and ideas about living and dying are most similar to yours?'
'What one thing would you most like to be remembered by?'
'Who do you think will miss you most?'
'Have you talked to your sister about how you would like her to cope with you not being there?'

Many patients adjust to deteriorating health in ways that differ from how they imagined it would be. This may be due to their own inner resources and possibly unexpected support from family and friends. As the patient's health deteriorates, providing opportunities to talk about the changes in their condition and relationships over time may be helpful.

Counsellor: John, tell me how you have managed this long period of illness as well as you have. What is it that helps you to keep going?

Patient: I just live from hour to hour and day to day. I've decided that if I let myself think about the future it makes it hard for me to be calm about what is happening to me now.

Counsellor: So how do you manage to keep out thoughts about the future?

Patient: I keep busy by seeing friends, and watch television a lot of the time.

• *Feelings of hope and hopelessness.* Two distinct aspects of hope in the terminal phase of illness, physical and emotional, may stem from the certain knowledge that the 'end will inevitably come'. Questions such as 'Will it be slow or quick? Will I be in pain, and how uncomfortable will I be?' reflect physical fears. Some measure of hope can be maintained at all stages of illness but careful choice of words is important if patients are not to be falsely reassured. One entrée into discussing the inevitability of death and introducing some hope is to find out from patients what they know about their condition and how they want to be cared for. For example:

Counsellor: What have the doctors told you about what's happening to you?
Patient: I have a feeling they've given up hope.
Counsellor: What makes you feel that?
Patient: They don't come to see me any more.
Counsellor: Would you like them to come more often?
Patient: I suppose so.
Counsellor: Has anyone else given up hope?
Patient: I'm in a daze now. I don't know what to think.
Counsellor: Is there anything you hope for?
Patient: Some quiet on the ward at night so I can sleep. More honesty from the doctors!
Counsellor: How do you think you can influence the doctors to be more honest?
Patient: Ask them more questions I suppose. Actually, I hope they don't say to me 'it's the end'. It's OK feeling it, I just don't want to *hear* it.

The second aspect of hope relates to the patient's emotional concerns. A patient's hope that he will be remembered after death, and how he will be remembered, is very different from the hope that he may live longer, have a less painful death and not lose control. One way is to encourage patients to talk about how they want to be remembered. An excerpt from a conversation illustrates the use of future–orientated questions:

Counsellor: Was there anything you particularly wanted to talk about today?
Patient: It bothers me that I'm still frightened in some ways.
Counsellor: Can you try and say what is frightening you now?
Patient: Not having control now.
Counsellor: Would talking to people about how you would like to be remembered help you to feel you had some control?
Patient: Perhaps. I want to be remembered like I used to be, which was very much in control of my life.
Counsellor: By whom would you most want to be remembered like that?
Patient: My son, also my parents. I hate them seeing me like this.

- *Saying 'goodbye'.* There are rituals for ending relationships. Saying 'goodbye' to someone who is dying can be the most painful farewell. It may be at this point that relatives and friends may seek the counsellor's support or advice. Brief but frequent visits to the patient, with short statements, may be all that is appropriate at this stage. However, if patients indicate that they might have any concerns, they should be helped to express them.

Counsellor: You say that your main concern is your worry that your father will 'go to pieces' when you die. Is there anything that will help you to not feel so worried?
Patient: No. I am ready to die and he won't let me go.
Counsellor: Have you been able to say this to him?
Patient: No. I couldn't.
Counsellor: Do the two of you usually have difficulty in saying what you want to each other?
Patient: Yes.

Counsellor: Do you think your father might 'let go' in his own time when he is ready? If he does it too soon, it may not be right for him.

Patient: Maybe I'll die before he 'lets go'.

Counsellor: Do you think that would be more difficult for your father or for you?

Patient: For him.

Counsellor: What would he have to do to show you he had 'let go'?

Patient: Not keep pushing food at me.

Counsellor: Do you think a father could *ever* let his child 'go'?

Patient: No! Maybe I should tell him I'm ready; that may help him a bit, which may help me.

Relatives can be reassured that just being there with the patient, sitting, holding a hand or reading conveys closeness and a sense of relationship. In some instances, relatives and friends feel afraid and do not wish to be with the patient at the time of death. They may need 'permission' not to witness the death. The nurse in the following example does not put any pressure on the husband of a dying patient to stay at her bedside.

Nurse: Sarah is not very well tonight. What do you want us to do if her condition deteriorates further?

Partner: I would like to know, of course. Actually in my mind I have already said 'goodbye' to her. I don't know if I want to see her worse or dying.

Nurse: That is OK. It's been a really tiring day for you. Why don't you leave things with us for a while? We will give you a call at home if things change. You can decide then what you want to do.

CONCLUSION

The terminal phase of illness holds special challenges for the counsellor. There may be physical, practical, psychological and emotional concerns that patients want to discuss or settle. As the patient's health deteriorates, the counsellor may need to focus more attention on the close family and friends. Professional and non-professional carers alike may find this phase of palliative care difficult if ideas and practices that accompany a 'good death' are not made clear.

This chapter has presented some ideas for responding to the complex emotional and practical concerns that may arise in the course of counselling the terminally ill. It stresses active engagement with the patient in the course of conversation. What is not conveyed is the appropriateness of sometimes sitting in silence with the patient, maintaining a physical presence but not engaging in unnecessary conversation. These are some of the most challenging moments for professional and non-professional carers. A counsellor's training and experience can help him to sit in silence with a patient. For others, the stillness becomes unsettling, though counsellors can help relatives to overcome feelings of helplessness when there is nothing more left to do and say, by encouraging them to read to the patient or listen to the radio with them. The message that is conveyed is that a presence can be more helpful and important than trying to solve a practical problem or make conversation in an emotionally charged situation.

Death ends a relationship in one sense but, at the same time, memories and ideas about the deceased may continue and affect those left behind. This paves the way for bereavement counselling, where required, and helps to promote emotional healing. The next chapter discusses bereavement counselling, which is linked to the theory discussed in this chapter.

CHAPTER 13

Bereavement Counselling

INTRODUCTION

It is at the point of the patient's death that counselling for those left behind (sometimes referred to as 'survivors') starts as a discrete activity. The process of grieving may last for many months or years. For some bereaved, one counselling session may be sufficient to clarify thoughts and feelings and reassure them that their reactions are normal. For others, several sessions may be more appropriate, spaced over time and possibly with longer intervals between them. Sessions over a few years may be indicated at important anniversaries (birthdays, dates of meeting and death). There are some bereaved people who need to be seen more frequently.

Timing is an important aspect of bereavement counselling. Friends, relatives and health care providers may sometimes complicate reactions to loss and bereavement by 'pushing' people to confront loss when they are not ready to do so. Losses experienced at one time in the life cycle may be experienced differently when similar events occur in, for example, old age.

It may be the painful feelings that come from loss and change following a death that prompt people to seek professional counselling. While death is a part of every life cycle, the untimely death of a child is a reversal of the natural order. Ill health can bring unexpected changes that take time and sometimes professional counselling to overcome. No assumptions should be made about the bereaved person's possible reactions; what is a loss for one person may not be a loss for another.

WHY OFFER BEREAVEMENT COUNSELLING?

The bereaved can be helped to discuss and reflect on the changes brought about by the loss. Information about the disease or death can also be provided, if it is relevant to the bereaved and there are unresolved fears for themselves or others. A counsellor can enable people to identify the effects of the death and address the loss, which is a way of looking towards the future. Although this process is distinct from that of 'coming to terms with the loss', it can at least help the bereaved to understand the loss in the context of day-to-day living.

The point at which people come for professional help for bereavement may signal that they have become 'stuck' in their loss or, on the contrary, wish to resolve difficulties and move on in their lives. It is helpful for the counsellor to understand whether there are other changes taking place that present as crises in the mourning process. Often, talking about the future may be as painful as talking about the past. Bereaved people can feel isolated because they are alone, or because others encourage them to 'look on the bright side'. Counselling can facilitate the expression of thoughts and fears which otherwise would not be spoken about. Where a death has been unexpected or difficult to accept, talking about it may help to make it more real for the bereaved.

Reactions to loss through death include feelings of grief, anger, guilt and sadness, which may be expressed in different ways. Some people find that they cannot stop crying; others have a desire to be left alone. These are by no means the only responses commonly associated with the death of a loved one. While still grieving, some may experience a measure of relief when death finally occurs, ending both the patient's suffering and the carer's distress associated with pending loss. While death may bring an end to the suffering for patients, it may also give rise to new and unanticipated problems. The special circumstance of a bereaved person having to live with the same life-threatening condition as the deceased means that fears evoked by the loss continue in their own lives. Sexual partners, for example, may also have been infected, and relatives with an inherited disorder such as Huntington's Disease or haemophilia may worry about their own health problems for the first time. Loss may also be complicated by social stigma when the cause of death is revealed. Cirrhosis of the liver from excessive alcohol use, or liver failure following an overdose of paracetamol, may carry with it a stigma not normally associated with loss.

Grief reactions may also be masked. If there is no open display of grief, it is difficult for others to know how a person is feeling, and they may therefore be uncertain about how to comfort or relate to them. Sometimes the bereaved continue to live as if the relative or friend has not died. If this apparent denial of reality is not addressed, it may become a problem that requires the professional help of a counsellor or therapist. The person may find it too painful to think about the loss, and fear becoming over-whelmed by their feelings. Such reactions to loss and death can, over a long period of time, affect people's ability to manage their daily lives. The intense feelings which some relatives and friends may experience at the time of death can give rise to emotional or psychological problems at a time in the future, if no attempt is made to place them in the context of the past, present and future. Delayed grief reactions can occur at any time after the initial period of loss, although the onset is most commonly associated with anniversaries such as birthdays and other significant dates and the occurrence of other personal losses. Counselling can help bereaved people to talk about events and painful feelings that might be difficult to discuss with relatives and friends, and is appropriate at any time that issues regarding loss affect the patient. Some people may never completely come to terms with a loss, particularly if it is the death of a partner or child. Loss of a partner can leave the remaining person feeling socially isolated, and this may indeed be the situation.

TASKS IN COUNSELLING THE BEREAVED

Clarity about the aims and tasks of bereavement counselling enhances its effectiveness. The main tasks include:

- Helping the bereaved person to *identify and address their main concerns.*
- *Enabling appropriate mourning* to happen without undue difficulties in daily living.
- Helping the bereaved review what has happened in the past and *develop ideas about the future* in such a way that the loss is balanced with some hope.

GUIDELINES FOR COUNSELLING THE BEREAVED

Themes to include in the structure of the session

The guidelines for bereavement sessions are similar to those described in Chapter 7, but in bereavement counselling there are some additional considerations, including:

- the events leading to the death;
- talking about the death and subsequent rituals;
- previous experience of loss;
- issues pertaining to how others have coped with the loss;
- beliefs about life and death;
- views about the past, present and future;
- the mourning process.

All these can be woven into the conversation in a way that is appropriate for the individual, the nature of the problem and the stage of bereavement that the individual has reached.

Check-list for the bereavement counselling session

It may be difficult for the counsellor to know what to focus on in a bereavement counselling session. The following issues might be of help in creating a framework or structure for the session:

- *Start the session* by identifying what made the bereaved seek an opportunity to talk or what it was that prompted a referral. The counsellor may also ascertain what the bereaved's expectations are for the session. Recalling memories and thoughts about the deceased can sometimes help the bereaved to start talking about their own feelings.
- *The events leading up to the death* and the circumstances of death affect people in different ways. Thus seeking information about the facts surrounding the death can help to start the discussion. Some of this information will be known to the counsellor involved with the patient and his contacts during the terminal phase of care. However, it may be therapeutic for the bereaved to talk about the events surrounding the death from a new perspective and to explore some of the following:

- how long the deceased person was ill before dying;
- who else the deceased and the bereaved talked to about the illness;
- from whom the deceased and bereaved got their support;
- whether it was an anticipated or sudden death;
- what provision was made for practical affairs before dying;
- how the dying person prepared others, if at all, for his death;
- what beliefs the deceased and bereaved had about life and, if known, about death and dying.

- *Talking about the death.* The way in which an individual died may leave memories that have an important effect on the bereaved. If, for example, the deceased choked to death, the bereaved may metaphorically remain 'choking with grief'. If the person died peacefully, the memory might be of a 'good' death. In circumstances where the death took place surrounded by those the patient most loved, the view may be that he was not 'lonely'. Conversely if the person died alone in the night, it might be more difficult for the bereaved to accept the reality of the death.

- *Rituals and events immediately after the death.* Bereavement counselling can, in its own right, take the place of a ritual for some people, as the conversations in counselling may keep alive memories of the deceased and provide a set time for expressing grief. Rituals that surround death, and the period after a death, help people to confront and deal with the pain of the event. Such traditional activities provide a context in which mourning can take place, as well as assembling friends and relatives who provide social support. Religious ceremonies and customs have their place in coping with loss. In the Jewish religion, for example, people mourn actively and in varying degrees of intensity for a year. The period of bereavement is circumscribed and the bereaved person is expected to stop mourning and resume a normal life after this period. Some traditions prepare a feast which includes the favourite foods of the deceased person. Keeping a lock of hair or maintaining the deceased person's possessions are forms of memorials. Other rituals include visiting the graveside or place of remembrance.

  The events that take place immediately after death may leave a lasting impression on the bereaved. The activities carried out can start or retard the mourning and healing process. Carrying out rituals may help the bereaved deal with overwhelming and incapacitating grief. An obvious ritual is for the person to visit the graveside with an explicit task (e.g. to read a letter in which important ideas and feelings are conveyed); other rituals may be uniquely appropriate to the person and their loss. These may include standing on a bridge and throwing a symbolic article into the flowing water, or returning to a significant place for the bereaved person, and to recite a poem. The possibilities are endless and the therapeutic effect is in terms of the power of the symbolism and association, rather than any objective criterion.

  Grieving can be prescribed with the aim of both intensifying and constraining thoughts about the deceased. One way is to suggest to someone overwhelmed with grief that he sets aside time each day to think about his relationship with the deceased. This ritual helps to give expression to the feelings of sadness, and helps the person to begin to cope better at other times of the day. The counsellor can further help the bereaved person by encouraging him to undertake small practical tasks when he is not focusing on his feelings of loss, and so begin to change his routine. The aim is not to disqualify the person's feelings, or to prevent him from grieving, but to help him to give expression to his grief as well as to continue with important daily routines. This can help the person to begin to put the loss and the overwhelming feelings that may accompany this into a more manageable perspective. The counsellor may also feel that it is appropriate for other relatives or friends to stay with the bereaved person until they can cope on their own. Information from the genogram (see Chapter 8) will help the counsellor to identify other sources of emotional and practical support.

Rituals may not be necessary or appropriate for everyone. Open discussion about how events were managed after the death can in itself be therapeutic. The following questions may help clarify the events after the death and any associations for the bereaved person:

- Who took main responsibility for organizing the funeral?
- Who made contact with family and friends?
- Who was the most difficult person to tell? What made it difficult to tell him?
- Was there a religious ceremony? What did this mean to them?
- Was anyone not told about the death, or not notified about the funeral? Who were they? What was the reason for not notifying them?
- What beliefs were held about the deceased and 'after life'?
- Who seemed most upset, and what were they upset about?
- Who did the bereaved see most immediately after the death?
- Who was most able to comfort the bereaved?
- Was there any relief? What brought about this relief?

• *Assess how the bereaved has been coping* by enquiring about how time is being spent. Giving the bereaved the opportunity to decide on the frequency of counselling sessions is one way in which to gauge the bereaved person's perception of how he is coping and the level of anxiety being experienced. Some examples of questions that can be used to help in this assessment include:

'How much of the time do you think about John?'
'You say that you think about John every evening just as you are about to go to sleep. Do these thoughts prevent you from going to sleep?'
'If you allowed yourself to forget his death for a while, what would you think about?'
'You say you'd feel disloyal if you didn't go to the cemetery. Where does this idea of disloyalty come from?'
'What memories of Frank do you most want to keep alive?'

• Consider *previous experience of loss* which may influence how the bereaved deal with a current loss. Helping them to make a connection with how they previously managed this loss may give them more confidence in their present ability to overcome the grief. Often the response is that they have never experienced a death. In this case links can be made with other important losses (divorce, emigration, pets, favoured belongings).

Counsellor: Have you had personal losses before?
Bereaved: Not the same as this. My father died suddenly four years ago.
Counsellor: How did you manage at that time?

Bereaved:	I was very shocked as he was very fit. It took me a long time to believe it.
Counsellor:	So was there anything from your father's death and how you coped that might help you now?
Bereaved:	I know that over time the pain seems to lessen. I was more prepared for Sarah's death because I knew she had cancer. Although I tried not to think it would end this way, I actually knew it would.

Where there have been multiple losses either in a family or of friends (an accident or infectious disease), 'shell shock' and emotional numbing may result. Helping the bereaved to express feelings and concerns, as well as linking them with their previous experience of dealing with loss, can help them to emerge from the shock.

Counsellor:	What makes it so difficult for you to talk about John?
Partner:	Just that he had to die.
Counsellor:	If you were to let yourself talk about John, what might be the easier things to talk about and what might be the most difficult?
Partner:	It is easier to talk about our relationship, which was really good. But it's also hard because there have been so many deaths among my friends and it might be Jeremy next.
Counsellor:	What have you learned from your experience of other friends that now might help you to deal with John's death?
Partner:	That somehow it seems that people are not afraid when it comes to the end.
Counsellor:	Then how can this help you with your own feelings?
Partner:	Knowing that people I have known were not afraid at the end gives me some strength.

- *Present and past relationships* influence the response to a death. It is common for the bereaved to feel initially that it will be impossible to enter another enduring relationship. Sometimes they are trapped by feelings of guilt that they should even consider future relationships. Helping the bereaved to identify and express beliefs, fears and guilt can be the start of enabling them to view these from different perspectives, and thus help to form the basis of release to move on in the future. Helping the bereaved person to look again at his or her relationship with the deceased sometimes rekindles the will to meet others. The following is an excerpt from a session with a bereaved partner:

Counsellor:	Sarah, you tell me you feel quite lost without Clive. How do you see yourself carrying on without him?
Sarah:	It is hard to think that I could ever make a close relationship again. I have a few friends. One in particular.
Counsellor:	How does Clive's death affect you present relationships?
Sarah:	I am frightened to get involved again in case I have to lose that person again.
Counsellor:	What was learned from your relationship with Clive that might help you to decide to have a new relationship in the future?
Sarah:	We were such good friends, even before we became lovers, and I know that is important. So maybe it is worth the risk.

- At the time of death connections with the *family of origin and choice* may be rekindled. This in itself can be a source of pain if the relationships were not good.

Using genograms to identify relationships and patterns of relationships across and between generations can be a powerful therapeutic intervention with the bereaved. It is a method of opening discussion about change, loss, and patterns of support and can generate interest in people's past and present and make them curious about their future. It makes talking about loss, relationships and emotional attachments clearer and more immediate. Young children as well as adults can be readily engaged in this task. For example:

Counsellor: How did you, as Eric's partner for all those years, get on with the family?

Partner: Hardly at all, because they didn't know about our relationship. They are very disapproving of people living together and not getting married. We kept it away from them as much as possible.

Counsellor: Now that his mother has been told that you were living together and were very close, has that changed things in any way?

Partner: At first she was very friendly and I used to phone her once a week just like Eric did.

Counsellor: You said that at first it was better; what has happened since?

Partner: I don't know but I guess she is mad that I was left his apartment.

Counsellor: How have you reacted to her being much less friendly?

Partner: I very seldom phone her.

Counsellor: So for whom is that more of a problem? You or her?

Partner: More for her. She's very lonely.

- *Beliefs* about loyalty to family members, sex, marriage, and parent–child relationships may be re-evaluated when there is a death, and may influence the bereaved's perception of how to manage relationships and live from day to day. The rituals surrounding death can serve to reveal, confirm or challenge these beliefs. Counselling can help people to express a belief, its origins, and how it affects the bereaved. Some further examples of beliefs:

No one will be able to grow and develop. Hidden behind a mother's grief may be the fear that she sees no future for the family.

A fear that 'too much upset' will lead to a breakdown or mental illness. Therefore it is better 'to keep the lid on'.

An idea that one has to be loyal to the beliefs of others such as parents and grandparents, by not showing emotion or talking about feelings.

The following illustrates how to identify beliefs:

Counsellor: You say that you feel bad about feeling some relief that your sister has died. Where does the idea come from that you cannot show some relief after her death?

Sister: It wouldn't seem right after all her suffering. My mother cried for six months after my father died. She was inconsolable.

Counsellor: What do you think that meant for all of you?

Sister: We were all too terrified to lighten things up. Mother would have thought that we were being disloyal. I would like to think that we needed to be like this to stop us all from cracking up.

- *Talking about the past, present and future* links the bereaved's beliefs and ideas with death and loss. The counsellor has a special task in actively addressing aspects of the past with the bereaved, which will help in looking to the future. For example:

Counsellor: Which of your memories about Charles are the most important for you now?
Mother: Charles' wish for independence and his love of life.
Counsellor: What will that mean for you in the future?
Mother: I am not very independent and he always wanted me to do more things on my own. I might remind myself of his strengths and try and get out a bit more.

The following example illustrates how the death of a father has affected the family, and how the counsellor helped the family to remember his beliefs and values.

Counsellor: We've spoken a lot about how this family has been different since your husband died. In what way is it the same?
Mother: My son continues to help me whenever he can.
Counsellor: How is this the same?
Mother: I suppose he saw his father always helping me, and his own mother, especially when she was so frail.
Counsellor: If your husband could see what was happening in your family today, what might his views be?
Mother: He'd be pleased that the children were remembering some of the things that were important to him.

- *The mourning process.* Adequate mourning is an essential part of the healing process. The counsellor may confirm that some of the bereaved's feelings of upset, grief or pain are expected, 'normal' and appropriate to that stage in the mourning process. Many people express great relief on hearing this. Positively encouraging mourning activities such as crying, wanting to be alone and thinking of the deceased a lot will allow the bereaved to grieve more freely and openly and accept the idea of death as a reality. It may also be useful to discuss mourning within certain time-frames, thus giving some structure to what could otherwise seem to be an infinite process. The counsellor may want to see the bereaved from time to time to assess for himself how the mourning process is proceeding. The counsellor can usually reassure the person that their reaction to loss is normal, and can help to put the mourning process into a time-frame that is appropriate to the patient.

Bereaved partner: I do still get upset. At times I don't know how I will manage from day to day.
Counsellor: I'd be surprised if you didn't feel that way. It is really quite normal at this stage.
Bereaved partner: I know. But it seems to go on and on . . .
Counsellor: How long do you think this will go on? What do you think will have to happen to tell you that it will be time to start going out more often with your friends?
Bereaved partner: I'm not sure. Sometimes I really want to go out more, but then I think it is not right. Maybe I'd be being disloyal.

- *Ending bereavement counselling.* The main aim of bereavement counselling is to help the bereaved to reach a point where they are able to look to and plan for the future more comfortably. The ability to do this is an important indication that the period of mourning is drawing to a close. Indications of this are that the bereaved may talk less about the deceased and start to think about new activities or relationships, or return to previous routines. Some examples of assessing the end of counselling include:

Counsellor:	What would tell you that your husband is beginning to see things differently since James's death?
Bereaved parent:	When he starts to go to the pub again and can talk to his old mates.
Counsellor:	We have spoken a lot about the things that have happened in your family since James died. What effect do you think this has had on the family?
Brother:	It has been difficult, but I think that it has brought us closer.
Counsellor:	In what way do you think it has brought you closer?
Brother:	We phone each other every week, and we get together at least once a month.
Counsellor:	Has there been anything good in that?
Brother:	I can't speak for everyone else, but I feel I have not been on my own in all this. Now I can talk to my mother about things that I have never been able to before. In fact, sometimes I think that I just repeat what I say here with you to the family. I was wondering if I really need to come so often.

CONCLUSION

Irrespective of the settings in which they work, all counsellors have some experience of working with people for whom issues about loss are most relevant. There are many different psychological theories about loss and its impact on individuals, couples and families. However, counsellors have to translate these ideas into therapeutic practice. It is sometimes especially difficult to counsel bereaved patients, because some may be inconsolable while others display no signs of their apparent distress. The ideas and skills described in this chapter offer a framework for practice and for dealing with some of the problems that may arise in the course of bereavement counselling.

In certain settings, such as hospitals, it might not be appropriate to offer ongoing bereavement counselling. It may be detrimental to the process of recovery for the bereaved to return to the place where the death occurred. It may be more appropriate for counsellors to refer a bereaved person to a colleague in another setting. In other circumstances the original counsellor may not be able to take on the specialist work that bereavement counselling entails, for practical or other reasons. Although aspects of bereavement counselling can be carried out by a range of health care providers, it is essentially a counselling task which demands specialized skills and for this reason should be provided only by those with the appropriate training and experience.

Giving bad news, counselling in terminal care, and bereavement counselling are activities that place enormous emotional demands on the counsellor. Chapter 19 describes how counsellors can learn to cope with their own stress and distress in the course of their work. Inevitably, counsellors will feel 'stuck' at certain points in the course of their work with patients. It is important to recognize that this is a normal occurrence, though the sources of 'stuckness' may vary. Chapters 14 and 16 describe possible sources of an impasse, and how to manage feeling stuck when counselling.

CHAPTER 14

Counselling the 'Worried-well' and Patients with Intractable Health Worries

INTRODUCTION

Some patients are either not reassured by doctors that they do not have an identifiable medical problem, or they have a medical condition but have become somatically fixated. They are referred to in the literature as respectively the 'worried-well' and somatizing patients. The problem directly affects the relationship between the doctor, patient and family. The impasse and consequent feelings of exasperation and hopelessness often result in negative views developing about these patients, who are perceived as wilful, resistant to change, rigid in their thinking, and a drain on professional and personal resources.

We recognize the difficulties presented by these patients but also view them as a challenge. Innovative approaches to counselling are required, as are collaborative working relationships with the patient's professional and family care-takers. Counsellors can gain acceptance as a member of the health care team through successful treatment of these cases. Professional colleagues usually recognize that they are time-consuming and can leave doctors and nurses feeling exasperated.

THEORETICAL CONCEPTS

Abnormal illness behaviour (such as hypochondriasis) is regarded in psychiatry as a syndrome of mental illness. The diagnosis is made when there is a perceived discrepancy between the patient's reaction to a medical problem and the nature of the medical problem, if indeed there is one (Mayou 1989). A prerequisite for making this diagnosis is that the patient has been thoroughly investigated by a doctor. Furthermore, laboratory tests and diagnostic procedures must have been accurately carried out so that the patient's responses can be considered against objective criteria. Nevertheless, patients are prone to make subjective interpretations of their condition which may be at variance with the opinions of health care professionals, who rely on the results of objective diagnostic procedures and laboratory tests. Where patients' conceptualizations of their condition, illness or symptoms differ from those of health care professionals, there is the potential for an impasse to occur in the relationship. This chapter describes how to identify and manage this impasse in counselling sessions.

These patients use somatic language to describe their difficulties, irrespective of whether or not these are physical or emotional problems (McDaniel *et al.* 1992). Bodily aches and pains and specific medical conditions become real for the patient. He may also go to great lengths to convince others that the symptoms are real. The attending doctor may attempt to reassure the patient or offer a psychological explanation (for example, 'these headaches are a sign of stress rather than a brain tumour'). However, reassurance is usually refuted. The 'worried-well' may fear that they have contracted a particular illness or they may complain that they already have signs and symptoms of disease, *when in fact there is no medical evidence for this*. The range extends from those who misinterpret somatic signs and then worry about their health (for example, someone who experiences the symptoms of indigestion and then worries that they have coronary heart disease), to patients with somatic delusions that can even mimic 'real' symptoms, such as in the case of pseudo-seizures.

Most people will at some time have transient worries about their health and minor symptoms. However, a small group of patients become fixated by these symptoms and worry about them incessantly. These patients are most likely to be referred to counsellors after doctors have failed to reassure them, in spite of repeated tests and examinations and logical explanations. They may be labelled as 'hypochondriacal', 'compulsive', 'obsessive' or 'hysterical'. Such labels rarely help to break the cycle of help-seeking behaviour and are not reassuring to the patient. The patient's drive for help and the doctor's response to this are depicted in Figure14.1.

The onset of the patient's worry may coincide with feelings of anxiety, depression or guilt. Counselling sessions frequently focus on uncovering possible 'causes' of the patient's disproportionate and unremitting worry, vigorously exploring the link between emotional problems and their somatic expression. The suggestion to the patient that somatic symptoms may be indicative of emotional problems is, however, often rebuffed. This is because somatic symptoms

- are a more socially acceptable presentation of problems and carry less stigma than psychological problems;
- are viewed by the patient as physical (and consequently amenable to diagnosis and treatment);
- can lead to secondary gains for the patient in the form of attention from increasingly frustrated professional and non-professional caregivers.

Pointing out these processes to the patient rarely alleviates the symptoms. The patient will deny consciously misconstruing his symptoms, and this can lead to a more polarized relationship between the patient and the counsellor. There is sometimes an ebb and flow in the patient's experience of these problems and consequently the certainty with which the conviction, or delusion, is held.

Events and psychological processes in the patient's life may be associated with a tendency to display psychosomatic manifestations of distress. Patients may include the following:

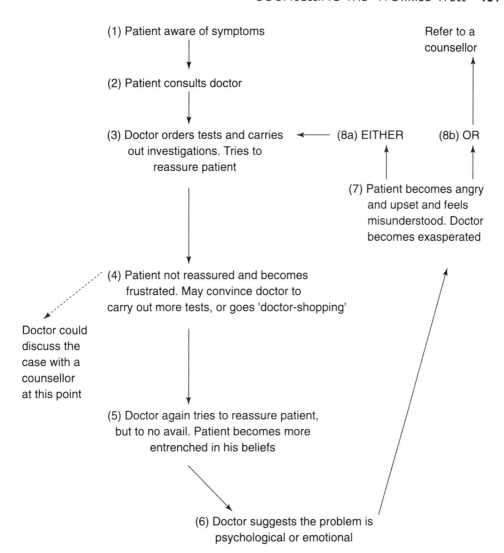

Figure 14.1 Cycle of doctor–patient interaction in 'worried-well' cases

- *Those with relationship problems.* A fear of illness can indicate difficulties about entering into, remaining in and ending relationships. The worry is a symptom which regulates the social and emotional distance in a relationship. For example, a lonely person may find some relief from solitude because caregivers take their somatic complaints seriously. The somatic presentation of a psychological problem may be viewed as a less stigmatizing means of gaining access to treatment, through which there is less risk of rejection for the patient. Thus an intractable worry about one's health may signal a call for professional help in a troubled relationship.
- *Individuals, couples and families going through life-cycle transitions.* Points of transition in individual, couple and family life cycles may exacerbate existing stress and relationship difficulties, which may be expressed as somatic problems. Examples are

parents of rebelling adolescents, couples facing the 'empty nest', individuals experiencing mid-life crises, people who have recent bereavement and those who have recently divorced or separated.

- *Those with past medical or psychological problems, or who have some connection with health care.* There may be an elevated risk for these patients because of their personal experience of health care. Those who have previously been treated for medical problems may be more likely to somatize than those who do not have a past medical history.

- *Misunderstandings of health education messages.* A small 'worried-well' group comprises those who may have misunderstood health education messages and believe themselves to be at risk of illness because of lifestyle, exposure to an infectious agent in foreign countries, or messages about self-diagnosis (as with women and breast cancer). Public health education through mass media campaigns (television, radio, newspapers) only convey limited information. Some people may then need to have a personal interview with an informed counsellor or health professional for their specific questions and anxieties to be addressed.

MANAGING THE 'WORRIED-WELL': THE COUNSELLOR'S DILEMMA

It is useful to have an overview of the management of these patients. The term 'worried-well' is an inaccurate definition for patients who are self-referred or have not previously seen a doctor. No patient referred for counselling can be defined as well by a counsellor until he has been examined and investigated by a doctor. Only after physical illness has been excluded can the patient be viewed as 'worried' *and* 'well'. Any worry about a patient's health should be taken seriously and it is essential to defer to medical colleagues to address the problem first.

A problem arises where the patient is not reassured by the doctor. If the counsellor then colludes with the patient's definition of the problem, he may reinforce the patient's problem. If, on the other hand, the counsellor tries to reassure the patient, he will be doing precisely what the doctor has already tried, and failed, to achieve. Although reassurance may temporarily alleviate the patient's worries, it is unlikely to solve the underlying problem. A more effective approach is for the counsellor to present both sides of the dilemma simultaneously, and to do so tentatively. This means on the one hand accepting the patient's view of himself as suffering from a physical illness, whilst at the same time cautiously introducing the possibility that these concerns about his health must be anxiety-provoking and stressful for the patient. This opens up the possibility of further discussion with the patient about the impact of illness. Developing these ideas within the counselling relationship helps to broaden the patient's view of his so-called illness without incurring the patient's resistance to being labelled as having a purely psychological problem.

Care must be taken to avoid directly interpreting the patient's behaviour exclusively in psychological terms at an early stage in the counselling relationship. Interpretation of the problem sometimes has negative connotations and may lead the patient to feel rejected and misunderstood, resulting in more help-seeking behaviour and even ending the counselling relationship. Equally, there is a possibility that seeing the patient for counselling in a health care setting, over a prolonged period, could inadvertently reinforce the problem by exposing the patient to a medical context.

GUIDELINES FOR COUNSELLING THE 'WORRIED-WELL'

The referral

The importance of the referral process is particularly relevant with somatizing patients (see Chapter 7). Most of these patients are unreceptive to a referral to a counsellor, which is entirely congruent with the nature of how they view their problem.

- The patient believes he has a physical rather than a psychological problem.
- The patient's anger, annoyance or dejection may be increased by the doctor's suggestion of a referral.
- The patient may feel abandoned and misunderstood, relegated to being emotionally disturbed and annoyed at the suggestion that his symptoms are either exaggerated or feigned.
- He may strongly resist a referral by intensifying the pursuit for a medical diagnosis, becoming more demanding of the doctor or seeking second and subsequent opinions from other specialists.
- The patient may even feign co-operation to project a receptive openness to any 'medical' investigations and avoid being combative with the doctor, confirming suspicions of psychological difficulties (Turk and Salovey 1995). Even if the patient is not outwardly defensive and 'resistant' to the referral and seems co-operative, the counsellor should assume that he may not be willing to begin to view his problem in psychological terms.

The first meeting with the patient is more likely to be successful if it includes the referring doctor, even if this is only for a part of the session (see Chapter 15). Discussion between the counsellor and doctor before the meeting can facilitate the referral. Seeing the patient at this first meeting in the doctor's consulting room prevents an abrupt shift in focus from the physical to the psychological. It conveys the counsellor's initial acceptance of the patient's medical definition of the problem. The presence of both the doctor and counsellor can also help to demystify the counselling process for the patient by clarifying what might be achieved through counselling. This can be done by:

- the doctor introducing the counsellor *as a part* of the clinical team, reinforcing the mind-body link;
- emphasizing the counsellor's expertise in helping people to cope better with illness and medical procedures, including knowledge of specialist skills to help them with their self-esteem, disruption to their life, relationships, distressing emotions (such as anxiety and resentment) and changes in roles and lifestyle;
- reassuring the patient, at this stage, that medical concerns will continue to be dealt with by the doctor and that the counsellor and doctor will exchange information about the patient's condition and progress.

All these details can enhance the chances of counselling having some positive effect on the patient's condition.

The initial stages of counselling

Counselling should start by getting the patient's view of his problem. Thereafter, acknowledging the devastating effects the patient's symptoms or condition have on his life can be a way of building rapport. This should include some discussion about the impact of the symptoms on the patient's relationships and career, and intrusion into leisure activities. The history of the onset, symptoms, significant events and medical investigations should also be addressed. It is important to limit discussion of this gradually from session to session, as otherwise the counsellor may inadvertently reinforce the patient's somatic fixation.

The main emphasis in the initial stages of counselling is to acknowledge the patient's distress, resist the temptation to reassure the patient and avoid offering psychological interpretations. This is achieved by assuming a collaborative and non-oppositional stance and by using medical language and medically styled interventions in counselling (McDaniel *et al.* 1992). These may include desensitization interventions, symptom diaries, and attention to the patient's sleep, diet and exercise routines. The counsellor should ask affirming questions about how the patient has coped with these symptoms and other unwelcome experiences and events in his life. Where possible, routine problem-defining questions should be asked which help the counsellor to construct a wider map of the problem. This may also lead to the counsellor completing a genogram with the patient and eliciting relevant information about the family and illness, and transgenerational illness meanings (see Chapter 8).

Some of the following questions can help the counsellor to explore these issues with the patient:

- When did this problem start?
- What do you think has caused this problem?
- What do you think the symptoms indicate?
- What have you done to help alleviate the symptoms? With what effect?
- Who else knows about this problem? And what are their views about it?
- Have you had other medical problems in the past? How did these affect you?
- What was happening in other areas of your life (e.g. relationships, work) when your worries/symptoms started?
- How have these concerns affected you (emotionally)?
- How have other health care providers been of help to you with this problem? (Always frame the question positively even if you suspect that the patient will criticize them for not taking him seriously.)
- How do you see your ideas about your symptoms being similar to or different from your doctor's ideas about them?

At the end of the initial stage of counselling, the patient should have had an opportunity to talk about his view of the medical problem and the impact this has on him. Unlike in some other counsellor situations, it may not be possible to discuss and agree on specific treatment goals. The reason for this is that the patient is likely to re-emphasize his somatic concerns, thereby diminishing the place of counselling in his treatment.

Main therapeutic interventions

Innovative therapeutic interventions are required to deal with the impasse that is likely to arise between the counsellor and patient in the course of counselling. It mirrors that which has arisen between the patient and the doctor. An impasse is marked by a 'more-of-the-same' situation (Watzlawick *et al.* 1974) in which any intervention by the counsellor results in 'no change' in the patient system. In counselling a somatically fixated or worried-well patient, a symmetrical relationship between the counsellor and patient can develop, characterized by an increasingly authoritative counsellor trying to convince an equally rigid patient that he is not ill, but to no avail.

Patient
'These symptoms must indicate that I am ill/infected'

Counsellor
'The doctor says that all the tests are negative, so you must be well'

Figure 14.2 Symmetrical relationship between patient and counsellor

This can become a 'game without end', with some variations. The interaction becomes repetitive and ineffective. Traditional theories about resistance in psychotherapy tend to blame the patient for the impasse. The counsellor may indicate what he perceives as the patient's resistance; or he may slightly vary his interactive behaviour, for example, by raising his voice or adopting a tone of greater authority. The view we take about resistance (be it to the doctor's opinion or to prescribed treatment) is derived from Kelly's (1969) work in psychotherapy. He suggests that the impasse between the counsellor and patient reflects the stuckness of the counsellor rather than the obduracy of the patient. In other words, the counsellor has not found the right 'key to the door'. To resolve this, the counsellor needs to become creative (and less predictable) in his problem-solving, rather than blaming or labelling the patient.

Cognitive-behavioural methods of intervention aimed at changing the patient's beliefs and behaviour and developing coping skills can be used (Turk and Salovey 1995). These interactions assume a fit between the patient's conceptualization of his problem and the rationale for the treatment being offered. As the patient is unlikely to accept that somatizing is a symptom of a psychological problem, he may resist cognitive-behavioural interventions until such time as his conceptualizations change. For this reason, they may be only partially successful with a limited number of these cases. Nonetheless, cognitive and behavioural interventions can be used in the course of a wider treatment approach, especially reinforcement (of more adaptive illness responses), exposure (to feared situations), extinction (of inappropriate illness behaviours) and fostering self-control (over maladaptive thoughts, feelings and behaviours), as well as biofeedback, relaxation training and distraction skills training.

The overall aim is to shift the patient's cognitive and behavioural repertoire away from habitual and rigid automatic thoughts and responses. (See 'Skills for managing an impasse in counselling' p. 137). A key feature is that the patient's physical and psychological symptoms can be translated into identifiable and concrete difficulties, rather than vague and uncontrollable ones. Such interventions focus upon the *individual's* beliefs and behaviours rather than on the relationship between the individual's beliefs in the context of his family, and the impact this has on the therapeutic system of professional carers. Further interventions can be used which are designed to encourage the individual to view the problem differently. An example may be to place the worry and its impact within the context of family relationships. Systemic interventions which reframe the problem (see Chapter 4) take the relationship between the beliefs of family members into account. These can be done with an individual and do not require other family members to be present in sessions. This form of intervention is particularly useful when the patient is unable or unwilling to change rigid beliefs. It is aimed at reducing resistance to change and dismantling these rigid beliefs in order for the patient to move out of his stuck position and to develop a new view of the problem. Other systemic interventions are described more fully on the following page.

The counsellor can construct a genogram with the patient (see Chapter 8) in order to explore family relationships and transgenerational illness meanings (Seaburn *et al.* 1992). When appropriate, this information will be woven into the therapeutic process and intervention.

The following case example illustrates the application of some of these ideas to working with a patient who had intractable worries about being infected with human immunodeficiency virus (HIV – the virus that causes AIDS) despite a series of negative test results. The patient self-referred to an HIV counselling service, and therefore a link with his doctor was not of primary concern in counselling.

Background

David, a 32-year-old warehouse supervisor, phoned an AIDS telephone hotline saying that he was concerned that he had become infected with HIV and given it to his wife Liz (aged 31 years). He had had sexual intercourse with another woman after he became drunk at a party a year ago. David reported that, apart from this one episode, he had always been faithful to his wife, and she likewise, for the ten years of their marriage. This was his only reported risk of HIV infection.

The couple had moved to London four years previously to find work. David reported that he wanted to move back to Wales because he was mixing with a 'bad' crowd here who encouraged him to drink alcohol, which his wife was opposed to. He believed that his wife wanted him to stay in London because it meant that she could work. He also reported that he had wanted children, but that his wife did not.

It was suspected during the course of the phone call that this man was excessively and somewhat inappropriately worried about his risk of HIV and that he required something other than rational explanations and information about HIV/AIDS. An appointment was offered to him to be seen by a counsellor in an AIDS Counselling Service, which he accepted gratefully. Up until this point, he had had no such offer from other hotline services, although he had been making calls to them on average four times a day.

David arrived half an hour early for his appointment and was found pacing around outside the unit waiting eagerly to be seen. Upon interview it transpired that David had read extensively about HIV/AIDS-related symptoms, tests and treatment in the process of checking

Skills for managing an impasse in counselling

A number of approaches can be used to break the cycle of 'Yes I am . . . No you're not' in counselling. Some of these are powerful interventions and should be used with sensitivity and care. Apparent resistance can be managed as follows:

1. **Comment on the apparent stuckness**
   I feel that each time I try to persuade you that you do not have a tumour, you seem to be quite convinced that you have. If you were the counsellor in my position, what might you say to a patient?

2. **Adopt a one-down, defeated position**
   (Somewhat theatrically, looking exasperated) Well, well, well; Steve, you seem to have got me here. I just can't think how I'm going to change your ideas. I just don't seem to be able to throw any new light on this. I'll need to think about this for a while.

3. **Solicit the patient's help**
   Do you have any ideas about what may help to convince you that you don't have a tumour and that you are not dying?

4. **Discuss the effect of the worry on relationships**
   How has this worry affected your relationship with your wife?

5. **Ask what might happen if the worry persisted**
   If this worry never went away, what effect might this have on you and how might you cope?

6. **Ask what might happen if things got worse (feared catastrophe)**
   What is the worst thing that could happen to you with this problem?

7. **Ask what might replace this worry**
   If, for some reason, you stopped worrying about dying, is there anything else you might start to worry about?

8. **Talk hypothetically about having the illness**
   You keep trying to convince me that you are terminally ill. You don't believe the doctors when they tell you that all the tests were accurate and reliable. Let's pretend for a few minutes that you are terminally ill. Let's talk about a day in your life as a terminally ill young man. How much of the day would you worry about dying? Who would you talk to about it? What plans would you make? What would you do that was not associated with your illness? How would this be different to what you are doing now?

9. **Discuss some advantages of worrying (reframe)**
   Has your worry resulted in anything good for you?

10. **Indicate that the patient has control**
    You will know when you are ready to stop worrying about your heart and be convinced that the test results were correct.

out his own risks and his wife's symptoms. He had become so conversant with the topic that he was now able to correct misinformation that he might receive from the helplines. He was also well aware that his exposure to risk of infection was low and that his two negative HIV antibody test results, taken three and nine months after the risk encounter, were likely to be accurate. Despite this knowledge, he was still convinced that he had given HIV to his wife. She had recently developed various aches and pains, and he attributed these to her having AIDS, although he was aware that these symptoms were atypical of AIDS. Furthermore, he was aware of the 'situational' nature of the symptoms, which disappeared when his wife visited her mother in Wales and returned when she came back to London. David had not told his wife of his infidelity.

David reported that his wife had said that she was finding his distress intolerable, but that she could not leave him because she feared he might kill himself. David had confirmed that he had considered suicide as a way of ending his worry, misery and guilt. However, he felt that he could not do this to his wife. He cried bitterly at this point. They were unable to leave each other yet were also becoming increasingly unable to be together. This position was to some extent reflected by the threat of HIV infection. David and his wife appeared to have little in common other than that they might now share the same virus. However, the virus which connected them might also separate them, through divorce, suicide or death from AIDS.

Counselling interventions

It was clear that HIV had an important place in their relationship. It had organized their beliefs and thinking. Intervention was aimed at enabling David to have a new view of the problem. His compulsion to read about HIV/AIDS and to phone hotlines repeatedly was reframed as his now being an expert in the field.

David: I've been phoning AIDS hotlines sometimes four times a day because I have been so worried about having HIV.
Counsellor: That's interesting, tell me, what have you learned from making these calls?
David: That people don't know as much as I do about HIV and AIDS. They tell me things that are wrong. I know they are wrong because I've read books about it. They don't know what a retrovirus is or how long it takes to sero-convert.
Counsellor: So, you have become an expert in AIDS hotline services. We don't know which are the better hotlines, so you probably know more about them than we do . . .
David: Yes, I could tell you all about them . . . (David proceeded enthusiastically to tell the counsellor about AIDS hotline services).

David had placed emphasis on discovering the truth about whether he had HIV. However, he only attemped to prove he had been infected. The problem was redefined by emphasizing the strength and the consequences of David's belief. It was suggested to him that irrespective of the evidence against his having HIV, he believed that he was infected and that the difficulty then was how to live with this belief, given that it seemed nothing could be done to change it. David's fear that he had given his wife HIV, because of his infidelity, was reframed as his caring and concern for his wife that she should have good health.

Reframing of the problem was aimed at providing David with a new view of his problem, one that placed it within the context of his relationship with his wife. The task of the counsellor is to provide a context for discussion of problem-solving and the patient's options, as a way of overcoming resistance to change, and to move the patient from the stuck position and facilitate new problem-solving.

In David's case, it would seem that the solution he found was for them both to move back to Wales. He phoned the counsellor a month after his visit to say that he had decided not to have another HIV antibody test because he could not stand the stress of it. He had stopped phoning helplines because he realized that they could not tell him any more than he already knew or might give him wrong information which annoyed him. When asked why they were returning to Wales, David laughed, saying that if his wife did have AIDS, then this was the best place for her to be. On another level, however, it was also the place where David said that his wife's aches and pains disappeared as well as the place where he would prefer to live.

CONCLUSION

Somatizing and worried-well patients present a unique challenge to health care providers in general and counsellors in particular. Successful treatment requires close collaboration between all professional carers, and innovative therapeutic interventions. Some patients may remain unresponsive to treatment and the possibility of a consultation with, or referral to, other mental health specialists (such as a clinical psychologist or psychiatrist) may then need to be considered. We have found that there is also a small group of these patients who, once in counselling, keep producing a worry about symptoms of their health in order to maintain access to, and contact with, the counsellor. This usually occurs when counselling is coming to an end. In such cases, the worry is a ticket of entry to psychological support systems. Unless the counsellor notes this, the patient will revert to the worry at the end of counselling sessions in order to re-engage the counsellor. It can be of some help in these circumstances to say to the patient: 'I will continue to see you for counselling even when you no longer have these worries'. (Some readers familiar with hypnotic techniques will recognize that this is in itself an intervention.) The main concern behind the patient's symptom is then suggested and other issues can be explored. Counsellors need to be sensitive to the different concerns of patients and the indirect ways in which patients may sometimes express these concerns. The principles of managing resistance have been outlined in this chapter and may be applied to other clinical situations in which an impasse develops.

CHAPTER 15

Models of Consultation and Collaboration

INTRODUCTION

Much has been written about how to improve the psychological care and treatment of patients, and most published work assumes that patients and counsellors have freely entered into working contracts. In many cases in health care settings, counselling evolves in a less straightforward way for the counsellor or patient.

From the counsellor's standpoint, numerous contextual issues must first be addressed. Clarification with referrers and other colleagues about the role and position of the counsellor in a specific case is an important first step. Failure to attend to relationships with the referrer or other health care professionals, not only at the start of the counselling service but throughout its duration, could undermine the service and even lead to its termination.

Some counsellors believe that counselling can help in all areas of patient care and management. In most health care settings counselling is secondary to medical and nursing care, however important and pressing the implications of the psychological and social components of an illness may be. The challenge for counsellors is to find a way into the health care system without posing a threat to colleagues. This chapter describes how different approaches to professional collaboration and consultation in health care settings can facilitate a wider range of interesting and creative ways of working with colleagues and patients, enabling counsellors to have a secure place in the health care team.

DEFINING CONSULTATION AND COLLABORATION

Starting with an assumption that a counsellor is not necessarily needed, or wanted, in a particular health care setting helps to anticipate resistance, scepticism, rejection or conflicting messages (i.e. 'Yes, we want a counsellor, but we don't really have much faith in what you can do'), irrespective of how welcoming medical and nursing colleagues may seem. It is important to differentiate first between the aims of consultation and collaboration.

- *Consultation.* A consultation in a health care setting can be (a) *with a large system* (e.g. team, ward, unit or professional group) about how they are managing a particular task or activity; (b) *with an individual or team* about their treatment and care of a particular patient; or (c) *directly with a patient* or family who have asked to see or been referred to the counsellor. Consultation may not involve direct patient contact.
- *Collaboration* is working with colleagues towards an agreed objective and is advanced through direct consultations with patients and colleagues.

Consultation and collaboration are closely connected. One of the aims of consultation is to improve interprofessional collaboration (Seaburn *et al.* 1996), which can lead to new referrals and more frequent requests for consultations. Collaboration through open discussion and a willingness to consult can help establish the position and credibility of the counsellor in the multidisciplinary environment. The entry of the counsellor into the team is potentially complex and may be time-consuming. The need for a counselling service may arise for a number of reasons, such as the following:

- Increasing workloads and administrative demands may make it difficult for doctors and nurses to address all of the patient's psychological needs, which may be complex and time-consuming.
- Some members of a team may have experience of, or have heard about, the usefulness of having a counsellor as part of the team.
- A suggestion is made by a counsellor that a service might benefit from having a counsellor to help solve and manage some of their patients' problems.
- An element of competitiveness may mean that staff pay 'lip service' to the idea of having a counsellor just because other teams are doing it.
- The team experiences benefit from referring to a counsellor and invites him to join it.

How a counselling service is introduced and developed will also depend on whether there are existing protocols for psychosocial care. The counsellor should adopt a non-oppositional stance, irrespective of whether the environment is receptive, cautious or hostile. This stance can help the counsellor to integrate into the team and gain acceptance from colleagues. This entails: having small goals; starting by learning about the unit; building up credit with one's colleagues; and avoiding criticism. Attitudes of hostility or caution may stem from myths or stereotypes about each professional group, either due to past experience or as a defence against the introduction of something different or new. Counsellors and health care professionals sometimes have stereotypic views of one another (McDaniel and Campbell 1986). These are listed below:

Doctors' and nurses' myths about counsellors:
- Providers of 'tea and sympathy'; a shoulder to cry on.
- 'Do-gooders' who cheer people up.
- Not properly trained, or unprofessional amateurs.
- Overly sensitive.
- What they do with patients is plain common sense.
- Glorified agony aunts offering a listening service.
- A last resort with difficult patients.

- Time wasters who sit and talk.
- Useful only for dealing with hypochondriacs and panic attacks.
- Outcome or effectiveness cannot be measured.
- They analyse too much.

Counsellors' myths about doctors and nurses:
- Preoccupied with boundaries and limits of competence.
- Do not share easily.
- Not open to new ideas.
- Offer only hi-tech and impersonal care.
- Bedside manner is superficial.
- Territorial and do not work easily with new colleagues.
- Medical model of practice is vastly different to the counselling model.
- Assume power and act in a patronizing manner.
- Use props (white coats, stethoscopes, beepers) to identify themselves and create distance.
- Stressed, and some could do with counselling.
- Believe that they already do limited counselling with their patients.

Some of these ideas may, at first, seem amusing or even ludicrous. The fact is that, however amicably members of some multiprofessional health care teams get on with one another, they may approach and deliver patient care differently and hold constraining and sometimes erroneous beliefs about one another. An awareness may help counsellors to practise in such a way as not to conform to these stereotypes and to avoid being defensive or oppositional when they are voiced. This will go a long way to building up collaborative working relationships with colleagues. The context or setting in which the counsellor works also affects the range of possible collaborative relationships that can be fostered. Different models of practice are described and illustrated below.

MODELS OF PRACTICE

For historical, practical and conceptual reasons, counselling services may develop differently in different health care settings. What may begin as a counselling service for children undergoing renal dialysis may be extended to all children in the renal unit, and later to all paediatric patients in the hospital. Similarly, a stress management and relaxation clinic for patients attending a GP surgery may in time become the basis for a primary care counselling service. By way of contrast, a counsellor who works initially as part of a generic hospital-based service may, in time, develop a close working relationship with one particular unit (for example, a paediatric neurosurgery department) and through the closer and more intensive relationship with the team, opt to work as a full-time member of that team. Others may have a range of different roles within the health care setting, leading to close collaborative relationships with a limited number of departments or units. One counsellor, for example, may work in the oncology department three days per week, as part of a team undertaking a limited trial of placing primary care doctors in Casualty Departments or Emergency Rooms for two sessions per week; he could then teach medical and nursing students communications skills for the remainder of the time. Counsellors can work in a number of settings:

- Separate from the health care setting (for example, in private practice), taking referrals from the hospital, clinic or health care setting.
- Within a doctor's surgery, taking referrals from any member of staff, or self-referrals.
- Within a hospital or clinic in a counselling or psychotherapy service, taking referrals from any department or unit.
- Within a hospital or clinic, taking referrals from a limited number of departments or units.
- Within a health care setting, but working as a specialist in only one unit or department.
- Within a community domiciliary service visiting patients in their homes.

Within each of these settings, the counsellor can organize his practice in a number of different ways, depending upon the needs of the service and his level of competence and experience. This involves direct or indirect patient or colleague consultations, or any combination of these. Counsellor practice can include:

- Consultations with patients only.
- Consultations with professional staff only about their care of patients.
- Consultations with professional staff about staff relationships.
- Consultations with both staff and patients.
- *Ad hoc* consultations with either staff or patients (i.e. consultation-liaison practice).

A well-trained and experienced counsellor need not have an extensive knowledge of a particular medical condition, although this helps in gaining the confidence of the team. However, an understanding of the context in which treatment and care is provided is a vital first step. Having a framework for consultation with other health care professionals in health care settings can help to achieve these aims.

CONSULTATION WITH PROFESSIONAL COLLEAGUES IN HEALTH CARE SETTINGS

Consultation with colleagues working in the same organization is a special professional situation which is common in health care settings. The unique feature of internal consultation is the relationship between the counsellor and the consultee, which adds another dimension to the consultation process. Seniority and shifts in relationships with colleagues may lead to requests for consultation. The request also implies a focus on what is happening not only to a patient, but also to the dynamics of the caring team, as well as other organizational matters.

Requests for a consultation stem from an idea that there is a dilemma or a need for specialist discussion about a problem. It may be that a lack of consensus over how to manage a problem has itself created a problem. Consultation begins when someone affected by the problem discusses the difficulty with someone else, be it in a formal consultation meeting, over the telephone after working on a difficult case, in a ward meeting, or in any other setting. It is the activity of discussing the problem, rather than where this takes place and for how long, that defines consultation. There is a tradition in medical care that complex problems are discussed with colleagues (who may be more knowledgeable or senior) or referred to them. So consultations about psychological problems with counsellors are commonplace in these settings. The relationship between the counsellor and consultee may be challenged when one consults with someone within the same organization, as illustrated in the case below.

A counsellor in a general hospital was asked by a doctor to offer ongoing consultation to an oncology team because the team worked in a stressful field, and a consultation could help to raise staff morale. One of the dilemmas faced by members of the oncology team was that, should morale improve, they would be expected to provide more psychological support to patients in the unit and this would require additional time and skills. The counsellor, on the other hand, had already been offering a support service to some patients. For this reason, the counsellor already had some views about staff relationships in the oncology unit and was aware that not all the nurses and doctors wanted to become involved in patient support and psychological counselling. The dilemma for the counsellor was that he had been asked by the head of the oncology unit to consult with the group. A reluctance to become involved in the management of problems between members of professional staff might ultimately result in fewer referrals being made to him, which might also impede the research project in the oncology unit which the counsellor was hoping to pursue.

What prompts a request for consultation?

Some teams in health care settings arrange for regular and ongoing consultations in order to prevent day-to-day difficulties from becoming major problems. Difficulties may emerge in working groups when there is an apparent inability to solve a problem, difficulty in responding to changes, or a lack of agreement over strategies for problem-solving. In health care settings, most problems have an impact on health service managers, in addition to clinical staff, because of the hierarchical structure of the organization through which accountability is arranged. Therefore the counsellor in this setting needs to address the wider implications of problems and solutions, and not limit views of the problem to the scenario which the consultee has described. The ability to add a new dimension to a dilemma or shift people's views about a problem is the basis of a successful consultation. For example:

A junior doctor came to understand in the course of consultation with a counsellor that, more than anything else, his career promotion was being held up because he did not pay sufficient attention to the impression he made on colleagues. He was consistently late for ward meetings, he seldom wore a tie and he wore his hair long. This was frowned upon in the conservative teaching hospital in which he worked. His own explanation for the difficulties he faced in his career centred around how colleagues on the ward were apparently 'sabotaging his work'. He later came to accept that he was partly responsible for sabotaging his career prospects and that this possibly stemmed from his ambivalence about whether he really wanted a career in medicine. Once he accepted the idea of paying attention to his personal presentation, the impression he made on others changed and he was accepted as a registrar three months later.

When consultation is requested, it is likely that the doctor or health care team requesting the consultation will have the view that they are on the 'losing side' in relation to a patient or another department or team. The need for consultation can therefore be prompted by a need to redress this in order to be seen as more competent or better placed in the professional hierarchy. Cost and practical concerns (e.g. highly confidential patient information) often preclude engaging a consultant or counsellor from outside the organization. Other possible reasons for requesting a consultation are as follows:

- The consultee wants to relinquish responsibility for a case or problem and intends to pass it on to the consulting counsellor.
- The problem is apparently 'highly confidential' and there may be a fear that 'dirty washing' will be openly displayed.
- The experience and expertise of the counsellor is valued.
- The counsellor may be more flexible about time than an external consultant, if he is from the same organization.
- There may be a belief that there will be greater loyalty and support if the consultant is from within the same organization.
- The consultee may experience feeling isolated in the hospital or clinic, and the counsellor may create a new connection or relationship.
- It may be more helpful to have someone in greater authority in the organization to confirm or reinforce a view or idea, or offer a different view.

Consultation is requested and occurs not only when there is a problem but also when people in a 'healthy' team are ready for more growth. Problems or events that typically prompt a request for consultation in health care settings stem from one of five possibilities, even though they may be linked. These are listed below, with each definition of a problem or issue followed by an example.

- *Problem with patients.* A medical specialist asks for advice from a counsellor about how to manage a patient who will not comply with treatment.
- *With patients and relatives.* A patient complains to a clinic manager about his treatment and care.
- *With managers.* The director of a medical disaster team is asked to redraft their operational plan and pay greater attention to the care and support of victims and their relatives. A counsellor is invited to comment on this aspect of the draft document and make suggestions for its improvement.
- *With colleagues.* High staff turnover in a diabetic clinic prompts senior medical and nursing staff to consult with a counsellor to see whether this problem might be caused by staff relationship problems or by how the service is organized and managed.
- *Within a team.* A new staff member joins a team in order to develop a new clinical and research project. A counsellor is invited to facilitate a team-building event.

There are many other examples of consultation work and it is important to stress that many of these are only indirectly concerned with patient problems.

How does a counsellor become a consultant?

Most counsellors who act as consultants to other staff undertake consultation in addition to, or as a part of, their clinical work. The following are five attributes of consultants which individually or collectively may have led to achieving this position:

- *Seniority* within the setting.
- *Authority* or seniority within one's profession.
- *Experience* in dealing successfully with similar problems.
- *Position* of impartiality by not being attached to any one unit.
- *Respect* for one's ability to think clearly and to solve problems.

The choice of consultant may be determined by the nature of the problem. If the problem is concerned with the patient's behaviour or relationships, it is more likely that a counsellor will be approached for a consultation. Consultation skills are rarely formally taught in universities or health settings. Initiation into consultancy work in health settings is usually through experience of problem-solving with colleagues, and as a result of close, collaborative working relationships. A typical opening scenario from a colleague seeking consultation may be: 'Can I discuss a clinical problem with you?' or, 'I'm having some difficulty writing up my proposal for more nurses in the community care programme. Would you have a look at my draft proposal?' Two central points underpin consultation: the definition of relationships between colleagues and the view of the health care setting as an organization.

Defining relationships through consultation

Consultation in the form of discussion or case review provides an opportunity for new views to emerge and for some relationships to be redefined. This is not to suggest that every piece of clinical work should be preceded by extensive consultation in relation to the task and outcome. This may be neither warranted nor practical. It is important, however, for the consultant in the health care setting to be clear about the nature of his relationship with the consultee, that is, whoever is clinically responsible for the case. There is a difference between a referral and a request for consultation over a clinical case. The counsellor may move between these positions in relation to a case. The counsellor's consultant position must be mutually defined: the consultee requests consultation and the counsellor agrees to consult. A colleague may, for example, refer a case and the counsellor may choose to consult his colleague about how he can develop his work with the patient rather than the counsellor take on the case himself.

Essentially, there must be agreement between the professionals that consultation will take place. As the counsellor may move between different positions, he needs to be flexible, adaptive and able to 'observe' himself in different interactive positions. Some different consultation positions are listed below.

- *Between colleagues.* A doctor asks a counsellor working in the same team for some advice about how to break 'bad news' to a patient.
- *Between units/departments.* Members of staff on the Intensive Care Unit request consultation from a counsellor for bereavement issues.
- *Between hospitals.* Senior members of staff in an infertility counselling unit are

engaged in consultation with colleagues in another district hospital who are in the process of setting up an infertility unit in their own hospital.

While the consultation task remains the same in each, the counsellor will have different relationships with a range of people, depending where they are in the hospital hierarchy. There is a tendency to be more formalized and thorough about setting up and conducting the consultation the further one is socially, hierarchically or physically (in terms of localization) from the consultee.

The hospital or health care setting is also an organization. It is sometimes helpful to think about how problems arise within organizations by drawing a parallel with problems in families. In a health care setting such as a hospital, a professional may react to a particular problem in such a way as to exacerbate the problem. They may seek allies (and thereby create enemies), become ill, act in a more autocratic way, leave the department, and so on. Similar processes can be observed in families confronted with problems. A hospital comprises many departments and disciplines. This inevitably leads to people having different views within departments and between the hospital and other institutions. These differences may stem from competing models of care, conflict over hierarchies and relationships, or different generations of workers who may not share the same values and approaches to the delivery of health care.

The aim of consultation is to elicit and address different views of problems and generate a climate in which new ideas, beliefs, alternatives, meanings and behaviours can emerge. In the same way as it is essential to have a structure or approach for counselling sessions with patients, it is desirable to have guidelines for conducting consultations with colleagues.

STEPS IN CONSULTATION

Planning the consultation

There are several stages in planning any consultation, though they are not necessarily rigidly applied. A colleague who asks for five minutes of time to discuss a case does not necessarily expect to be taken through each stage. The initial stages of consultation which are described in this chapter amount to a 'map' conveying a procedure for setting-up and organizing consultation session. The structure offers some guidance in the consultation procedure and it is especially useful where there is apparent 'stuckness' or difficulties in the consultation. The counsellor may have overlooked some steps or procedures and this may have lead to confusion about the consultation task.

The stages are listed below:

• Understanding the request for consultation and defining the problem;
• Developing ideas about the consultant–consultee relationship;
• Discussing a consultation contract;
• Conversations about the problem;
• Feedback and re-evaluating the contract;
• Case closure.

The first stage – understanding the request for consultation – has already been described in this chapter. Some of the next stages are described in more detail below.

Understanding the consultant–consultee relationship

A list of questions to help consultants clarify and define the consultant–consultee relationship include:

- Is there consensus in the consultee's department that the consultation should be requested?
- Is there an expectation that the consultation will uphold a particular view (i.e. he will not feel that he can introduce new or potentially controversial ideas)?
- Does the counsellor have some autonomy and flexibility in relation to the consultee?
- From the point of view of their professional backgrounds, is there likely to be some measure of fit between the counsellor and consultee?

A further step is to understand as much as possible about the effect it might have on established relationships if the consultation goes ahead. This includes clarity about whether the consultee is trying to create an alliance with the counsellor (bring him closer), hand over work or a task (redefining it as a liaison relationship), or perhaps discredit him by sabotaging the consultation (push him away). Posing the following questions to oneself is a useful way to speculate about these processes:

- What relationship do I already have with the consultee that may affect the nature, course and outcome of consultation?
- If I choose not to participate or accept the consultation request, what might happen with regard to the problem and with regard to my relationship with the consultee?
- What other parts of the organization might be affected by my participation, and how might they view my involvement in this problem?
- Are there any particular 'cultural' or organizational rules which would impede the work; for example, as a counsellor, can I bring into the conversation anything about the doctor–patient relationship with the doctor?
- If the problem were to deteriorate, how would I relate to the consultee?
- Given that this consultation is offered on the basis of 'good will' and is not being paid for, how will this affect our contract and respective obligations?
- What levels of the hospital system (e.g. senior management) might need to be involved and how might this affect my position in the institution if I had to engage them in our consultation?
- Should I become 'stuck' in the course of the consultation, with whom can I consult without breaching confidentiality relating to my work with the consultee?
- How will I deal with confidential information relating to the case that may be important for the process and outcome of the consultation?
- To whom am I ultimately accountable, and does this person have the authority to enter into consultation and institute any changes?

Three different positions can be covered in moving from liaison to consultation, and these are illustrated below. In the first position (A) the counsellor accepts the referral and sees the patient; in the second (B) a link is made with the referring person and together they see the patient; in the last (C) the referrer keeps the case, undertakes the counselling and consults the counsellor over difficult cases.

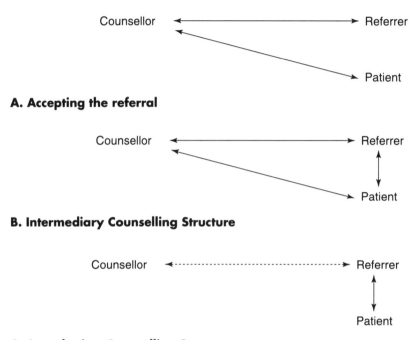

A. Accepting the referral

B. Intermediary Counselling Structure

C. Consultation–Counselling Structure

A difficulty arises when the referrer experiences problems and the consultant notes that the clinical work that remained with the consultee is not adequately carried out. It may be undermining to colleagues to revert back to a liaison structure. In these situations we suggest trying a few joint sessions and seeing the patient together with the colleague. We define this as a learning experience for us, but we hope to pass on some of our skills. Before the session we agree that one person will interview the patient and the other will observe and consult. If there are points which have not been addressed, the consultant will be free to point these out to his colleagues during the session. In this way, the clinician retains control over the questioning and the session. This method of joint consultative session has proved helpful in general medical problem-solving, in case management and in developing and enhancing relationships with colleagues.

Discussion with the consultee

Once some ideas have been developed about the relationship with the consultee, a meeting can be arranged to discuss any of the points listed above which might impede the consultation process. Prompt attention to a consultation request in a hospital setting can enhance a good relationship. Some requests may relate to life and death issues and circumstances may change rapidly. Prompt discussion may help to resolve problems that could deteriorate further if left for any length of time.

A meeting is arranged with the person who requests the consultation in the first instance. Some meaning has to be given to the meeting and for this reason one might define the purpose of the meeting as follows:

Counsellor as consultant:	Dr Smith, thank you for coming up to my office this morning. I think we agreed to meet for fifteen minutes and to arrange for another meeting if we need some more time. As you may recall, I said to you over the phone that before I could undertake consultation meetings with you and members of your department, I would first like to think over some ideas about my working with you over this problem. The reason for this is that, in my experience, the success of consultation depends upon several things. These include being clear about my role, my task, and my relationship with you now and in the future. I think that it is especially important to think these over because we need to consider whether I am the most suitable person to be working with you on this. Firstly, do you have any thoughts on this?
Consultee:	Well actually I'm very pleased you've brought this up. It was not an easy decision for me to approach you, particularly because I know that you're very busy and also because, frankly, Dr Jones (the co-director) had some thoughts that maybe we should be approaching someone outside the hospital.
Consultant:	How did it come about that you asked me?
Consultee:	Dr Jones and I had heard about your work in the Rheumatology Unit and in fact it was he who first suggested we get in touch with you. I think he got cold feet, though, when he thought that if things 'went wrong', so to speak, it would make it difficult to refer patients to your counselling team in the future. I suppose he was trying to protect our good working relationship.
Consultant:	If there were any disagreements or problems in our relationship, how might you handle the situation?
Consultee:	I know that I could always talk to you. Perhaps Dr Jones would be more inclined to blame me and also remind me that we might have been better off with someone outside.
Consultant:	What made him choose not to come to this meeting? (and so on)

Discussing a contract

Making a contract is the basis of an agreement between the consultee and the counsellor as to what will be discussed in the course of the consultation and how long it may take, and to clarify professional boundaries. It is also important to establish whether the consultee has the authority to enter into a contract. The consultee might be asked, for example:

To whom do you report? Is he aware of our meetings? Do you need his permission in order to be discussing these problems with us? How might it affect things with him if you were to set aside two hours a week in clinic time to meet with us?

Some provision must be made for flexibility within this. For this reason, the contract does not set out conditions or fixed endpoints, but rather guides the consultant–consultee in the relationship until the contract is renegotiated by virtue of new and evolving problems or ideas. The contract might take some of the following points into account:

- There is an agreement to meet for consultation.
- There is an agreement to participate in and contribute to the meetings.
- The consultant can ask for something from the consultee.
- The consultant may work with a team of colleagues.
- What is said in the context of consultation is confidential to the consultation context.
- Each person takes responsibility for what they say.
- Consultation is to be distinguished from any other collaborative clinical work between the teams or any members of the teams.
- Meetings will take place at a specific time in a specified place for a specified length of time.
- Certain people will be expected at meetings. Procedures are agreed in the event of any one of them not being able to attend or if someone has to leave the meeting.
- Financial arrangements pertaining to the consultation are agreed.

Once the contract is agreed, the consultation can proceed. However, in a health care setting, not all problems discussed between colleagues are formally negotiated or take place in a designated place, at a prearranged time. Consultations can be *ad hoc* and take place at the nurses' station, in ward meetings, in corridors or over the telephone. It helps, however, to keep a contract in mind even if there is no formal agreement or definition that consultation is taking place. An approach by someone for help with ideas for writing a letter to a colleague is an example of this.

Conducting the consultation – tasks

The process of consultation is inextricably linked to the tasks of the consultant. The consultant's tasks, including consultation skills, can be set out as follows.

Consultation can help to define, clarify and solve problems through a conversation between the consultee and consultant. The consultant helps to create an environment in which change can occur. While change may be sought, the consultant may have no control over the direction of change or decisions made by the consultee. Questioning is particularly helpful for gathering information and exploring initial ideas. Examples of questions to a consultee in relation to general medical problems are listed below:

'How has it come about that there has been a shift in emphasis from in-patient to out-patient care?'

'What was happening at around the time this was upgraded from a unit to a department?'

'Can you tell us something about community care arrangements?'

'If a patient were to become ill out of hours, what arrangements have you made for staff cover?'

'What are the particular aspects about working with this group of patients that might be different or stressful?'

'How is the handover to the new staff organized?'

'What do you think is unique to your work with this group of patients which sets your needs apart from other units in the hospital?'

'Who outside of this unit most recognizes this?'

Formulating hypotheses

An initial task of the consultant is to consider carefully his place in the wider health care system. Sometimes, the consultant recognizes that it is neither appropriate nor possible to offer consultation. This may be due to his level of competence, position within the system, or decision not to work with a problem or consultee. Should he choose to proceed with the consultation, it helps to make a hypothesis or calculated guess about problems before each subsequent consultation session. This is based on available information (e.g. who requested the consultation, with what in mind) and helps to focus the questioning for each consultation interview.

Hypotheses can be formulated as soon as a request for consultation is made. Descriptions of the problem, as well as gaps in the story, are pieces of information that can be drawn on by the consultant. The hypothesis evolves as more information becomes available and the consultation proceeds. It is also helpful to reflect on how and why the consultants have come to understand the problem in a particular way. We ask the question: 'What has been happening to influence our own thinking in this particular way?' Hypothesizing can be of strategic value to the consultant and the consultee. This in turn helps the consultee reduce his bias towards any one person or idea as the consultee, his context, and all those connected with the problem are taken into consideration.

Some initial questions to the consultee about the hypothesis in a first session may include the following:

What has prompted the request for consultation?

Why now?

When did the idea of consultation first come about?

What is happening in and around the unit?

Who first spoke about this problem in the unit?

Have new staff recently joined the unit? Has someone recently left?

What will inform us that the case can be closed and that we no longer need to be discussing this problem?

'Dreaded' issues

Identifying and talking about 'dreaded issues', or what people fear the most about their having a problem (see Chapter 11), is a technique used in consultation. The fear may be in relation to the consequences of the problem not being solved. Similarly, in a consultation there may be issues or outcomes that are 'dreaded' by the consultee. These may include a fear of dismissal, being ignored in decision-making, or not being put forward for promotion. Hypothetical and future-orientated questions are an effective way to address these fears ahead of time.

The following examples of questions might be used in order to help the consultee discuss his fears:

'Who is ultimately responsible for this case?'

'What implications would there be if the patient were to die/commit suicide?'

'What would be the worst possible thing that you could imagine happening in this case?'

'What, in your view, is the difference between secrets and confidentiality?'

'What recent changes in staff have there been and what changes do you anticipate?'

'What has to happen in order for you to feel that you have done the best you can?'

'If this problem persists, how do you see things for yourself in relation to this unit?'

Ending the consultation and arranging follow-up

The process of hypothesizing, consulting, reviewing the feedback and contract continues until there is agreement that the initial (or revised) goals of consultation have been reached, or there is agreement, for whatever reason, to end the consultation. At the end of the consultation, the consultant and consultee need to discuss:

* If or how they will work together in the future.
* What follow-up is to be arranged (if any).
* What changes there might be in their relationship.
* What will remain unchanged.
* What procedure will be followed if the problem recurs.
* What feedback (if any) about the consultation needs to be presented to a third party.

This process provides an opportunity for the consultant to avoid being redrafted in to carry out more work, even after the contract has ended, and for the re-creation of the appropriate boundaries between colleagues.

CONCLUSION

Counsellors working in health care settings may be called upon to consult with their professional colleagues. The consultant's relationship with the consultee is different to that which the counsellor has with a referrer. However, the consultant still draws on similar skills to those he uses when seeing patients. These include skills in problem identification, examining different possibilities and outcomes, addressing 'dreaded issues', reframing, and using questions as a method of conducting the consultation interview. An important difference is that the consultant must also pay special attention to his role and position within the system. He is usually a part of the wider health care system with which he is consulting. This has implications for whether he can consult with certain individuals, teams or units, and the extent to which he can reasonably be impartial and helpful. Inevitably, there will be situations in which the consultant considers he is 'stuck' or unable to move the consultation in any direction. It may be that confidential information discussed in the course of consultation impedes the clinical work of the consultant. Seeking consultation from others within or outside the hospital is a significant step towards resolving this impasse.

Consultation skills make it possible for counsellors to relate differently to some of their professional colleagues. They also pave the way for developing collaborative work with colleagues. Where joint consultation sessions are held with patients and doctors (as well as nurses), they learn more about counselling skills and techniques and counsellors acquire a better understanding of complex medical issues. In turn, patients benefit from better co-ordinated care. Where counsellors consult with their professional colleagues, they can apply their problem-solving skills to the wider system, in this case, the health care system. This chapter has described how the role of the counsellor extends beyond that of receiving referrals and liaising with referrers, to include consultation and collaboration within the health care setting.

CHAPTER 16

Moving on from Feeling Stuck in Counselling

INTRODUCTION

Problems at work are as inevitable as those in one's personal life. Sometimes, the one leads to the other. For example, a difficult day at work may result in being short-tempered at home. Counsellors are trained to be reflective practitioners, learning to identify problems and their possible source, and to work towards their resolution. This can extend to addressing the extent to which the counsellor may himself have caused, maintained or exacerbated a problem. This chapter examines possible sources of 'stuckness' in counselling in health care settings and some ideas and strategies for overcoming these.

WHAT IS 'STUCKNESS' IN COUNSELLING?

'Stuckness' in the counselling process can be defined as a block to progress, either from the counsellor's or the patient's point of view. During the counselling process, there are usually episodes in which either little or no progress is made with a patient or indeed there is evidence of some repression of problems or difficulties. Our training includes learning how to recognize when the counselling process has become stuck and to work with the patient in order to free the therapeutic process from an impasse. Perceived lack of progress in counselling is usually viewed as normal, even though it sometimes implies that the patient is resisting the counsellor's (preferred) idea or intervention. Stuckness can occur at any stage in counselling, from the point of first contact – or even before, if there is some disagreement as to whether counselling should in fact take place – right up to the last moments when terminating a case. Stuckness is usually characterized by a lack of progress in counselling. Indications of this include:

- going over familiar issues without evidence of any progress in how the problem is viewed;
- obvious boredom or missed sessions by the patient;

- the counsellor not looking forward to a counselling session;
- the counsellor becoming hostile or argumentative with the patient.

Unchecked, it can lead to patients dropping out of counselling, the patient's problems being unresolved or becoming intractable, the counsellor acquiring a bad reputation in the hospital or clinic setting, and even counsellor 'burnout'.

Stuckness need not denote a problem in counselling. Some counsellors may view it as an opportunity to reflect on the process with the patient and move beyond the impasse. Others see it as an ideal time to talk about the idea of 'resistance' in the counselling process. Counsellors may sometimes even consciously 'create' an impasse or stuckness as a therapeutic intervention in order to focus the patient on his ambivalence or reticence to change.

CAUSES OF STUCKNESS

There are numerous possible causes of stuckness in counselling. The more obvious ones stem from the patient's reluctance to change, but there are both contextual and personal issues for the counsellor to consider when trying to identify these possible causes.

Patient issues

A number of events or processes may impede the progress of counselling for a patient and these may differ from one situation to another. The following are short examples to illustrate this:

- The patient does not share the same view of the problem and its possible solution with the counsellor (or other health care professionals) and therefore does not comply with or accept treatment.
- The patient does not want to be referred to a counsellor and transfers the responsibility for problem-solving onto the counsellor as an act of aggression.
- Illness has brought about changes in the patient's relationships. Issues raised in the course of counselling can add to the patient's experience of uncertainty, role confusion and anxiety in addition to relationship changes brought about by his illness.
- The patient feels unable to make important decisions for himself either because his illness has drained his capacity to solve problems creatively, or there is little incentive to change. This impasse is often transferred to the relationship between the counsellor and patient.
- Issues about loss are painful to talk about and not a part of everyday conversations. The patient is unsure of how to talk about his feelings or the effect of revealing them to a comparative stranger in counselling sessions.
- Denial of problems can be used as a means of coping with them (either consciously or unconsciously).
- The patient is frustrated by the slow pace of counselling and was hoping for practical solutions, rapid results and evidence of progress, including possibly a 'cure'.

- The patient's needs are not identified or not met, leaving him feeling frustrated, vulnerable and dissatisfied.

Problems arising from the counselling setting

For the counsellor, there may be processes within the work setting which directly or indirectly lead to feelings of stuckness in counselling sessions. These may include some combinations of the following:

- Accepting a referral without first assessing whether it is a suitable case for counselling and failing to identify or address confounding problems or dynamics which may impede progress.
- Insufficient feedback between different members of the health care team, especially between the counsellor and others, resulting in uncoordinated care and mis-understandings and lack of congruence over approaches to treatment and care.
- Having too much to do and too few resources (usually time), leading to a lower standard of care or treatment and the making of unwise decisions.
- Inflexibility on the part of the counsellor, who is determined to preserve a traditional model of counselling as practised in an 'ideal' setting, which is viewed as curative and the antidote to change, pain and chaos in the patient's life.
- Not paying attention to changes in the patient's condition, prognosis, treatment, level and context of social support, mental state or ability to attend counselling sessions.

Issues relating to the counsellor

Unresolved personal responses to illness, loss or disability may occur and limit the effectiveness of the counsellor. Other personal issues may include the following:

- Inappropriate reactions to a patient's problems, such as giving unrealistic re-assurance, stemming from insufficient therapeutic skills and training, lack of supervision, and fatigue.
- Over-identification with the patient (becoming too close emotionally), which may lead to breaking professional boundaries, such as giving a patient the counsellor's home telephone number 'so that he can call at any time he needs to talk'.
- Under-identification with the patient (becoming too distant emotionally), which may lead to inflexibility on the part of the counsellor, a lack of empathy or the patient feeling that the counsellor is 'cold' and 'uncaring'. This can include having a narrow view of the relationships people choose and how they conduct themselves within them.
- Acting in a way that implies judgement of the patient, his lifestyle or the strategies he uses to cope with his illness. This could manifest as overt criticism of the patient, instructing the patient to make different decisions, or implied criticism com-municated non-verbally (e.g. frowning, shaking one's head or a look of exasperation). This can also present where the counsellor feels that he has to take sides with either the patient, his family or other colleagues.
- Becoming didactic in consultations with patients and instructing the patient to act in a particular way. This may arise where the counsellor feels anxious about dealing

with the patient's uncertainty or where the counsellor is frustrated, impatient or overworked.

- Always treating the patient's problem or symptoms without attending to any of the patient's emotional needs. This may arise where the counsellor has a preferred style or approach to counselling that exclusively involves problem identification and problem-solving. It may also occur where the counsellor feels unsure how to respond to a patient who cries or says very little.
- Feeling under pressure to solve every problem, offer definitive answers to questions and create a sense of certainty. The counsellor may also blame himself (erroneously) for failure in counselling.

RECOGNIZING POSSIBLE SIGNS OF STRESS IN THE COUNSELLOR

It is important for the counsellor to be able to recognize when he is stressed, and how this may interfere with the counselling process. The following questions can help the counsellor to identify the presence and possible source of stress which may lead to stuckness when counselling patients:

- Take your 'emotional temperature': are you overly sensitive, or emotionally cold and distant? Ask, 'What is going on here?'
- Have you established an unhelpful pattern in how you communicate with patients and colleagues (e.g. are you constantly argumentative or dismissive?)?
- Have you become predictable in how you respond to patients and different problems? Have you lost a feeling of challenge and desire to respond flexibly?
- Are you frequently tired and irritable (e.g. overwork or personal difficulties)?
- Are the boundaries between your personal and professional lives sometimes unclear? Do you take too much work home, or come in to work when it is not necessary to do so?
- Are there significant changes in your leisure pursuits (e.g. too much drinking and no exercise)?
- Are there significant changes in your family and personal relationships?
- Do you feel a sense of achievement in your work, or does the constant experience of loss take its toll on you?
- Are you affected by ill health, disability or loss in yourself or your personal relationships?

STUCKNESS WITHIN THE COUNSELLING RELATIONSHIP

The emphasis thus far has been on patient, counsellor and contextual factors which affect progress in counselling. This assumes that counselling has started and that the counsellor and patient are both committed to the session or course of sessions. Stuckness may also occur at the point of referral and even before there has been agreement to meet for counselling. The chances of this happening in a health care setting are high for a number of reasons:

- The referrer may not have clearly explained the reason for the referral or gained the patient's co-operation and consent for the referral.
- The patient may not recognize (or may not *want* to recognize) that there are psychological and relationship issues which need to be examined in the course of counselling.
- The referral may literally be 'a dump', that is, a gesture by another health care worker who is either exasperated, frustrated or uninterested and refers a patient to a colleague only 'to get him off his back'.
- The counsellor may feel that the problem is not of a psychological nature and is therefore inappropriate for his service (e.g. the patient requires help with housing, income support or sickness benefits).

Failure to address these issues will at some point result in an impasse in counselling. The algorithm (Figure 16.1) may help in deciding whether counselling can or should proceed.

STUCKNESS ARISING FROM CONFLICTING ROLES AND RELATIONSHIPS BETWEEN PROFESSIONALS

Although all health care professionals may share a common mission of helping to treat and care for their patients and family, they may differ in how they demonstrate their caring for patients and how they relate to them. Doctors and nurses have 'hands on' contact with their patients. In contrast, physical contact between counsellors and their patients is not accepted as usual practice. Not only may there be different approaches to care, but competition and rivalry between professional care-takers can also undermine the counselling process. This may result from feelings of envy or misunderstanding over the aims and goals of a particular treatment approach. Two examples illustrate possible problems.

> In the following case, it became clear that the counsellor's omission of not explaining to nurses on a ward that counselling sessions might make the patient seem more upset for a short while led to their anxiety that counselling was actually making the patient more upset. Lack of liaison or feedback to the nurses resulted in their protesting to the referring doctor that the counsellor was upsetting the patient and making it more difficult to care for him. In this case, the patient was being investigated for Crohn's disease and had been admitted for tests by his doctor. One consequence of the patient's anxiety about being in hospital was that he developed abdominal pains and diarrhoea, possibly relating to symptoms of anxiety and distress. The nurses believed that these symptoms were exacerbated by counselling sessions in which the patient spoke about his extreme worry about being diagnosed with the condition and the effect that this could have on his family life and career. Figure 16.2 illustrates the effects of the problem between the nurses and counsellor.
>
> This misunderstanding could have easily been avoided if the counsellor had explained to the nurses and to the patient that psychological problems sometimes get worse initially, especially if the patient remains anxious about the outcome of the tests and investigations. Instead, in this case, poor liaison resulted in the patient becoming more distressed, his being

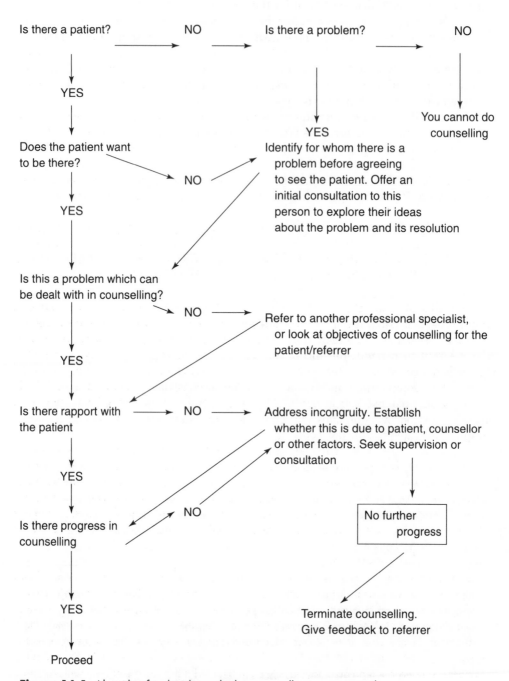

Figure 16.1 Algorithm for deciding whether counselling can proceed

prescribed sedative medication, and possibly too a deterioration in the relationship in both of the professional groups most directly involved.

It is possible that two professional groups each with a remit for psychological care (in this case, a health advisor in a sexually transmitted disease clinic and a hospital-based counsellor) could have conflicting approaches to patient care. The patient had recently been diagnosed with hepatitis B, which he had probably contracted after sexual contact. When the patient wanted reassurance that he would soon recover fully, he visited the health advisor who readily gave him reassurance. However, symptoms of ill health, including jaundice, night sweats, lethargy and fatigue made the patient acutely anxious. He was prone to have panic attacks at home. Sessions with the counsellor focused on helping the patient talk about his fears, develop strategies for coping with panic attacks, and cope better with his illness. As soon as the patient felt better and did not experience panic attacks, he would seek out the health advisor for further reassurance sessions until the next cycle was repeated. This is depicted in Figure 16.3.

The second case example indicates the split in the health care team between the 'good' and 'bad' care-takers, and consequently the dilution of focus and intensity in counselling. Collaborative work, or an agreement that only one of the professionals would work directly with the patient, could help to avoid such splits and their consequences. It could be argued that in this case the split was not unduly harmful to the patient because reassurance did not necessarily exacerbate the patient's symptoms. Indeed, reassurance may have been containing for the patient and helped to strengthen his ability to cope. Nonetheless, it could also be reasoned that a deterioration in the patient's condition could have led to a breakdown in the relationship with the health advisor, who would no longer have the confidence of the patient. Although different mental health professionals may be involved in any one case, it is preferable to limit direct patient contact to only one counsellor, or for others to be invited in on an *ad hoc* basis similar to the role of a consultation–liaison psychiatrist in a general hospital.

Counsellors may work hard to establish effective and collaborative professional relationships with their colleagues, though this task is seldom complete. There is frequent change of personnel in most health care settings, particularly in teaching hospitals and even between shifts. New staff may not understand the role and position of the counsellor, while others, by virtue of their perception of hierarchy among professionals and between different groups of professionals, may not recognize that of the counsellor.

In this case example, the counsellor had worked closely with the consultant haematologist to develop a comprehensive care and treatment service for patients with sickle cell disease. The team comprised nurses, a medical social worker, a physiotherapist, and a junior doctor on rotation. All new patients were seen initially by the consultant haematologist and then by the counsellor. This arrangement changed soon after the appointment of a registrar in haematology. He felt that patients only needed to be referred to the counsellor when they displayed obvious signs of psychopathology. In practice, no new patients were seen by the counsellor in the first two months of the registrar's appointment. The counsellor first discussed this with the registrar, who remained adamant that he would not routinely refer new cases to him. Feeling exasperated, the counsellor then discussed the problem with the

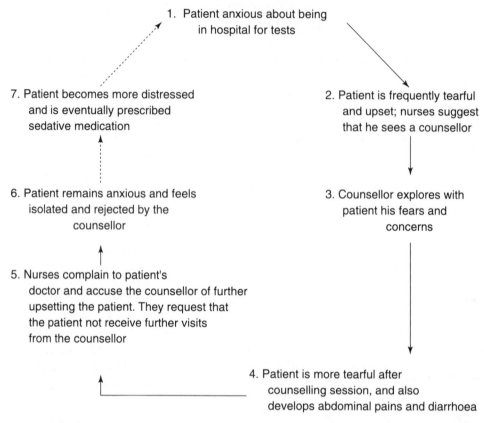

Figure 16.2 Misunderstandings between professionals giving rise to management problems with the patient

consultant haematologist. Although the consultant was sympathetic to the counsellor, he did not want to interfere with the practice of the registrar whom he relied on to reduce his workload. The problematic triangular relationship remained unchanged until a patient committed suicide eight months later. The registrar asked the counsellor for help with counselling the bereaved relatives, one of whom was also being treated for sickle cell disease. This tragic event coincidentally resulted in a closer working relationship between the registrar and the counsellor. It provided an opportunity for the two professionals to discuss how the counselling service could best be introduced to patients in the future, and led to fortnightly case meetings attended by all members of the unit to discuss patients' psychological and social problems. By virtue of the professional hierarchy, only the consultant haematologist could have insisted on his registrar referring all new patients to the counsellor. Even so, the registrar might have remained sceptical and referrals to the counsellor might not have been well made. Experience has taught us to be patient and use every opportunity to define and redefine the position, role and tasks of the counsellor. Impatience leads to resistance and ill-feeling between colleagues.

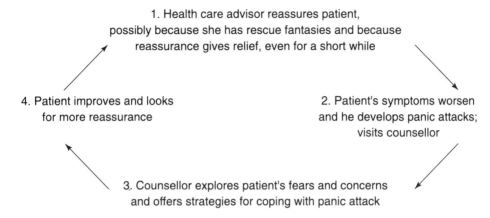

Figure 16.3 Cycle of misguided psychological interventions and care

AVOIDING AND MANAGING STUCKNESS

Having some strategies and procedures for dealing with an impasse or stuckness in counselling can help to avoid these situations and manage them when they occur. Highlighting possible sources or causes of stuckness is a first step towards its resolution. An initial task for the counsellor is to reflect on the situation confronting him by answering a series of self-reflective questions about the case or problem. Some examples of questions are as follows:

- What appears to be the problem?
- What is my reaction to this problem?
- Is this a problem I can solve by myself or does it require the help or intervention of others?
- Why does this problem occur at this point in time?
- How can I best deal with the problem?
- What is the worst possible consequence of this problem? What might happen if the problem is not addressed?
- What is expected of me (by the patient, referrer, colleagues, line manager) in relation to this problem?
- What is the least that needs to be done to bring about change?
- If other colleagues were in a similar position, what might they be inclined to do?

It is also helpful to consider other ways of resolving an impasse in counselling. This can be achieved in a number of ways:

- *Arrange for consultation or supervision.* Another counsellor or consultant may view the problem differently, or at least be able to advise on alternative options for solving the problem. The act of describing the problem to another professional familiar with complex interpersonal and organizational dynamics may itself prove helpful. A consultant or supervisor can provide useful feedback about what you may be doing to cause, maintain or exacerbate problems. It does not necessarily imply that the counsellor failed to discern his role in a problem; it is difficult to observe and be objective about a process of which one is a part.

- *Discuss the problem with a line manager.* Although one's supervisor may also be a line manager, these functions are often separated in health care settings. Indeed, counsellors working in health care settings may not have the support of a sizeable group of similarly trained professionals. This in itself may present a problem for the counsellor (and managers), who may be unclear about tasks, expectations and accountability associated with this work. Nonetheless, someone within the management structure is likely to have been designated a line manager with whom counsellors can discuss professional or organizational problems. In a GP practice, this could be the senior partner or practice manager. In a hospital, this may be the head of therapy services, a consultant psychologist, psychiatrist or psychotherapist, or a senior member of nursing or medical staff. It is not necessary that a line manager comes from the same professional background. Most health care professionals who have had management experience will be familiar with problems stemming from professional rivalries, service provision and resourcing, and those stemming from caring for patients and their families. Consultation with a line manager could prove an efficient way of reducing stuckness.
- *Arrange a team meeting.* Given the importance of interprofessional collaboration and the potential problems that arise when this does not work well, other colleagues may be directly or indirectly affected by progress (or the lack of it) in counselling. Most medical specialities have regular patient case discussions or ward rounds. Although professional colleagues usually welcome our attendance at these meetings, this position is not achieved easily and sometimes requires a sensitive approach and persistence to ensure that counsellors are viewed as a permanent part of the team. This can take years to happen and patience is required as other health care staff gradually come to understand the counsellor's role and what can be offered. This process is slower and more difficult if the counsellor is not attached to any one speciality and consults to teams across the spectrum of specialities. Nonetheless, *ad hoc* meetings with key personnel or with a team with which one has loose links are an obvious way to explore and resolve problems. It also provides a further opportunity to clarify the role of the counsellor and strengthen professional relationships.
- *Arrange for personal therapy.* If there are personal problems which interfere with counselling, especially those relating to loss, health concerns or disability, personal therapy can help to address and resolve some of them so that they do not affect the patient's treatment and the counsellor's well-being.

CONCLUSION

An impasse can arise in counselling for a number of reasons. It may be caused by difficulties in the counsellor–patient relationship, between the counsellor and the referrer or other professionals, as a consequence of organizational dynamics and pressures, and because the counsellor is inadequately trained or stressed at work. A self-reflecting counsellor is usually able to identify the source of the impasse and recognize the stuckness that may follow in counselling sessions. Counsellors have long recognized that the complex interpersonal dynamics in counselling sessions and the practice of counselling make it inevitable that an impasse will occur. Solutions are to be found in (a) reflection upon these dynamics; (b) recognizing and understanding the relevant influence of contextual and organizational issues in counselling; (c) more effective team collaboration; (d) supervision or consultation; and (e) sometimes, the counsellor's own course of personal therapy.

CHAPTER 17

Counselling for the Prevention of Ill Health

INTRODUCTION

The physical and mental health implications of being diagnosed with an illness, particularly if it is chronic, degenerative, associated with disability, terminal, or transmitted to others (serious infection or genetic conditions), mean that prevention should be uppermost in the minds of health care professionals. This includes the prevention of disease and disease progression, somatic manifestations of stress, mental health problems and social or relationship/family problems.

Diagnosis of a physical illness can affect individuals and their families in a number of ways. One important effect is the potential for worry and anxiety about the diagnosis, investigations, treatment or prognosis. The patient may not have any signs or symptoms of disease; just 'knowing' is sufficient to stimulate fearful thoughts. These thoughts, in turn, affect the individual's behaviour and the concomitant physiological 'fight or flight' response of the sympathetic nervous system. Initially, the individual engages in the *alarm* phase of the stress response, preparing to attack or defend against the perceived threat (Selye 1956). The individual is able to maintain this response in the *resistance* phase for a considerable time before submitting to the *exhaustion* phase following prolonged exposure to stress. Cardiovascular and immune function changes may occur to make the individual more vulnerable to illness and symptoms. Psychologically, an exhausted individual may lose motivation, feel helpless, lack confidence, withdraw from others and become depressed. This compounds the illness process, as well as the person's motivation and approach to treatment and healthy living.

Mrs Davis was diagnosed with multiple sclerosis but told 'not to worry' by her doctor until serious symptoms occurred. Mrs Davis found this very difficult to do and became increasingly anxious and worried. Two years later she was referred for psychological treatment of anxiety when she said she was having difficulty coping. Had she been referred early, post-diagnostically, for preventive counselling, she could have been taught anxiety management strategies as well as had the opportunity to discuss her fears and feelings about her diagnosis and consider the implications for her and her family. By increasing her sense of control and ability to cope with different scenarios, she might not have needed crisis intervention. Her adaptation to diagnosis and disease progression could also have been improved with preventive intervention.

As has been stated, many of the above mental and physical health complications arise from the individual's cognitions and fears, rather than the disease process itself. How can illness, stress, anxiety and depression be prevented?

THEORETICAL BACKGROUND

Current psychological models of health-risk behaviours and precaution adoption include the Health Belief Model (Becker 1974), Theory of Reasoned Action (Fishbein and Ajzen 1975) and the Precaution Adoption Process (Weinstein 1988). They are cognitive individualistic models, focusing on the individual's thoughts and beliefs.

The Health Belief Model

The Health Belief Model indicates that a person's perceived vulnerability to a health threat, their perceived severity of the threat and the cost benefit of adopting a preventive action are central to whether an individual adopts a more healthy lifestyle. However, the limitations of this model include the assumption that humans are able to make rational and logical decisions about their behaviour and that their individual beliefs are robust and not easily influenced by the beliefs of significant others.

This model suggests that, for preventive counselling work, the counsellor needs to understand the individual's perceived vulnerability to health risk, their beliefs about the severity of that threat and the cost benefits of changing their health-risk behaviour or adopting a preventive behaviour. Hypothetical future-orientated questions can be used to elicit the individual's beliefs and as such bring this cognitive process to conscious awareness for discussion with the counsellor and significant others. It may be that in so doing, the individual will be able to make a rational decision based on the available evidence, rather than an irrational one fuelled by emotion and confusion.

Theory of Reasoned Action

The Theory of Reasoned Action is, as the name suggests, a model which relies on logical and rational thought-processes that influence human behaviour. In particular, this model proposes that health-risk behaviour and precaution adoption are related to the individual's intentions, which in turn are linked to the private attitudes the individual holds about a particular behaviour and also their beliefs about subjective norms and how other people might view this particular behaviour. The model encompasses a social comparison component and places greater value on shared belief systems. This model has similar limitations to the Health Belief Model, but it can account for seemingly irrational health behaviours when one considers these behaviours in the context of peers, family or culture. An example would be smoking or drug use, which may be a peer-led activity that is socially sanctioned. Although the individual may know logically that these behaviours are a health risk, he is able to continue engaging in them by rationalizing their use or denying their adverse consequences. For some individuals the need to be accepted socially or to fit into the family, for example, is seemingly greater than their need to survive. Indeed, working clinically with patients who are having difficulty changing their health-risk behaviours, we have often found that the individual has to reconstrue their whole existence, and not just a simple behaviour, in order to be able to adapt and change. Frequently it includes involving significant others, who are integral to the maintenance and change of health-risk behaviours and precaution adoption.

The Precaution Adoption Process

This model similarly focuses on individual thought-processes, but in addition it describes the adoption of healthy behaviours in accordance with five stages of development. These are:

1. Knowledge
2. Risk Acknowledgement
3. Personal Risk Acknowledgement
4. Intention to Act
5. Action

The model proposes that individuals have to know about a health risk as the first stage toward adopting a preventive measure. In this respect education is fundamental to behaviour change, but unlike many health education programmes, this model suggests that education alone is not sufficient for behaviour change. The second stage of this model indicates the need for individuals to understand the risk attached to certain behaviours. This is different from stage 3, when individuals are required to acknowledge their own personal risk. Many people who are trying to change their health-risk behaviours find that moving from stage 2 to stage 3 is a frequent stumbling block. They may well know about a health-risk behaviour and accept that it is risky, but not feel that they themselves are personally vulnerable. Lifestyle studies indicate that people overestimate their ability to avoid health hazards and underestimate their risk of becoming personally vulnerable. This is a somewhat rose-tinted view of one's health actions.

Stage 4 is similar to Fishbein and Ajzen's (1975) model in that it identifies intentions to act as key predictors of subsequent action. Again, many individuals find that moving from stage 4 to stage 5, the action stage, is difficult. They may well intend to do all sorts of things (e.g. stop smoking, reduce alcohol consumption, use condoms) but when the time comes they are not able to follow through their intentions. Again, one key factor which may influence people's intentions to engage in a particular behaviour may be the views and beliefs of significant others. In a study looking at condom use by college students to prevent HIV and other sexually transmitted diseases, it was observed that although students may have condoms with them at the time of intercourse with a new partner (and *intended* to use them), there were many students who in fact did not use them. It would appear that communication between the couple, and the use of alcohol and drugs, were major influences on whether or not a couple used a condom, even though they may have intended to do so.

The implication of the above models for preventive counselling is that the counsellor needs to understand the individual's beliefs in the context of their relationships with others. In particular, it may be useful to include partners, parents or children when considering the obstacles to behaviour change and determining what would have to happen in order for a person to adopt a more healthy lifestyle. A family consultation can have the added advantage of disseminating the health education message to other members of the family, as well as activating the patient's natural support network to ensure change and subsequent maintenance of behaviour change.

DEVELOPING A SYSTEMIC APPROACH TO PREVENTION OF HEALTH PROBLEMS

A systemic approach to preventive counselling and the use of 'motivational interviewing' strategies (Miller and Rollnick 1991) may be particularly useful for helping individuals to understand their individual beliefs in a social context (their partner, family, peers, colleagues at work, and culture). By using hypothetical and relationship-based questions, individuals can start to develop a different view of how their beliefs and behaviour fit into the wider context of their relationships with significant others. The reciprocity of the relationship becomes apparent as the person understands that the 'ping-pong' of ideas between himself and others generates a new belief system, one that has synergy and a dynamic which is greater than any one person's individual contribution. The patient can develop an understanding not only of how others influence his beliefs and behaviour, but also of how the individual's thoughts and actions affect these other people. It may become clearer to the patient and his family, or work context, what would have to happen in order for the individual to develop a healthy lifestyle. By developing the 'group mind', individuals are better able to understand and develop their role in order to assist the adaptation process. Rather than the individual changing whilst the context remains the same, the patient and context are both influenced as new behaviours are established.

Two main advantages of a systemic approach are that they include significant others who influence the patient's thoughts and actions, and that behaviour change remains the responsibility of the patient and his family. The systemic counsellor provides a context in which change can occur. It is a non-directive approach and, ultimately, choice remains the prerogative of the individual. This approach is different from other person-centred therapies, however, in that in asking hypothetical and relationship-based questions, new material and ideas can be brought into conversation, rather than reflecting back old materials and old ideas – possibly maintaining the 'stuckness' of the patient (see Chapter 16). Past, present and future questions can also be useful to change the emphasis from looking at what went wrong to looking at what would have to happen for things to be right, and developing a more solution-focused approach.

THE ROLE OF THE COUNSELLOR IN PREVENTION

Early intervention

The main aim of a preventive approach to counselling is to pre-empt problems and assist the patient to be proactive in their coping responses. Rather than react to crisis, the patient can discuss the implications of investigations, treatment and their prognosis in a hypothetical way with the counsellor in order to prepare themselves psychologically for difficult situations or bad news and mobilize their coping resources and natural support network. Ultimately, preventive counselling aims to assist the patient and his family in their adaptation to illness. If preventive counselling is successful, then therapy as such is not required. Preventive counselling offers the opportunity for early detection of problems, circumnavigating crisis situations and encouraging a relatively stable path for the patient through this adaptation process. Reducing stresses at source will in turn impact on the individual and his family to reduce anxiety, stress-related symptoms and depression.

Instigating the counselling or consultation process pre-diagnostically, or as soon as practicable thereafter, is vital if one is to work preventatively with patients. The counsellor needs to introduce himself to the patient to promote personal contact and accessibility with the patient. An initial meeting is a prime opportunity to develop a link upon which a therapeutic relationship can be based in the future, and to inform the patient of possible areas in which the counsellor may be helpful. Information-giving is also part of preventive counselling, for example about genetic diseases, the effects of smoking, or contraception, and is integral to the counselling process in health care contexts. Myths about therapy and counsellors can be dispelled and patients' questions answered. Below are some of the questions the counsellor might ask at the initial meeting:

'I understand that you have recently been told by your GP that you have MS . . . What do you understand about this illness?'
'How has it affected your thoughts and feelings?'
'What has helped you to cope these last few weeks?'
'Who have you talked to about it?'
'What worries you most about this illness?'
'How can we best help you at this point?'

Stress management

Stress management techniques can be taught to patients and their families using group presentation, information sheets and audio-tapes that can be used in everyday life and without supervision. The individual is taught to recognize the interaction between their thoughts, feelings and behaviour, especially the connection between worrying and fearful thoughts, sympathetic nervous system arousal and stress behaviours. Relaxation training is an important part of any stress management approach, teaching the individual how to counteract the effects of sympathetic nervous system arousal. Other important components in stress management include problem-solving, decision-making, coping, effectiveness training and other individual-based methods of reducing stresses at source or the impact of stress on the individual.

Less common are systemic approaches to stress management which include family and organizational interventions. This may reflect the difficulty of trying to identify sources and consequences of stress within the family or work place, or implement systemic interventions. For some patients it may be particularly helpful to address how their stress is affected by, and in turn affects, the family or their work setting. Stress and anxiety are context bound and in this respect could be modified by changing the context in which they arise.

> A counsellor was asked to offer staff support to ward nurses who, according to their manager, were stressed by 'their workload and the emotionally charged nature of patient problems'. The manager wanted them to 'off load' onto the counsellor. The counsellor could have offered one-to-one counselling or group counselling but instead decided to look at the context in which stress was arising for these nurses. It transpired that the nurses most affected were night duty nurses who tended to work in isolation, without support and supervision. These were also the nurses least likely to be able to attend a support group. Instead, the counsellor had a consultation with the manager to look at what the manager could do to improve the supervision and support of these nurses, reduce isolation and improve time management and work delegation practices. The impact on the ward nurses was favourable. Morale increased and reports of stress decreased. The nurses no longer felt they needed a counsellor but rather looked to each other for support and guidance. The manager was also pleased with her improved management skills and decided to apply for an in-house nurse management training course.

Couple and family consultation

Patients often worry about family reactions to their illness and may decide not to tell their loved ones about their condition, which involves keeping secrets and reducing the patient's opportunity for a social support buffer against stress. Frequently the patient's rationale for not telling the family is that they do not want to upset them, or fear that a family member may try to move in and take over the patient's life. How the family respond to illness will inevitably affect the patient's own adaptation, his beliefs about the illness, ability to cope, experience of symptoms and mood state. Conversely, the way in which the patient responds will affect the family. The circularity and reciprocity of this dynamic provides the context in which the illness is managed. Family consultation may be particularly useful to help expose family beliefs about illness, coping and healthy lifestyle changes, and to see how these beliefs translate into behaviour and relationship patterns in the family. Where a family feels stuck, this new view may be liberating and help the family to challenge old beliefs, change responses and support the patient.

Wife:	John is so depressed about his heart condition. He goes to bed early every night and is grumpy. He used to be so attentive.
Counsellor:	In what way was he attentive?
Wife:	You know . . . in bed and everything . . . lovemaking.
John:	(looks out of the window)
Counsellor:	(to engage John) John, were you aware that Jill misses your attention?
John:	Yes I suppose so, but I worry about what it will lead to.
Counsellor:	What do you think it might lead to?
John:	. . . in case I have another heart attack.
Counsellor:	What has Dr Green told you about lovemaking after someone has had a heart attack?
John:	That it's OK for me to.
Counsellor:	Do you believe it is OK?

John: No.

Counsellor: Jill, what do you think would help John to feel more reassured about his health . . . ?

Where individual family members feel isolated, they can be helped to feel connected and better able to understand each other's views and beliefs. Where families feel that too many changes are happening too quickly, a sense of homeostasis and stability can emerge during family consultation. Family consultation can provide an environment in which to discuss issues which might otherwise have remained a family secret; provide an opportunity for people to say what support and care they would like from others; address dreaded issues such as disability or terminal illness; and look at family beliefs and trends in health-risk behaviours and precaution adoption. Families can be involved in helping patients adopt more healthy lifestyles and in planning their care. Including the family can prevent feelings of exclusion and secrecy, or expecting relatives to make decisions on the patient's behalf.

Social support

Research has shown time and again (Leiter 1990) that social support is a major influence on reducing anxiety, stress, and depression. Preventive counselling in health should always involve promoting access for patients to their natural support network, including family, friends and voluntary agencies. Empowering the individual to look to their own natural resources is preferable to encouraging a dependent relationship with the patient. If the patient feels that the only person he can confide in is the counsellor, then the counsellor's absence may make the patient feel impotent. The counsellor is also at risk of occupational stress and burnout if he feels unable to share the patient's care with other individuals and promote patient responsibility for adaptation to illness.

   Promoting social support may include consulting with the patient to help him establish who it is best to talk to in the family, how he can do this, when he can do it and what the possible responses might be. Preventive counselling may include role-playing situations of disclosure, or reacting to negative or upsetting responses. Using hypothetical questions and role-play, the patient is encouraged to consider a variety of possible outcomes so that he feels better able to cope. The following are examples of such hypothetical questions:

'How would you tell your mother about your illness? If I were your mother . . . what would you say?'

'You say you are afraid of worrying her, how would this affect you and your relationship with her?'

'Your mother could respond in many different ways . . . if I role-play some different responses, could you see how you might respond . . . ?'

Role-play and rehearsing difficult or feared situations play an important part in prevention. They can facilitate problem-solving and communication, helping to prevent illness (for example, familial or sexually transmitted diseases), worry, stress, isolation and depression.

Social support for some individuals, especially if they are isolated or unable to access their natural support network, may involve voluntary and statutory agencies. Having a daily purpose and being with others can help inoculate the individual against isolation, being consumed by negative or worrying thoughts, and depression.

Some individuals will enjoy the opportunity of meeting other people who have the same illness, and may be unaware of how to do this. Other patients fear meeting others with the same disease and would prefer to develop a non–illness-related social network. It may be helpful for some patients to think about courses they might enjoy or voluntary work with which they could become involved, particularly for those who find paid employment difficult, in order to increase their social network. This might also have the advantage of increasing the patient's sense of achievement and distract him from worrying or negative thoughts.

Lifestyles

Promoting healthy lifestyles is an important part of preventive intervention. Most people know what constitutes a healthy lifestyle, but feel that for one reason or another it is difficult for them to change the habits of a lifetime. In particular, some people would like to reduce their smoking behaviour or alcohol consumption, increase exercise and relaxation, or adopt a healthier diet or safer sex. Preventive counselling can include looking at the individual and family beliefs which prevent the individual from making lifestyle changes. The individualistic cognitive models described earlier in this chapter are particularly useful for considering underlying beliefs which inspire behaviour and obstacles to change. Understanding 'what went wrong', however, is limited in its intervention, and sometimes a more useful and solution-focused question to ask is 'What would have to happen in order for things to change?' – this could be addressed to the patient or significant other.

> Counsellor: If Peter were to give up smoking, what would help him not to start again?

> Counsellor: What would help you to use condoms with your partner?

A major benefit of considering lifestyle changes with the patient is the increased sense of control and options it can give patients. With patients for whom medical treatments are limited or unavailable, complementary therapies and self-help programmes can be encouraged. Patients in such situations can feel that they are actively helping themselves – albeit in a small way – and promoting optimum health in the face of illness, disability and their own mortality.

Children, families and prevention

Healthy and unhealthy lifestyles are frequently learned in families and handed down through generations. Cultural, political, medical and religious influences may affect the family beliefs about health and illness; other important influences for children, other than parents and siblings, include peers and the school environment. Drug and alcohol use and smoking, for example, are behaviours which are often tried out during the adolescent years in some cultures. Some children role-model their behaviour on that of their parents or an older sibling or significant other, learning both healthy and unhealthy ways of living. Peers are also very influential, using peer pressure to encourage peer unity and peer-led behaviours such as substance abuse. Prevention, then, needs to involve consideration of the context in which health behaviours are learned or changed. Including other family members as part of the consultation process is important if children and other family members are to understand the context in which health beliefs and lifestyles develop and change. Likewise, prevention programmes and interventions need to generalize across settings to include home, school and work environments, and not simply health care settings.

CONCLUSION

Many counsellors who work in health care settings are inundated with referrals when patients have problems or reach crisis level. Rarely is there an opportunity to work preventatively with patients unless contact is made at an early stage prior to investigations or after diagnosis. Where it is known that patients with particular diagnoses are likely to develop anxiety, depression or other psychological or relationship problems, it would seem to make good sense to offer early intervention, whether it be individual, family or group based. The counsellor is then in the optimum position for pre-empting problems, developing patient coping skills and resources prior to crisis and, in some instances, assisting in the prevention of distressing circumstances. The patient and family can be better prepared and supported for dealing with difficult and distressing situations, unpredictability, uncertainty, fear, confusion and despair. They are less likely to feel stress, anxiety or depression if they can be helped to feel more in control and better able to resolve stressful situations, learn techniques to reduce signs of stress and anxiety, develop their repertoire of coping responses, access social support and develop health-promoting behaviours as described in this chapter.

CHAPTER 18

Language Use and Stereotyping of Gender-specific Diseases

INTRODUCTION

Developing a sensitivity to gender-biased language is important for counsellors when talking with patients and their families. This is a useful way to recognize our own, and the patients', personal applications and understanding of the meaning of gender-biased words. Sensitivity to the potential of language as a collaborative resource can help keep gender-biased language from creating barriers between patients and health care professionals, since these words can add to patient pathologies. Attention to gender-biased language also highlights the recursive relationship between patients' biomedical and psychological symptoms and social experiences. When symptoms are described in words better suited to describing relationships, a counsellor will often discover the patient's non-medical concerns (Latz 1995). For example, patients talk about 'Who will do the shopping, cooking, laundry, who will change the bed, where will I get money to pay for outside help?' These are examples of patients' non-medical concerns surrounded by talk about how relationships are affected by patients' health issues. This recursiveness is important to note because patients' biomedical issues are not without psychosocial implications and psychosocial implications are not without biomedical issues (Bloch 1988).

The circular relationship between psychological and biomedical issues deserves serious attention. Patients typically receive symptom evaluations through the biomedical lenses that set up an either/or situation of, for example, biomedical or psychosocial indicators. A biomedical lens often assesses patients as parts rather than as a whole system (e.g. cardiovascular, respiratory, male/female reproductive) and addresses gender-related health issues by using gender-biased language to gather patients' symptoms. These words often indicate stereotypic gender behaviour, e.g. 'tomboyish', 'hysterical', 'macho', 'stoic', and do not provide for patients' personal experiences which cannot be sequentially or coherently documented in notes and research results. This can lead to the exclusion of physical symptoms, causing health care professionals to over-focus on the psychological components of patients' ill health.

A biopsychosocial approach of both/and (rather than either/or) offers counsellors a way to address patients' biomedical issues and their psychosocial implications (McDaniel *et al.* 1992) at the same time. The biopsychosocial 'lens' views a medical situation systemically, addressing this recursion in a way that a biomedical or psychosocial lens is unable to address alone. For example, anxiety in a patient may indicate ongoing psychological distress or may simply express situational anxiety over being ill. The systemic viewpoint also recognizes that each lens has its own appropriate professional language and approach for developing treatment plans for patients.

Health care professionals rarely have much training in identifying and managing the psychosocial gender-role aspects in patients' illnesses. Imprecise or exclusionary language, such as that which diagnoses gender-same diseases, can lead health care professionals to misunderstand conditions that relate specifically to one gender and not the other. Treatment of a specific disease is often prescribed according to concepts applicable to the majority of the population rather than the presenting individual. One gender's information, aetiology, or experience is often ignored or misapplied to the other gender's considerations. For example, women are two-thirds of the 'patients with chest pains and normal coronary arteries [yet are perceived to] have predominantly psychiatric disorders' (Rutherford and Braunwald 1992: 1346). In cardiovascular disease, male patient orientations for symptomatology, aetiology, procedures, diagnoses and treatment plans have been applied to female patients' experiences, to the detriment of female cardiac patients' biomedical symptoms. Such inaccuracy leads to over-identification, as well as inappropriate treatment, of female cardiac patients' psychosocial symptoms, so that female patients presenting with less definitive cardiac symptoms have 'an exaggerated preoccupation with personal health . . . and panic disorder' (Rutherford and Braunwald 1992: 1346).

Female patients' medical concerns, experiences, and language may be different from those of male patients, yet these differences are often unaccounted for in typical medical care. A case example:

Counsellor: You were 33 when you first were noticing symptoms. Is that correct?

AC: That's correct.

Counsellor: And it was heaviness in the chest?

AC: Heaviness and pain right in the centre of the chest. I was going to school at the time, and uh I had two children. One was two years old and one was six years old. And I was waiting for my husband to come home. Then I rushed to school and I kept saying . . . as I'd run up the steps because my class was always up two flights of steps . . . I kept saying 'the books are getting heavier. I'm like really in pain here' [points to chest]. And finally, uh, one night about two o'clock in the morning, I had to call a neighbour to come be with the kids. Because the pain was excruciating. And I went into the neighbourhood hospital . . . And they diagnosed me as having a heart attack which I really . . . and I had gone to doctors before this. They ruled out angina and they said it could be hiatal hernia, it could be gall bladder. They never even . . . suspected heart disease.

Counsellor: How long ago was that . . . how long did it take for the symptoms to develop to this point? And that they still talked gall bladder?

AC: Not long. I would say three or four months. It went very fast.

Counsellor: So you first experienced chest pains and then it progressed, and then they ruled it out, but for three months you were sick?

AC: I was . . . nobody – nobody diagnosed it correctly, basically, and trying to take tests for hiatal hernia and gall bladder tests. And then finally um when this thing happened in the middle of the night, I went into the hospital and I had a heart attack and I was there and I just didn't believe it. [drops voice] I have heart disease. I just was so sick, and in shock.

Gender-biased words and terminology can have a powerful influence on the medical experiences of patients with diseases that are biomedically defined as being gender-specific, for example, heart disease, lupus, sexually transmitted diseases, impotence, infertility and cancer. Defining any disease as gender-specific means that there is very little in the way of research procedures and symptomatology directed towards the gender excluded, yet both genders can be susceptible to these diseases.

LANGUAGE USED IN BIOMEDICAL SETTINGS

The gender-biased language of traditional biomedical research methods favours the masculine experience. This can readily be seen in language used to describe the research outcomes of the Framingham Heart Study, which began in 1948 and concluded in 1968. The biased clinical language that is commonly used often assumes behaviour, e.g. hysterical or emotional, which prejudices observations of patients. Gender-biased clinical observations that are reported with gender-biased language in traditional medical terminology reflect only the male values of autonomy/ distance rather than relationship/interdependency, which are female values.

For example, the Framingham Heart Study demonstrates how gender-biased terminology can imbalance a study's focus. This has led to a popular belief that cardiovascular disease is a gender-specific disease – male – and that women are not at risk from cardiovascular disease until after menopause. Similar misguided beliefs also affect men, as in the case of breast cancer, a gender-specific disease classified as female; because of gender-biased assumptions, e.g. men are not at risk, no symptomatology, treatment plans or self-examinations have been applied to men with this disease.

Gender-biased language and terminology can affect health care professionals' assumptions and observations of patient behaviour, which are then expressed in patients' clinical reports. Again, the Framingham Heart Study is an excellent example of gender-biased language and terminology being used in reporting clinical outcomes that profiled women participants as cardio-hypochondrial with benign chest pains. These concepts of gender-biased terminology in turn entered the public's popular language and applied inappropriate meanings to women's behaviours, experiences and symptomatology.

For example, if a health care professional perceives a woman as a 'whining cardio-hypochondrial' patient with 'benign chest pains', it can mask real physical problems. Actual symptoms can be dismissed and the focus may be more on the woman's psychosocial symptoms. Gender bias in health care professionals' clinical language easily assumes stereotypical behaviour (e.g. hypochondrial or hysterical), which then defines symptomatology and the diagnosis, possibly leading to distorted treatment plans.

Counsellors may also notice that women patients tend to use language that is better suited to describe relationships than biomedical symptoms when talking with health care professionals, who tend in response to use sequential language with women patients.

Women sometimes report their psychosocial and biomedical symptoms to their health care professionals through gender-biased language. Female cardiac patients typically speak the language of relationship and report their symptoms in great detail, while health care professionals typically speak the language of pathology which fosters distance and autonomy, as illustrated in the words of a patient below:

> I couldn't get through a day. I worked part-time. I wasn't working a full-time day, and I couldn't figure out why I was just so exhausted all the time. And I would come – I'd finish my day, I'd go to bed, I'd take a nap, I'd drag through the evening, then the next day it would start over. Up to then – I had a few really hard chest pains but who doesn't? And one was while I was bending over – I remember that was in March when my brother was visiting. I went to bend over just to pick up one of these curbstones – I didn't think I was coming back up. I was in so much pain in my chest and I had shortness of breath. And it scared the life out of me. I didn't know what was going on. I decided it's time for a physical. I was just tired of feeling tired, and I went for a physical with the GP. It was . . . so this GP just started treating me pretty much . . . thinking that I had . . . I was pre-menopausal and some other strange things. He prescribed tranquillizers. I was sitting there hysterical, crying and saying I can't get through the day, I can't walk from here to the car without feeling totally fatigued, my chest was aching, I had shortness of breath. And I just didn't feel well. And for me to say . . . at that point in time . . . I was not a person that didn't feel well . . . I had it. I wanted some answers. You know, at least start some course of treatment.

The incidence of stereotyping by health care professionals through the use of gender-biased language is higher for women than men and affects health care professionals' decisions to treat the reported medical condition. Health care professionals may be tempted to associate any patient's use of dramatic, florid language and detailed description of their symptoms with hypochondria and hysteria. This is especially true for female patients but the problem also affects male patients. A general lack of focus on the language patients use contributes to treatment imbalances, assignment of psycho-pathologies, and miscommunication between patients and health care professionals. Such biomedical miscommunication between health care professionals and their patients is of major concern for insurance providers, since miscommunication is the most cited reason in medical malpractice suits.

Health care professionals who pay attention to the use of language by patients and their families could reduce the chance of miscommunication and alter patients' medical experiences by shifting perceptions about the nature of the illness. For example, if a female patient with cardiac problems also expresses depression, anxiety and stress, these could be reinterpreted to the patient's benefit. These accompanying systems could be reframed by counsellors as a normal part of the patient's recovery. Counsellors would be able to appreciate such apparent pathological indicators as an untapped resource or a natural expression of cardiac patients' biomedical and recovery experiences. Such a perception could frame the psychosocial side of cardiac experiences into a less pathological framework and might subsequently require less medically aggressive treatments, e.g. prescriptions for mood-altering medications, for these patients.

A less pathological approach to psychosocial symptoms of depression, anxiety and stress, framing them as cardiac companions, fits well for cardiac complicated women. This term establishes an alternative reference for symptoms as indicators that may not be a permanent part of patients' lives and certainly not as another disease or mental illness that needs to be cured. Systemic terminology allows the possibility of turning previously assigned cardio-psychopathology into a resource, especially for female cardiac patients, that could assist in their recovery and strengthen aspects of the female cardiac patient and health care professional. Another example of shifting a pathological view of psychosocial symptoms is illustrated by a patient who had inoperable cancer:

> This patient's oncologist noted apparent depression and suggested to the patient that an additional prescription could relieve this situation. The patient was angered by the health care professional's suggestion. So the doctor referred this patient to a counsellor. The patient, when speaking with the counsellor, said, 'I have never been depressed in all my life and I won't be treated for something I never had and don't have now.' The counsellor asked the patient what she thought her doctor was referring to. The patient responded, 'I guess because I was telling him that I was sad, frustrated, with no energy. I find that I'm always thinking about my garden.' The counsellor responded, 'So are you more frustrated than depressed?' The patient nodded in agreement; she said, 'This is the time I prepare my soil for Spring planting and start my seeds. It used to take me only two days and now it is taking me two weeks. I'm behind and I won't be able to catch up. I find myself worrying about depression and additional medication. Which is taking more of my time and energy. My poor garden.'
>
> 'So are you perhaps frustrated about your garden and that you are not able to do anything about it?' 'Yes,' she replied. The counsellor suggested that depression to her is just her being a frustrated gardener. The patient agreed and said she was going to tell her doctor on her next visit.

Just as anatomy is indispensable to the medical field, listening-and-talking is indispensable to the field of counselling and psychotherapy. In fact, the above example demonstrates that health care professionals live so completely in their appropriate language that they 'cannot imagine its absences, so [they] cannot consider its presence' (Percy 1991: 420). For counsellors, language is the major resource in encounters with patients, family members and medical colleagues. Most health care professionals, patients and family members lack a way to evaluate their language practices with each other.

Counsellors can collaborate with other health care professionals to bridge communication gaps with patients when speaking about the psychological aspects of patients' illnesses to their families. This can positively influence and interrupt cycles of miscommunication. Counsellors are trained in language skills that identify and introduce change into patients' physical experiences and the health care professionals' perceived psychosocial implications. The counsellor can interrupt this recursive cycle by listening to, and using, the patients' and health care professionals' languages. This strategy provides the support necessary to improve patient compliance, creates patient-oriented treatment plans, and increases the patient's ability to cope with lifestyle changes.

Counselling in health care settings focuses on discovering patterns of interaction in patients' and other health care professionals' language, actions, or inactions with each other and with the patients' family members. Language which becomes communication, according to Bateson (1972), creates predictability, redundancy, meaning and pattern. This insight may help counsellors to understand patients' language. Gender-biased language colours perceptions and views female patients, for example, as story-tellers, ramblers who are unable to stay on the subject, do not produce a predictable pattern of communication and leave crucial diagnostic information undetected. Male patients tend to speak in a language of coherence/sequence which is the same language style in which health care professionals were trained, making the detection of diagnostic information easier. In other words, the use of language in any conversation only has relevancy to the listeners. If one side of a conversation's language is unheard, the teller and the experience will be under-emphasized.

THE IMPLICATIONS OF GENDER BIAS FOR COUNSELLING IN HEALTH CARE SETTINGS

The power and importance of gender-sensitive language in health care settings persuades and dissuades the listener as to the value and validity of patients' stories about symptoms. Language helps patients and their families give meaning and understanding to a medical event. Counsellors who are aware of language's persuasive power also become sensitive to how different cultures may view a vast array of biomedical problems. The following examples will convey that the use of language in medical conversations has relevancy to sensitive and aware listeners.

Language using gender-specific/biased words conveys not only information but also gender-specific behaviours to counsellors and health care professionals. This type of word use and language suggests stereotypical behaviours. The following are excerpts of the typical language found in the talk from three women's interviews (Polly, Mary and Lynn) with a counsellor. Each case example shows predetermined gender-specific behaviour of women, and the popular response of health care professionals to women with cardiovascular disease.

Counsellor: So when you talk to the doctors, how do you talk to them?
Polly: I usually tell them, I know you're probably going to think I'm crazy. I'm just concerned about this because I have this history. And if it's not that, you know, fine. If you tell me that this is gas and it's not chest pain or if you tell me that I'm having, uh, palpitations because I'm drinking too much caffeine, you know, then I'm happy.

The above is an example of how patients set up a gender-specific stereotypical response. The interview continues with the patient speaking about medical follow-up.

Polly: They – young people – they don't follow up, they don't – they don't go for their routine exams, they [doctors] don't see a lot of young people. And usually, if a young person comes in with, say, what they believe is a cardiac problem, [the cardiologist will dismiss] it usually as an emotional problem. And doctors [cardiologists] tend to think [if a young person states that] if you say well, I was having chest pain, that you – you've either been exercising or if you're dizzy or whatever that is, it's really not a cardiac-related problem. You know, that it's really something else. Because they find that a lot. You know, and I've seen it. They found it a lot, um, like when I first, um, had the valve replaced . . .

Mary: Sometime in May, I was – I had relapse – I was, um [this patient just had by-pass surgery], I was, um, in the hospital for three nights just to monitor me, see what was going on. Again I didn't know if it was the anxiety more than anything but they [health care professionals] monitored me for three months and then I was in the emergency room again. If you do what you're supposed to do. I didn't do what I was supposed to do because I was so depressed from it all.

Lynn: The fact that I can get it out. There are many nights when I can't sleep and I lie in bed and I cry to myself. And I cry because all of a sudden I'm feeling fine tonight, so I shouldn't. You know what I'm saying? I'm not saying that the end result was not beneficial to me. Of course it is. I'd have to be a moron to say that it was not beneficial as far as I'm concerned. And pills aren't the answer.

These examples indicate that language is a powerful influence that shapes the medical experiences of female patients. 'Language is what bewitches but language is what we must remain within in order to cure bewilderment' (de Shazer 1994: 3). Language is a principal way in which humans express, explain, process and participate in experiences of life, situations with family members, social contacts and dealing with health care teams. Language also offers a blocked reality because it is arbitrary, it is unstable, and its meanings change depending on multiple variables, e.g. who is speaking, who is listening, and the context. Use of language and choice of words influences health care teams' decisions to order diagnostic tests and develop treatment plans.

When gender-biased terms are used, initial symptoms may be misinterpreted, symptoms may be overlooked, and when the disease diagnosed as a gender-specific disease, the resulting disbelief of diagnosis places the patient into an 'it could be worse' frame of reference. Gender-biased language used by health care professionals makes it easy to discard any recursion between the medical and psychological symptom systems. Language and treatment that would support a more biopsychosocial view – for example, talk about death, scars, loss of control, companionship or the lack of it, relationships with doctors, and concerns for recovery – are often ignored.

GENDER-BIASED LANGUAGE AND PSYCHOSOCIAL SYMPTOMS

The perception that the severity of physical symptoms may be perceived differently depending on the gender of the sufferer places both genders in a potentially recursive cycle because women with less definitive cardiac symptoms, as the following case study shows, are seen by health care teams as stress-filled, nervous, or psychosomatic.

'I don't cry for no reason'
A cardiologist referred Luz, a 63-year-old female cardiac patient, to the in-house counsellor for psychotherapy. The patient scheduled her initial counselling session between her series of diagnostic tests. The counsellor invited Luz into the office and began the session by asking her

why she thought Dr Mayes referred her to a counsellor. Luz said that she was having a hard time since her heart attack in April. She explained that she was afraid all the time and cried often.

The counsellor sat facing the patient and asked Luz to tell about her recent medical events. Luz cleared her throat. The counsellor said, 'Just tell me the events as you recollect them.' Luz began by saying that she didn't realize she had been having a heart attack. Her pains began in January. She thought they were just signs of indigestion because an antacid provided her with relief and her pains stopped. Until she was hospitalized and the doctors said she had a heart attack, it never occurred to her or her husband that these pains were early signs of possible heart trouble. She tearfully continued to say she had always been healthy and had only been in the hospital for the deliveries of her two children. Softly crying, she mentioned that even up to the week before her hospitalization she thought that she was just having digestive problems brought on by her eating habits or her gall bladder.

On Wednesday something changed. The pains did not become intense but the antacid provided only temporary relief and then only momentary relief. By Friday, as she was driving herself home from the hairdresser, she decided she needed to have a doctor check out her pain. Her husband took her to the emergency room but she was sure it was nothing.

The counsellor asked Luz if the pains ever increased in intensity. She said no, that it was just a steady ache by that time and more annoying than anything else. The counsellor asked her to describe the pain in relationship to the only pain reference she had, which was her labour pains. Luz replied that the pain never became that intense or unbearable. She began to cry fully now and said that she still finds it hard to believe that she had a heart attack.

Luz said that she should be grateful because, so far, her series of tests showed nothing unusual. She asked, 'So why am I crying?' The counsellor suggested that some people just cry more easily than others. The counsellor asked Luz if she cried easily. She said, 'No, I don't cry for no reason.'

Another example is found in the following case study.

It didn't hurt

Three weeks ago Charlie received a diagnosis of breast cancer. It was the last diagnosis he expected from his doctor. Charlie noticed a lump on the left side of his chest about a year and a half ago. He really did not know how long the lump had been there before he noticed it. He did not think too much about the lump. Because it didn't hurt, Charlie thought it didn't need immediate attention. If Charlie had been a woman he would have had several mammograms, starting in his late thirties. He would have known how to make routine self exams and that he needed to report any changes immediately to his doctor.

Charlie only thought to mention it a year and a half later to his doctor during his last routine check-up because he noted a visible change a few weeks before his appointment. The nipple on his left side had changed position on his chest. His primary care physician advised him to have a surgeon check it out. Charlie made an appointment with the surgeon for two weeks later. The surgeon told Charlie, 'It could be a calcification, a benign tumour, or cancer, but I won't know until I surgically go in to biopsy it. I will remove it either way but especially if it is cancerous.' The lump the surgeon removed from Charlie's chest proved to be cancerous. The surgeon has referred Charlie to an oncologist to set up his treatment course for his breast cancer.

Charlie was not negligent about his health care. He was ignorant of preventive measures for, and symptomatology of, breast cancer because there is not an aetiology for men. Breast cancer is generally defined as a female disease. Charlie is an innocent victim of health care professionals defining a disease as gender-specific, and the potentially deadly popular beliefs that arise when a disease is defined as gender-specific. He found out that cancer, and more importantly breast cancer, like cardiovascular disease, is a gender-same disease and a health concern for both sexes. Defining a disease as gender-specific fosters a false sense of security and symptom ignorance for both women and men.

Counsellors with language awareness can recognize that the talk of patients and their families is filled with idiosyncratic meaning and application. This sensitivity to language illuminates areas that are important to patients and their families by highlighting problem-solving and decision-making skills, as well as language patterns that create meanings of medical experiences for individual patients and their families. A communication and relationship problem can arise when counsellors and health care professionals become entangled with what appears to be inappropriate language to describe medical symptoms.

Health care teams' professional training seeks to enhance the real sequence of patients' medical events and give these medical events an objectivity independent of language. The health care teams' professional language is one of pathology, which fosters distance and autonomy, but it is not the preferred language used by most patients and their families. Counsellors can develop the ability to recognize that they, health care professionals, patients and patients' families are 'languaged creatures and see everything through the mirror of language' (Percy 1991: 419–20). The language of health care professionals' training is one of coherence/sequence and makes sense in a health care setting but it differs from that of non-health care professionals.

CONCLUSION

The language of patients and their families will communicate agitation through losing track of sentences, wandering off the subject, digressions and personal details. This is an acceptable language form that often provides patients and their families with a way to understand and give meaning to their recent medical events. In essence, patients and their families can be saying to you and health care teams that 'This is how I, not you, make sense of my world, the people I interact with, my medical event, and my disease.' This chapter suggests to counsellors and health care professionals that both female and male biomedical symptoms may not be heard because the talk of the health care setting can become entangled with idiosyncratic language in which patients' physical symptoms can become submerged. This opens the door for health care professionals to focus too intently on psychosocial interactions and allows counsellors and health care professionals to be drawn into situations that can lead to miscommunication.

A recursive cycle of frustration for overworked health care professionals, symptomatic patients and concerned family members is not useful in an overloaded health care setting. Counsellors and health care professionals can make the effort to reflect, take time to listen and consider the differences in their own, the patients' and their families' language, releasing an untapped resource with diagnostic potential. A problem which often arises in medical interactions is that patients and health care professionals perceive each other as insensitive, unable, or unwilling, to provide and receive the best possible medical treatment and care. If, instead, counsellors and health care professionals are sensitized to the gender psychosocial conditioning that gender-biased language attaches to patients and their behaviour, such potential problems will have little effect on diagnoses and treatment plans.

CHAPTER 19

Work Stress and Staff Support

INTRODUCTION

This chapter provides an analysis of occupational stress and burnout in health care workers. It is important for counsellors to have some understanding of stress and burnout among health care professionals for personal reflection and because they may be called upon to help their colleagues to manage their stress and to cope with the effects of burnout, and also because the source of some of the problems that they encounter at work may be occupational stress among colleagues.

Burnout has been construed as the end stage of prolonged exposure to stress at work (Chernis 1980). The health worker, however, has mostly been viewed in isolation from his context and many stress management interventions are employee-focused, treating the worker rather than the context in which stress arises. This runs counter to research evidence suggesting that organizational stress-prevention programmes are more effective than individual coping initiatives (Cooper and Cartwright 1994). A systemic approach takes account of the context in which stress arises, the reciprocity and dynamic nature of work relationships, and how change in one part of the team effects change in another. Stress in this chapter will be considered as being organizationally mediated rather than as a clinical problem requiring individual clinical intervention.

AN INPUT–OUTPUT MODEL OF HEALTH WORKER STRESS

An overview of the stress and burnout literature in health care reflects an input–output model of the sources and consequences of stress and burnout (Schaufeli *et al.* 1993). The *input* includes work stressors such as working with distressed patients, large case-loads and occupational risk or hazard. The *output* includes cognitive, emotional, behavioural and physiological manifestations of stress such as loss of concentration, memory problems, angry outbursts and frequent illness.

A transactional model of occupational stress (Cox and Mackay 1981) considers how the external stressors become internalized physiologically and the impact this has on health and behaviour. The mediating mechanisms of interest in this model are the individual's (i) perceptions of stress and (ii) access to coping resources.

The stressors are primarily thought to emanate from patient contact and organizational mechanisms (Schaufeli *et al.* 1993). Pervasive in the 'caring professions' are frequent encounters with emotionally charged and stressful situations. This chronic exposure may take its toll on the health worker, particularly if the employee is not adequately trained and supported to deal with these situations.

Some health workers may be particularly vulnerable to stress and burnout, having come into this work because of personality attributes or personal agendas and histories. Burnout is more likely in empathic, sensitive and dedicated workers, but also occurs in those who are over-enthusiastic, idealistic and prone to over-identification with patients.

Much of the stress and burnout research in health care workers has focused upon the emotionally challenging nature of working with patients. But professional relationships can be equally emotionally challenging. Although the buffering effects of positive collegial relationships and social support are well documented (Leiter 1991), much less is known about how relationships at work mediate stress and stress prevention.

The effects of occupational stress include worker irritability, anxiety, low morale, increased use of alcohol, increased illness and accidents, decreased performance, depression, suicide, interpersonal relationship difficulties and 'burnout' (Cooper and Cartwright 1994; Shaufeli *et al.* 1993). In human, economic and legal terms, occupational stress is costly. In addition, patient care and relationships with colleagues at work and family are likely to be compromised by worker stress.

Counsellors are particularly vulnerable to stress factors at work because many work in relative isolation (e.g. do not have counselling colleagues), have restrictive confidentiality boundaries (e.g. contain information within the therapeutic relationship) and are often exposed to emotive issues and human distress. For those who work in medical settings and multidisciplinary teams, there is the added stressor of developing common aims, communication, defining roles, and sharing work and responsibilities with colleagues. A systemic approach can address the dynamics of work-place relationships with colleagues, patients and significant others and offer a different view of stress and stress prevention.

SOURCES OF STRESS IN A HEALTH CARE CONTEXT

Cary Cooper (1983) has identified six major sources of stress in the work place. These are: job-specific stressors such as physical risk from infection; role within the organization, including role ambiguity, conflict and territoriality; career structures and processes; interpersonal relationships at work; organizational structures; and the effects of work pressures on family life.

Most jobs have an element of health-risk factors, role ambiguity, interrelationship problems and career limitations, and they impinge on family life, etc. Are there specific and unique factors for counsellors working in a health care setting?

Traditionally, stress and burnout research in health care has focused on *job-specific stressors*, including the emotionally challenging nature of the work, the fear of contagion, and heavy workload (Cooper 1983). Counsellors are frequently exposed to emotionally charged situations and the upset of patients and their significant others. They are also often approached by health care workers for support and understanding in the absence of other (formal) staff support mechanisms.

The *impact of health care work on family life* has also been documented in the literature. Worker stress may increase if the family hold negative attitudes about the patient group or the nature of the work, or are unable to provide social support as a buffer against stress and burnout (Leiter 1991). Counsellors may feel bound by confidentiality boundaries to refrain from looking for support from family, and may also be 'emotionally drained' and have few resources left to offer support at home.

The *organizational structure* is an important source of stress. The National Health Service in the UK, for example, has undergone substantial organizational change in recent years. Development of the purchaser/provider environment and the re-organization of departments and staff have involved considerable organizational change and development. These have generated a potential source of stress for employees as they adapt and develop new identities, roles and tasks at work and deal with the loss of colleagues, teams, career plans and, in some cases, their jobs. Funding of services may mean that one service is favoured over another and this may manifest as interpersonal and interdepartmental conflict. Counselling is a recent addition to the mainstream structure and many counsellors work in isolation, even if they are seen to be part of a multidisciplinary team. They are often managed by non-counselling professionals and may have no counselling peers as part of the service in which they work. There is no formal counselling structure, counselling payscale or job description within the UK National Health Service structure, yet the number of posts for counsellors is increasing. This situation can lead to ambiguity, conflict and confusion; another source of stress for counsellors.

Involvement in the process of organizational development and decision-making may be an important buffer against stress and burnout, by increasing workers' sense of control. A systemic approach addresses these contextual features and provides a framework for developing a supportive organizational structure for counsellors.

Career structures and processes are affected by organizational change and provide a context for worker stress. Some health workers may be more vulnerable to stress because of the increasingly limited nature of their posts. There is an increasing tendency to offer 'limited posts' for economic reasons. They may be time-limited (short-term contract), cost-limited (vulnerable to reduced funding and cost-improvement initiatives), or career-limited (have limited career progression and development opportunities). Counsellors may be vulnerable to stress because their post lacks security, planning, decision-making, development opportunities, career enhancement, personal development, achievement and satisfaction. This may result in decreased morale, boredom and burnout.

The psychological, medical and social implications of illness necessitate multi-disciplinary and multi-agency collaboration. Health care teams often rely on collaboration and co-ordination. They do not always have clear leadership structures, objectives or ascribed roles and tasks. The role of the counsellor, if not explicitly defined and agreed, can result in *role ambiguity and conflict*, a precursor of occupational stress and burnout.

Developments, change and uncertainty within the NHS provide ample scope for *interpersonal relationship* ambiguity, confusion and conflict. Similarities and differences between health workers (and teams) are not always seen in terms of complementarity. Similarities may be viewed as duplication, 'treading on toes', competition and redundancy. Differences may be viewed as autonomy, segregation, territoriality, conflict and blame. Workers engage in 'fight or flight' communications and responses (the first stage in the stress response).

Poor management, supervision and collegial relationships may contribute to stress and burnout. Good work-based relationships may buffer the individual against stress (Leiter 1991). Counsellors may be advantaged by professional recognition of the need for supervision. However, they may be disadvantaged by their relative isolation and absence of a counselling management structure and counselling peer support.

THE DEVELOPMENT OF BURNOUT

Chernis (1980) views burnout as a transactional process between external work stressors, internal worker strain and mediating psychological mechanisms. In this respect it is similar to a transactional model of stress and occurs in stages as follows:

- The first stage is where work demands exceed personal resources.
- The second stage is characterized by an emotional and physiological response to this discrepancy, resulting in anxiety, tension, fatigue and exhaustion.
- The third stage involves changes in attitude and behaviour, including a detached stance towards patients and a more self-absorbed, self-gratifying approach to work.

Burnout could be construed as a disengagement from stressors associated with working in human services. This process could be a coping mechanism or defence on the part of the worker, to reduce exposure to stressful encounters with patients. Burnout can be characterized by emotional exhaustion, depersonalization and reduced personal accomplishment associated with working in social or caring professions such as teaching, health services and police work (Maslach and Jackson 1986). Emotional exhaustion is a feeling state of being overstretched or taxed by the demands of human services. Depersonalization refers to an attitude of uncaring or callousness towards recipients. Reduced personal accomplishment is the sense of decline in competence or achievement in working with the public.

THE EFFECTS OF STRESS ON THE HEALTH WORKER AND WORK ENVIRONMENT

Health worker stress will have an impact on (i) collegial relationships, (ii) team and organizational functioning, and (iii) patient care. These effects will in turn have repercussions for the individual employee and so on in a circular fashion. The consequences of stress are also the sources of stress.

Cause–effect analysis in stress and burnout research provides a linear view or narrative of occupational stress. The interpersonal context of stress, however, is obscured. This is particularly relevant when considering the dynamic nature of workplace relationships and how the stressor and buffering effects of the same relationship can fluctuate over time and across situations. It is not simply a matter of people; stress is context bound.

A systemic perspective on organizations is concerned with the context and process of organization and team functioning, alliances, conflict and disengagement. The organization (team) is viewed as an entity in flux, which at any one point in time may be seen to have a sense of stability or homeostasis about it. There is a degree of 'balance' and 'fit', such that activity in one part of the organization is likely to have a ripple effect on other parts of the organization. In turn, these changes will impact on other areas of the organization, creating a reflexive relationship. In practice it is hard to know which is the chicken and which is the egg. Both, however, are necessary to the evolution of the other.

Systemic analysis is concerned with the 'feedback' process, e.g. how staff influence the organization as well how they are influenced by it. Systemic interventions aim to create a contextual view of stress at work. Through consultation with a systemic consultant, there may be increased awareness of interpersonal dynamics and communication patterns within the work group. So, for example, instead of the health worker focusing on patient or colleague characteristics as the source of stress, he can develop a new view – an understanding of the relationship between counsellor and patient or counsellor and colleague, for example, and how these relationships 'fit' together and interact within a given context. It is the stressor and buffering effects of relationships and the contexts in which they take place, rather than individual characteristics or attributes, which are important from a systemic perspective. Intervention might include feeding back observations (questionnaire and behavioural) of the dynamics of the interpersonal relationships and communication patterns of the work group to the work group. Change remains the prerogative of the team or organization, including management.

The stressor and buffering effects of organizational relationships are the important focus, rather than simply what the organization has done to the health worker. Intervention focuses on the employee–employer fit, and may include team and management development and employee assistance initiatives as part of a balanced package.

The systemic counsellor may have a role in one-to-one counselling as employee assistance and in facilitating staff support groups. For his own medical team, however, the ability to be neutral and to be viewed as neutral is thereby compromised. An external facilitator is more likely to be successful in facilitating team development and communication within the counsellor's own 'work group'.

ORGANIZATIONAL APPROACHES TO STRESS

Current initiatives in health care settings to reduce stress at work include stress management workshops, training in relaxation and coping skills, individual counselling and staff support groups (Cooper and Cartwright 1994). Employee assistance, stress management and counselling initiatives may increase individual coping skills but also reinforce the worker pathology narrative of occupational stress. These interventions aim to support or change the worker, rather than change the context in which stress arises or reduce stress at source. Likewise, group support initiatives may provide a forum for listening to 'blame' and 'worry' stories rather than effect change within the organization.

Research evidence indicates that organizational interventions are likely to be more effective than individual programmes. It may be that organization-based initiatives enhance the buffering effect of positive collegial relationships (Leiter 1991). Some interventions such as team building or management development, however, may improve interpersonal relationships and communication at work and so reduce stress at source.

How organizational interventions are planned and delivered is vital to their appropriateness and success. A request for intervention needs to be viewed systemically and metaphorically rather than as a literal request. What does the intervention mean to the managers, to the employees and to the organization as a whole (including the person being asked to intervene)? What effect is it likely to have; who is likely to benefit and who will not?

Work group, team and organizational interventions require organizational analysis and interpretation. Organization-trained facilitation is required to promote worker understanding of work relationships, ensure a constructive atmosphere and prevent staff from becoming negative and destructive, targeting scapegoat individuals. Organizational development interventions are not group or family therapy (although some principles may remain in common).

GUIDELINES FOR REDUCING STRESS AT WORK FOR COUNSELLORS

The following guidelines outline ways in which the counsellor can develop optimum work conditions for reducing occupational sources of stress. These principles are derived from the above theoretical and research observations and can be applied to other health care workers.

- Try to avoid working in isolation. Establish links with other health care professionals as well as counselling peers.
- Define team confidentiality parameters and access consultation and support with colleagues.
- Have a clearly defined job description and negotiate your role within the wider team (and encourage colleagues to do likewise).
- Have a clear accountability and management structure and seek to clarify ambiguous links with your manager.
- Negotiate caseload with your manager and referrers to clarify acceptable numbers and appropriateness of referral requests and service provision.
- Be prepared to adapt your working style to accommodate changes in patient numbers, patient needs and referrer or management needs.
- Have regular supervision and access staff support and development initiatives. If none are available, look to create them in consultation with your manager and peers.
- Have regular review sessions with your manager to review your work and set workable objectives.

CONCLUSION

Greater understanding of the context in which stress manifests and is mediated at work is needed among health care professionals. This includes the stress-inducing and stress-reducing roles that work-place relationships play in moderating occupational stress and burnout. Collegial relationships, power dynamics, team functioning and communication will be important areas in the future for organizational stress research and prevention in health care teams. The development of stress measures for counsellors and other health care workers needs to take account of work-based relationships in the broadest sense and to include relationships with colleagues as well as patients, and the recursive nature of the sources and effects of stress. Organizational stress-prevention programmes may offer more appropriate and effective staff support and development initiatives if they take account of the context in which stress is mediated rather than pathologizing the health care worker. Interventions aimed at improving organizational (and team) development and functioning, interpersonal communication and supportive work relationships might be particularly useful.

A systemic approach to organizational development aims to encourage workers to keep in mind the functioning of the organization as a whole, rather than focus exclusively on the individual. Organizational or team consultation creates a context of curiosity in which change may occur – according to the skill of the facilitator and the wishes of the team/organization. Counsellors can facilitate or provide a context for change and staff support, while maintaining team responsibility for the problem and its resolution. It is unlikely, however, that counsellors will be able to facilitate this process within their own team because of lack of objectivity. However, counsellors could be instrumental in organizing external facilitation, encouraging the view that stress is organizationally mediated rather than evidence of individual failing.

References

Anderson, H. and Goolishian, H. (1988). Human systems as linguistic systems: Preliminary and evolving ideas about the implications for clinical theory. *Family Process*, **27**, 371–93

Bateson, G. (1972). *Steps to an Ecology of Mind: A Revolutionary Approach to Man's Understanding of Himself*. New York: Ballantine

Bateson, G. (1979). *Mind and Nature*. New York: Dutton

Beck, A. (1976). *Cognitive Therapy and Emotional Disorders*. New York: International Universities Press

Becker, M. (ed.) (1974). The Health Belief Model and personal health behaviour. *Health Education Monographs*, **2**, 324–508

Bloch, D. (1988). The partnership of Dr. biomedicine and Dr. psychosocial. *Family Systems Medicine*, **6**, 2–4

Bowlby, J. (1975). *The Making and Breaking of Affectional Bonds*. London: Tavistock

British Association for Counselling (1990). *Code of Ethics and Practice of Counsellors*. Rugby: BAC

Buckman, R. (1984). Breaking bad news: why is it still so difficult? *British Medical Journal*, **288**, 1597–9.

Byng-Hall, J. (1995). *Rewriting Family Scripts*. New York: Guilford Press

Campbell, D. and Draper, R. (1985). *Applications of Systemic Family Therapy: The Milan Approach*. London: Grune & Stratton

Campbell, D., Coldicott, T. and Kinsella, K. (1994). *Systemic Work with Organizations*. London: Karnac Books

Carter, B. and McGoldrick, M. (1981). *The Family Life Cycle*. New York: Gardiner Press

Cecchin, G. (1987). Hypothesizing, circularity, neutrality revisited: an invitation to curiosity. *Family Process*, **26**, 405–13

Chernis, C. (1980). *Staff Burnout: Job Stress in the Human Services*. Beverley Hills, CA: Sage

Cooper, C. (1983). Identifying stresses at work: recent research developments. *Journal of Psychosomatic Research*, **2**, 369–76

Cooper, C. and Cartwright, S. (1994). Stress management interventions in the workplace: stress counselling and stress audits. *British Journal of Guidance and Counselling*, **22**, 65–73

Cox, T. and Mackay, C. (1981). A transactional approach to occupational stress. In E. Corlett and J. Richardson (eds), *Stress, Work Design and Productivity*. Chichester: John Wiley

de Shazer, S. (1994). *Words were Originally Magic*. New York: W. W. Norton

Diller, L. (1986). On giving good advice successfully. *Family Systems Medicine*, **4**, 78–90

Doherty, W. and Baird, M. (1983). *Family Therapy and Family Medicine*. New York: Guilford Press

Edwards, M. and Davis, H. (1998). *Counselling Children with Chronic Medical Conditions*. Leicester: BPS Books

Engel, G. (1977). The need for a new medical model: a challenge for biomedicine. *Science*, **196**, 129–36

Fishbein, M. and Ajzen, I. (1975). *Belief, Attitude, Intention and Behavior: An Introduction to Theory and Research*. Reading, MA: Addison-Wesley

Griffith, J. and Griffith, M. (1994). *The Body Speaks: Therapeutic Dialogues for Mind–Body Problems*. New York: Basic Books

Hoffman, L. (1981). *Foundations of Family Therapy*. New York: Basic Books

Hoy, A. (1985). Breaking bad news to patients. *British Journal of Hospital Medicine*, **8**, 96–9

Josse, J. (1993). Use of family trees in general practice. *Postgraduate Update*, May 1, 775–80

Kelly, G. (1969). Man's construction of his alternatives. In B. Maher (ed.), *Clinical Psychology and Personality: The Selected Papers of George Kelly*. New York: John Wiley

Kleinman, A. (1988). *The Illness Narratives: Suffering, Healing and the Human Condition*. New York: Basic Books

Kubler-Ross, E. (1969). *On Death and Dying*. New York: W. W. Norton

Latz, M. (1995) At the heart of patient's stories: a therapist listens to cardiac companions. Unpublished doctoral dissertation. Nova Southeastern University, Ft Lauderdale, Florida

Legato, M. and Colman, C. (1991). *The Female Heart: The Truth about Women and Coronary Heart Disease*. New York: Simon and Schuster

Leiter, M. (1990). The impact of family resources, control coping, and skill utilisation on the development of burnout: a longitudinal study. *Human Relations*, **43**, 11067–83

Leiter, M. (1991). The dream denied: professional burnout and the constraints of human service organisations. *Canadian Psychology*, **32**, 547–55

Lloyd, M. and Bor, R. (1996). *Communication Skills for Medicine*. Edinburgh: Churchill Livingstone

Maslach, C. and Jackson, S. (1986). *Maslach Burnout Inventory Manual* (2nd ed.). Palo Alto, CA: Consulting Psychologists Press

Mayou, R. (1989). Illness behaviour and psychiatry. *General Hospital Psychiatry*, **11**, 307–12

McDaniel, S. and Campbell, T. (1986). Physicians and family therapists: the risk of collaboration. *Family Systems Medicine*, **4**, 4–10

McDaniel, S., Hepworth, J. and Doherty, W. (1992). *Medical Family Therapy*. New York: Basic Books

McGann, K. (1994). Sex bias in the treatment of coronary artery disease: equity and quality of care? *The Journal of Family Practice*, **39**, 327–9

McGoldrick, M. and Gerson, R. (1985). *Genograms in Family Assessment*. New York: W. W. Norton

McLaughlan, C. (1990). Handling distressed relatives and breaking bad news. *British Medical Journal*, **301**, 1145–9

Miller, R. and Bor, R. (1988). *AIDS: A Guide to Clinical Counselling*. London: Science Press

Miller, R. and Telfer, P. (1996). HCV counselling in haemophilia care. *Haemophilia*, **2**, 1–4

Miller, R., Beeton, K., Goldman, E. and Ribbans, W. (1997). Counselling guidelines for managing musculoskeletal problems in haemophilia. *Haemophilia*, **3**, 9–13

Miller, R., Bor, R., Salt, H. and Murray, D. (1991). Counselling patients with HIV infection about laboratory tests with predictive values. *AIDS Care*, **3**, 159–64

Miller, W. and Rollnick, S. (1991). *Motivational Interviewing: Preparing People to Change Addictive Behavior*. New York: Guilford Press

Papazian, R. (1994). Trace your family tree: charting your relatives' medical history can save your life. *American Health*, **13**, 80–5

Percy, W. (1991). *Signposts in a Strange Land* (ed. P. Samway). New York: Farrar, Strauss & Giroux

Rolland, J. (1984). Toward a psychosocial typology of chronic and life threatening illness. *Family Systems Medicine*, **2**, 245–62

Rolland, J. (1994). *Families, Illness and Disability*. New York: Basic Books

Rosser, S. (1992). Re-visioning clinical research: Gender and the ethics of experimental design. In H. Holmes and L. Purdy (eds), *Feminist Perspectives in Medical Ethics*, pp. 127–39. Bloomington and Indianapolis: Indiana University Press

Rutherford, J. and Braunwald, E. (1992). Chronic ischemic heart disease. In E. Braunwald (ed.), *Heart Disease: A Textbook of Cardiovascular Medicine* (4th edn), pp. 1292–364. Philadelphia: W. B. Saunders

Salt, H., Callow, S. and Bor, R. (1992). Confidentiality about health problems at work. *Employee Counselling Today*, **4**, 10–14

Schaufeli, W., Maslach, C. and Marek, T. (1993). *Professional Burnout: Recent Developments in Theory and Research*. Washington DC: Taylor & Francis

Seaburn, D., Lorenz, A. and Kaplan, D. (1992). The transgenerational development of chronic illness meanings. *Family Systems Medicine*, **10**, 385–94.

Seaburn, D., Lorenz, A., Gunn, W., Gawinski, B. and Muauksch, L. (1996). *Models of Collaboration: A Guide for Mental Health Professionals Working with Health Care Practitioners*. New York: Basic Books

Selvini Palazzoli, M., Boscolo, L., Cecchin, G. and Prata, G. (1980a). Hypothesizing, circularity, neutrality: three guidelines for the conductor of the session. *Family Process*, **19**, 3–12

Selvini Palazzoli, M., Boscolo, L., Cecchin, G. and Prata, G. (1980b). The problem of the referring person. *Journal of Marital and Family Therapy*, **6**, 3–9

Selye, H. (1956). *The Stress of Life*. New York: McGraw Hill

Sharp, K. (1994). All in the family? Your medical history. *Current Health*, **20**, 29–33

Tomm, K. (1987). Interventive interviewing. Part 1: Strategizing as a fourth guideline for the therapist. *Family Process*, **26**, 3–13

Turk, D. and Salovey, P. (1996). Cognitive behavioural treatment of illness behaviour. In P. Nicassio and T. Smith (eds), *Managing Chronic Illness: A Biopsychosocial Perspective*, pp. 245–84. Washington, DC: APA Press

Watzlawick, P., Weakland, J. and Fisch, R. (1974). *Change: Principles of Problem Formation and Problem Resolution*. New York: W. W. Norton

Weinstein, N. (1988). The precaution adoption process. *Health Psychology*, **7**, 355–86

Wright, L., Watson, W. and Bell, J. (1996). *Beliefs: The Heart of Healing in Families and Illness*. New York: Basic Books

Index

Aborigines 19
abortion 76
accidents 97, 110
accountability 89
AIDS, *see* HIV/AIDS
Ajzen, I. 167–8
alcohol abuse 82
Anderson, M. 13
angina, *see* cardiovascular
  disease
anxiety 12–13, 47, 52, 55, 80, 81,
  91, 99, 120, 159, 171, 176,
  178
appetite, loss of 47
arthritis 106, 110
asthma 71
attachment theory 4, 12
avoidance 48

bad news, giving 97–108
  approaches to 100–1;
    conselling options 101–7;
    theoretical background
    98–101
Baird, M. 9
Bateson, G. 31, 180
Becker, M. 167
beliefs
  constraining 11; exploring
    25–9; facilitative 11;
    reframing 31–9, 73, 125–6,
    169
Bell, J. 5, 11, 25
bereavement 2, 99, 109
  counselling 119–28;
    guidelines 121–7

biomedical
  issues 55, 175–6; settings and
    language use 177–80, 183
biopsychosocial
  approach 175–6, 181; systems
    perspective 9–11
bone marrow transplants 91
Bor, R. 60, 82, 91, 92
Bowlby, J. 12
brain injury 55
Braunwald, E. 176
British Association of
  Counselling 79–80
Buckman, R. 97
burnout, staff support and
  185–91
Byng-Hall, J. 12

Callow, S. 82
Campbell, D. 32
Campbell, T. 141
cancer 55, 87, 110, 179
  breast 105, 107, 177, 182–3;
  lung 22
cardiovascular disease 22, 71,
  91, 166, 175–9, 180–1,
  181–2
  giving information 93–6;
    studies 177
care, provision 50
Carter, B. 12, 109
Cartwright, S. 185–6, 189
case histories
  bereavement 123–7; change
    and preservation 38;
    confidentiality 80, 81, 84;

consultee discussions 150;
counselling session 64–78;
counselling tasks 40–6;
dependence and
  abandonment 37; exploring
  and defining problems 48,
  52, 56–7; family secrets 86;
  focused counselling 68–9;
  gender biased language
  181–3; gender specific
  diseases 176–7, 178, 180–1;
  genograms 72, 77; giving
  information 90, 92, 93–6;
  health care consultations
  144–5; hope and
  hopelessness 35;
  idiosyncratic
  communication 19–20;
  issues in terminal care
  111–17; life and death 33;
  meaning systems 23–4;
  openness and secrecy 34;
  prevention of ill health 166,
  170–3; relationship with
  family 36; separateness and
  involvement 37; stuck in
  counselling 159–63;
  temporal themes 35;
  wanting to know 34;
  the worried well
  136–9
Cecchin, G. 12
Chernis, C. 185–6, 188
children 104, 173–4
Crohn's disease 137
chronic fatigue syndrome 13

clinical
  interview 12; language,
    gender-biased 181–3;
    observations, gender-
    biased 177–8; psychology 2
clinics, out-patient 4
Code of Ethics and Practice 79
cognitive individualistic models
    167
cognitive-behavioural theory
    4–5, 8, 13, 55, 135
collaboration 9
  and consultation models
    140–54; defining a
    consultation 140–2; hints
    for improving 15–17
communication
  giving bad news 97–108;
    giving information 87–96;
    mis-communication 29–30,
    179; patterns 29–30, 183;
    problems 3; skills 97–108,
    143
complementary therapies 27
concentration, lack of 47
confidentiality 1, 4, 27, 79–86,
    90, 111
constructivist approaches 4
consultation 9
  and collaboration models
    140–54; contracts 150–1;
    definition of 140–2;
    dreaded issues 97–108,
    153; formulating
    hypotheses 152–3; in
    health care settings 143–57;
    models of practice 142–3;
    steps in 147–8; tasks 151–2
contracts 150–1
conversational skills 7
Cooper, C. 185–6, 189
counselling
  aims 62–3; beliefs about
    illness and 18–30;
    bereavement 119–28;
    blocks to progress 155–65;
    check list 64; collusion with
    patients 49; competence
    58; definition 6, 9; giving
    bad news 97–108; giving
    information 87–96; guiding
    principles 62; implications
    14; levels of 14–15; for loss
    and terminal care 109–18;
    practice guidelines 63–8;
    for prevention 166–74;

principles and aims 60–9;
    session 64–8; stress and
    burnout in 185–91;
    theoretical concepts 60; use
    of questions 60–1; the
    worried well 129–39
*Counselling Children with
    Chronic Medical
    Conditions* 7
counsellor
  role and task 1–8; specialist 4,
    14
Cox, T. 185
cultural background 51, 99
curiosity 12
cystic fibrosis 71

Data Protection Act 85
Davis, H. 7, 12
death and dying 109–18
  see also loss; reframing beliefs
denial 48
dependency 114
depression 13, 51–2, 56–7, 77,
    82
desensitization 13
developmental issues 12, 50,
    185–91
diabetes 34–5, 91–2, 94, 145
diabetic ketoacidosis 71
diagnosis 6–7, 87–96, 103, 166
disability 99, 110
disclosure 100–1
disease, stigma and
    discrimination 22–5
disfigurement 99, 110
doctors, myths about
    counsellors 141
Doherty, W. 9, 11, 72, 130, 134,
    176
Draper, R. 32
drugs 56, 91, 103
dying, fear of 47
dysphasia 99

Edwards, M. 7, 12
Engel, G. 9
enurisis 72
epilepsy 99, 110

facilitative beliefs 11
family
  see also relationships;
    consultations 171–2;
    history 70–3; life cycle 71,
    73; secrets 83–4; systems 2,

4, 9–11, 19–22, 25–6, 28,
    51, 55, 70–8, 136, 168–9;
    tree, *see* genograms
fatalism 48
fatigue 30
female disorders, *see specific
    conditions*
Fisch, R. 135
Fishbein, M. 167–8
flat effect 47
Framlingham Heart Study 177
Freud, S. 2

gender-specific diseases
  stereotyping 175–84; and
    biomedical settings 177–80;
    implications for
    counselling 180–1;
    psychosocial symptoms
    181–3
genetic
  counselling 71; screening 55,
    87
genograms 19, 64, 94, 123
  basic symbols 75;
    constructing 73–7;
    theoretical background
    70–3
Gerson, R. 70, 74
Goolishian, H. 13
Griffith, J. 13
Griffith, M. 13

haemophilia 14, 71, 91, 120
headaches, persistent 13
health
  beliefs about 11; education
    132; minimal fundamental
    unit 9; promotion 4, 87;
    psychology 2; risks 168;
    worker stress 185–6
Health Belief Model 167
health care
  consultation and collaboration
    models 140–54; counselling
    tasks 40–6; giving bad news
    97–108; giving information
    87–96; limitations 55;
    practice, confidentiality in
    82–6; problems 4–5;
    providers 2–3;
    relationships 29–30,
    129–39, 140–54, 155–65,
    185–91; settings 1–8,
    14–17, 180–3; stress
    185–91

heart disease, *see* cardiovascular disease
hemiparesis 99
hepatitis 91, 92, 99, 103
Hepworth, J. 9. 11, 72, 130, 134, 176
herpes 99
HIV/AIDS 4, 14, 22, 26, 55, 82, 87, 89, 91, 98–9, 103, 107, 110, 146, 148, 168
Hoffman, L. 5
humour 48
Huntington's disease 120
hypochondria 130, 178
hypotheses 60–9, 152–3, 167, hysteria 178

ill health
    counselling for prevention 166–74
        role of the counsellor 169–74; systemic approach 169; theoretical background 167–9
illness
    see also meaning systems; abnormal behaviour 129–31; adjusting to 97–108; advent of 12; beliefs about 11; causation 25–9; communications 19–22; coping skills 2, 19, 22; counselling the worried well 129–39; disclosure of 70, 82; giving bad news 97–108; loss and terminal care counselling 109–18; objective reality 5; prevention 87; stigma and discrimination 22–5; stress association 4; terminal stages 90; typology 12, 50
immunosuppressive drugs 56
impotence 57, 177
infertility 4, 14, 26, 87, 177
information giving 87–96
    guidelines 92–6; issues covered 93; rationale 88–9; skills and techniques 97–108; specific issues 88; theoretical considerations 91–2
informed consent 92, 95, 103
insomnia 13, 47

Jackson, S. 188

Josse, J. 72

Kaplan, D. 134
Kelly, G. 135
Kleinman, A. 19
Kubler-Ross, E. 109

language 13
    in biomedical settings 177–80; and gender specific diseases 175–84; gender–biased 181–3
Latz, M. 175
legal implications 89, 91, 112–13
Leiter, M. 172, 186–8, 190
leukaemia 56, 110
life
    -cycle issues 12, 131–2; -styles 91, 173
litigation 3, 16
Lloyd, M. 91, 92
Lorenz, A. 134
loss
    and bereavement 2, 4, 88; bereavement counselling 119–28; fear of 47, 50, 99; and terminal care 109–18
lupus 177

McDaniel, S. 9, 11, 72, 130, 134, 141, 176
McGoldrick, M. 12, 70, 74, 109
Mackay, C. 185
McLaughlan, C. 104
male disorders, *see specific conditions*
Marek, T. 185–6
Maslach, C. 185–6, 188
Mayou, R. 129
meaning systems 19–22
    exploring beliefs 25–30; stigma and discrimination 22–5; theoretical background 18–22
medical
    concerns, non- 175
    conditions 1, 47, 49
    counselling, systemic 47–9; genograms 70–8; meanings 13
medico-legal issues 2–3, 97, 103
Milan Associates 60
Miller, R. 60, 87, 89, 91, 169
Miller, W. 169
miscarriage 76

MRI (magnetic resonance imaging) 55
multiple sclerosis 14, 166

neurology 91, 99, 142
nurses, myths about counsellors 141

oncology 4, 14, 51, 143
open wards 4
organization development 185–91

paediatrics 14, 142
pain management 13
Palazzoli, S. 11, 60, 65
Papazian, R. 76
paralysis, conversion 13
pathology, language of 178–80, 183
patients
    causes of illness 25–7; confidentiality and secrets 79–86; consultation and collaboration 140–54; counselling tasks 40–6; counsellor collusion with 49; dissemination of information 27–8; experience of illness 26–7; gender specific diseases 175–84; giving bad news 97–108; giving information 87–96; health problem prevention 169–74; illness and counselling beliefs 18–30; problem systems 54–8; receiving bad news 1, 25–9; reframing beliefs 31–9; refusing medication 2; stuck in counselling 156–8, 137; understanding problems 53–4; working with medically ill 11–14; the worried well 129–39
Percy, W. 179, 183
physical illness, psychological processes 2
post-modern ideas 5
Precaution Adoption Process 168
privacy, lack of 2
problems
    conceptualizing 5, 7; context of 11; definition framework 49–53, 55, 63; dreaded

problems *continued*
issues 97–108, 153;
exploring and defining
31–9, 47–59; giving bad
news 97–108, 153;
reframing beliefs 31–9;
showing understanding
53–4
prognosis 27–9
psychiatric disorders 176
psychodynamics 55
psychological
aspects to patient care 2,
161–2, 140–54; issues 47,
50, 175, 187; problems 31,
47–9, 54–8, 73, 132–9, 144;
responses 99; symptoms
181–3; theories 2–5
psychosocial
assessment 62; care 141;
categories 74; implications
175–6; symptoms 181–3
psychotherapeutic
approaches 4–6; counselling
14, 135, 179; framework
49–53; interventions 3, 7,
14, 31–9, 73
psychotherapy, role of medicine
and 2

questions 12, 60–1

referrals 2, 29, 47–9, 56–7, 64,
93, 133, 140–54
reframing beliefs 31–9, 95, 136
change and preservation 38;
dependence and
abandonment 37; hope and
hopelessness 35; life and
death 33; openness and
secrecy 34; relationship
with family 36;
separateness and
involvement 37; temporal
themes 35; theory 31–3;
wanting to know 34
relationships
bereavement counselling 124;
consultant–
consultee 148–50; with
family of origin 36–7,
124–5; health issues and
99, 168–9, 175; loss and
terminal care counselling

109–18; problems 3, 45, 73,
131; professional 155–65,
185–91; reframing beliefs
31–9
relatives, receiving bad news
97–108
renal teams 91
respiratory diseases 175
rheumatoid arthritis 94
rituals 17, 19, 122–3
Rolland, J. 12, 72, 110
Rollnick, S. 169
Rutherford, J. 176

Salovey, P. 133, 135
Salt, H. 82
Schaufeli, W. 185–6
schizophrenia 71
Seaburn, D. 134, 141
secrets 79–86, 93, 111
seizures, non-electrical 13
Selye, H. 166
sex 76
sexual abuse 82
sexually transmitted diseases 87,
161, 175
sharing information 1
Sharp, K. 76
social support 27, 172
sociogram 73
solution-focused approach 5–7
somataform disorders 13
somatic symptoms 13, 71
somatizing 133, 135
spinal injuries 14
staff suport and burnout
185–91
stepfamilies 71
stigma and discrimination 22–5,
55, 120
stress 22, 100, 178–9
coping with 44, 127–8;
development of burnout
188; effects of 188–9;
health worker 185–6;
management 141, 170,
185–91; organization
approaches 189–90;
recognizing signs 158, 188;
reducing 24–5, 67, 91, 190;
sources 186–8
stuck in counselling 155–65
avoiding it 137, 163–5; causes
156–8; professional

relationships 159;
recognizing stress 158;
referrals 158–9
suicide 82
supportive counselling 14
surgery 91
symbolic representations 19
symptoms
gender-biased 175, 180–1,
181–3; invisible
manifestations 99
systemic
approaches 5–6, 8, 71,
169–74, 185–91; medical
counselling 47–9

Telfer, P. 91
terminal care, counselling for
loss and 109–18
theoretical
approaches 62; concepts
9–17
Theory of Reasoned Action 167
therapeutic
interventions 135–9;
neutrality 16; processes 73;
systems 51–2
therapy 29
democratic process 5;
narrative 13; personal
165; systematic perspective
3
time
-limited counselling 3, 13–14;
and longevity 13
Tomm, K. 12
treatment 27–8, 50
treatment noncompliance 22
tuberculosis 91, 99
Turk, D. 133, 135

viral haemorragic fever 55

Watson, W. 5, 11, 25
Watzlawick, P. 135
Weakland, J. 135
Weinstein, N. 167
'worried well'
counselling guidelines 133–9;
counselling the 129–39;
counsellor's dilemma 132;
theoretical concepts
129–32
Wright, L. 5, 11, 25